S0-AYT-466

# VETERAN'S GUIDE TO BENEFITS

# Veteran's Guide to Benefits

## 2nd Edition

P. J. Budahn

STACKPOLE
BOOKS

Copyright © 1997 by Stackpole Books

Published by
STACKPOLE BOOKS
5067 Ritter Road
Mechanicsburg, PA 17055

All rights reserved, including the right to reproduce this book or portions thereof in any form or by any means, electronic or mechanical,
including photocopying, recording, or by any information storage and
retrieval system, without permission in writing from the publisher. All
inquiries should be addressed to Stackpole Books, 5067 Ritter Road,
Mechanicsburg, Pennsylvania 17055.

This book is not an official publication of the Department of Veterans
Affairs or the Department of Defense, nor does its publication in any
way imply its endorsement by these agencies.

*Cover design by Wendy A. Reynolds*

Printed in the United States of America

10  9  8  7  6  5  4  3  2  1

PRAIRIE CREEK PUBLIC LIBRARY DISTRICT
501 Carriage House Lane
Dwight, IL
60420-1399          ILDS #3
TELEPHONE:  815 584-3061
FAX:            815 584-3120

**Library of Congress Cataloging-in-Publication Data**

Budahn, P. J. (Phillip J.), 1949–
    Veteran's guide to benefits / P. J. Budahn.—2nd ed.
       p.      cm.
    Includes index.
    ISBN 0-8117-2975-3
    1. Veterans—Services for—United States.  2. Military pen-
sions—United States.  3. Consumer education.  I. Title.
UB357.B83     1997
362.86'0973—dc21               97-17038
                                     CIP

# CONTENTS

# INTRODUCTION

A unique band of people is scattered throughout the United States. They can be found in every major city, each suburb, and the smallest towns. They are on the farm and in the shopping mall, occupying every imaginable rung on the social ladder—and a few that are unthinkable—from the boardroom to the soup kitchen.

And though there are twenty-six million people in this group, they're considered a special band of people by the general public, by the government, and most especially, by themselves.

Of course, I'm talking about the men and women who have served their country in the military.

They have shared the mixture of excitement and dread during those long nights before reporting for their first day of training. They have experienced the indignities of boot camp designed to change them from civilians into members of the armed forces. And together they have known the hardships of moves and separations from loved ones, the bafflement of fitting into strange new environments, and the fear of realizing that if troops must take to the field anywhere in the world to protect the security or interests of the United States, they're the ones who will go.

When the day came to take off their uniforms, they assumed a new, special status, one that set them apart from the rest of the citizenry, one so special that it will probably be written in their obituaries even if they live for many decades after their discharge.

They are called "veterans."

For their sacrifices to the nation, the veterans of military service are entitled to a vast array of programs and benefits. A nationwide network of hospitals and clinics, a competitive edge when it comes to getting government jobs, financial help in paying for education, special business loans, regular monthly pensions for disabilities—these are among the programs that have been put in place for people who have served in the military.

It is while confronting this wide selection of programs and benefits, however, that veterans realize they have another bond with each other: They're all confused.

There are so many programs to choose from, and each is different. Programs for veterans are a mishmash, and each has its own eligibility criteria.

This confusion helps explain why most veterans never take advantage of the benefits they've earned by serving in the military. Only one veteran in twenty-five ever steps into a VA hospital, according to official estimates, while seven out of eight never claim any sort of veterans benefit.

*Veteran's Guide to Benefits* was designed to take the guesswork out of being a veteran. In simple English and clearly organized chapters, it spells out the basic facts about each major program—who's eligible, what's available, and how to get benefits. This book also highlights common misunderstandings about the various programs.

Not everyone interested in veterans benefits is a veteran. Spouses have their own needs, and some are married to veterans who are too ill to fight their own way through the legalistic jumble around many benefits. It helps to know what to expect—or not to expect—from veterans benefits when doing long-range family planning. Although most veterans benefits go directly to the veteran, widows and widowers of some veterans have a legal right to their own government pensions.

For them, this book proudly carries the stamp "spouse-friendly." This means also that others who are interested in veterans benefits but unacquainted with the special language of the military or the jargon of the Department of Veterans Affairs can use this book to gain a practical understanding of programs available to the men and women who served their country.

Whether you hung up your uniform decades ago, are a member of the reserves or National Guard, or are still on active duty and planning your transition back to the civilian world, you should know what you as a veteran are entitled to receive.

Several obstacles make it tough to learn about any federal benefit or government program. The initial problem involves language. Rule books are written by lawyers and experts, not by ordinary people. Even after you've figured out what a sentence means in simple English, you can't be sure if a legal detail has any practical consequences.

And, in a final insult, once you've ascertained what a rule book is really saying and whether a given detail has importance in the real world, often it's another struggle to figure out how each detail applies to people in your specific circumstances.

*Veteran's Guide* will help you overcome those obstacles to understanding your veterans benefits. The language here is straightforward, and practical advice is found throughout. Few readers will want to study every page, so, like any user's guide, this book is designed to give you quick access to the information you need.

Early portions of this guide summarize the veterans benefits for seven categories of veterans and for spouses: Just-Plain-Veteran veterans, Exit Bonus veterans, disabled veterans, low-income veterans, "Bad Paper" veterans, special veterans, military retirees, and spouses and survivors. You're in the "Just-Plain-Veteran" category unless one of the other categories applies to you.

Later chapters contain detailed information about each benefit and program. Each chapter is organized around a major topic, including health-care programs, disability pay, home loans, educational programs, and resolving problems with the military.

At the back of the book is a collection of specialized information. It includes a state-by-state summary of facilities operated by the Department of Veterans Affairs, plus a state-by-state listing of state-run veterans homes.

*Veteran's Guide* is a road map to your veterans benefits, but even the best map can't predict what roads will close, which bridges will be built, or where a new street will run. Changes in veterans benefits are made every year by Congress, the Department of Veterans Affairs, and other government agencies.

The information in *Veteran's Guide* came from many sources, including federal law, publications of the Department of Veterans Affairs, the VA staff in Washington, veterans organizations, veterans advocacy groups, and countless veterans, active-duty servicemembers, and spouses. The author is grateful for their help, but they are not responsible for any errors.

So before making a major decision based upon the information in this book, verify it through official sources. Generally, future changes tend to broaden programs, so the information here should be viewed as a conservative, bare-minimum description of programs and benefits.

A major exception is health care. The country grappled with plans for a national health-care system throughout the early 1990s, and some of those debates continue within the VA's health-care system.

When it comes to VA medical benefits, it may be useful to consider this edition of *Veteran's Guide* as a snapshot of the rules that was taken in the late 1990s. Later editions will update the picture and fill in more details.

A grateful nation has created a host of benefits for the men and women who devoted a portion of their lives to military service. Now, it's your job to figure out what you can get and how you get it.

*Veteran's Guide to Benefits* is here to help you.

# ONE

# Basics on Veterans Benefits

For many people, an understanding of veterans benefits is often confused by family folklore, by their own philosophy about the role of government, and by memorable "horror stories."

> About one out of every three adult males in the United States is a veteran.

If Great-Uncle Fred's financial future seemed secure for the rest of his days after he was wounded during the Korean War, you may approach your own discharge with unreasonable confidence, certain that your new status as a veteran will smooth out the bumpy spots in life.

Or, what is unfortunately more common, you may remember that Great-Uncle Fred was bitter for the rest of his life because he felt betrayed and abandoned by his government after he took off his uniform.

For most people leaving active duty, the truth is somewhere in between. Being a veteran won't open every door, solve every problem, or provide a lifelong income simply because you had a rough time in the military. Neither is it true that the American people have turned their collective back on the men and women who once served in uniform, canceling benefits in the name of austerity and walking away from obligations through simple indifference.

> The federal government spends more than $40 billion yearly on veterans.

Either stereotype can be dangerous to someone approaching the issue of veterans benefits for the first time. You're not likely to persevere if you think all the benefits have been sacrificed to balance the federal budget (which hasn't happened). Nor are you likely to stick it out if you believe veterans should be wards of the government for the rest of their lives (which happens only to those with the severest service-related disabilities).

The "good old days" weren't as generous as they seem, and the present era isn't as miserly as the headlines sometimes indicate.

Veterans benefits weren't established to solve every financial problem faced by everyone who ever served in the armed forces. They were created, at specific times, by lawmakers intent on solving specific problems. Some benefits linger on the books long after those problems disappear.

Whatever the origin, the rules underlying all veterans benefits were written to make important legal distinctions. Those rules aren't always clear to laypeople. It takes time, effort, and patience to figure out where you—or a loved one—fit into the bureaucratic categories.

For many veterans benefits, the important factor is the type of discharge you received. For others, the key question is when you were on active duty. A few even depend on where you served. Income is the major determinant of eligibility for other veterans benefits.

It may soothe some frustration to understand why this

happened. A certain amount of the confusion about the rules for veterans benefits stems, ironically, from too much zeal on the part of Congress and the executive branch in trying to help the men and women who served their country in uniform.

Lawmakers have always been eager to improve existing programs or to create new ones. With each improvement, the fine print in the eligibility rules changes to correct some oversight or to address a problem that is beginning to emerge.

Because many veterans programs have been around since the end of World War I, it's inevitable that the rule books should become the legal equivalent of a patchwork quilt. To follow the thread linking most programs, it's helpful to keep in mind the five basic rules for veterans benefits:

1. *Your discharge papers are your ticket to most benefits.* Saying that you're a veteran may get you a free beer in a bar, but it won't open the door to any meaningful veterans benefits. You must prove that you're a veteran. The basic proof required for most veterans benefits is your official discharge papers. They've had many names over the decades, but in recent years they've been technically called "DD Form 214."

You get your discharge papers (which are actually just one document) on your last day on active duty. Be sure to keep them someplace safe. Many veterans rent a safety-deposit box at a neighborhood bank just to store this valuable document. Others take it to the clerk of courts in their hometown, who will preserve a copy among the court's official records, making it easier to get copies later.

Whatever you decide, make sure that other family members know where your discharge papers are. You might not be able to help them when they need to find them. And if you don't know where your discharge papers are, decide *today* to get a copy. Don't put it off. For details about getting copies of your discharge papers, see the chapter entitled "Tying Up Loose Ends with the Military."

2. *The burden is on you to show that you're eligible for a benefit.* The most important benefits—free medical care, VA pensions, home loans, and educational benefits—cost the government money, and money wrongly spent on benefits for ineligible people means there's a little less money left to pay for benefits for eligible, deserving veterans.

The same scrutiny befalls the spouses of veterans who attempt to qualify for certain benefits. They will be expected to produce marriage certificates before receiving any benefits offered to the spouses of former servicemembers.

Remember that paperwork "gatekeepers" guard the entrance to every major veterans program. Ultimately, those gatekeepers help you by ensuring that scarce federal resources aren't being wasted on ineligible people. Still, that knowledge won't always make it easier to deal with frustration and delay. But at least it makes some of the "paperwork exercises" a little less crazy.

3. *Getting approved for some benefits takes time.* Qualifying for VA disability compensation or a VA pension can take months, sometimes even more than a year. Fortunately, however, for some of the major veterans benefits, it takes only a few minutes to pass through all the gatekeepers. So long as you have your DD Form 214 or other discharge papers, you should be able to get rapid approval to buy a home using a GI Bill home loan or to draw on your GI Bill educational benefits at school.

VA medical care falls somewhere between the extremes. Most patients at VA hospitals and clinics are there because they've already qualified for VA disability compensation or VA pensions. Those in immediate need of emergency medical care, of course, get it. But they also may get a bill from the VA hospital for those services. VA hospitals are for the neediest veterans and for those with medical problems that have been officially rated as service connected.

Don't wait until you're ill before figuring out whether you might qualify for free treatment in a VA medical facility. Take the time, while you have the time, to find out how the rules apply to you.

4. *Everything changes.* Officials in Congress, the White House, the Department of Veterans Affairs, even the Pentagon are constantly refining the rules that affect veterans benefits.

Solving problems, resolving inequities, and meeting the limitations of budgets are among the factors that keep veterans benefits in a constant—though largely minor—flux.

> Change is a certainty for VA programs. Make sure you have the latest details.

As the United States approached the late 1990s, however, a sentiment for change touched the nation's medical system. It was called "health-care reform," and it held the potential for sweeping changes in the programs available to veterans. Whatever does, or doesn't, happen on the issue of health reform will have an impact on the VA medical system.

Former servicemembers and their families should remember that all explanations of veterans benefits will eventually become outdated. Even *Veteran's Guide.*

As the title of this volume states, this is a "guide," not a bible. Even the best road map changes, but that's no reason to keep your car in your driveway forever.

5. *There are plenty of experts to help you.* In every department store, some salespeople are better than others. Their skills and personalities cover the human spectrum. Some of them will appeal to you, some will turn you off, and to most you'll be indifferent. Despite their diversity, those salespeople will share a common trait: They're all interested in selling you something.

Keep that in mind when you're dealing with the employees of the Department of Veterans Affairs. They're as diverse as any group of people, but they also share a common trait: They have those jobs because they want to work with veterans. For the latest in information and for personalized help in obtaining veterans benefits, there's no substitute for a VA employee.

At most VA medical centers, the folks with the most comprehensive information are called "veterans benefits counselors." VA regional offices and benefits offices are also good places to go for help and information.

A list of all these VA facilities is found in the back of this book. Also in the back is a listing of major veterans groups that offer free, professional assistance to any veteran who requests it. That work is done by full-time staffers known as "service officers." Frequently, VA offices will refer veterans to a service officer for help in filing a claim for benefits.

You don't have to belong to a particular veterans group to consult its service officer. They exist to help all veterans, not just members.

# TWO

# KINDS OF VETERANS (AND SPOUSES, TOO)

---

**In This Chapter:**

- *Just-Plain-Veteran Veterans*
- *Exit Bonus Veterans*
- *Disabled Veterans*
- *Low-Income Veterans*
- *"Bad Paper" Veterans*
- *Military Retirees*
- *Special Veterans*
- *Spouses and Survivors*

---

Unique programs, valuable benefits, and important services are available to meet the needs of those who have served our country in the military, but getting them requires that would-be recipients take an active role. You must be your own "veterans' advocate." You must know what's reasonable to ask for, and which fights you can never win.

That's where *Veteran's Guide* comes in. It will help you to familiarize yourself with the benefits available to you, or to your veteran. To make that self-instruction a little easier, this chapter has divided veterans into seven major categories.

## JUST-PLAIN-VETERAN VETERANS

Most benefits for most veterans are, mostly, straightforward. There is an established array of programs. Eligibility rules have been constant. And it doesn't take a legal wizard to figure out who gets what.

Complications begin to arise when veterans have specific problems—a disability or an adverse discharge—that put them into a legally distinct category for qualifying for veterans benefits.

The benefits for those special cases are outlined later in this chapter. Here we'll look at a summary of the major programs and benefits available to what we'll call the "Just-Plain-Veteran" veteran. And since no discussion of a government program would be authentic without a newly coined acronym, let's call them the JPV vets.

What's a JPV vet? It's the typical man or woman who joins the military, serves a tour or two in uniform, and then returns to the old hometown, without any complications or problems connected with his or her military service. Most veterans are JPV vets.

Specifically, the JPV vet meets all of the following conditions:

- Not eligible for retirement.
- Not receiving exit bonus.
- Not disabled.
- Had received an honorable or general discharge.

The JPV vet qualifies for the basic package of veterans benefits offered by the federal government. And if you qualify as a JPV vet, you've passed through the first set of rules on the road to some of the most important veterans programs—health care in a facility run by the Department of Veterans Affairs, and possibly a VA pension.

The benefits for all veterans are built on the basic benefits package of the JPV vets. Here's a summary:

## Transition Benefits

- *Exit bonus:* No.
- *Final physical:* Yes.
- *Final dental checkup:* Yes.
- *Time off for job and house hunting:* Yes, but determined by the individual services.
- *Job-hunting classes, counseling, data banks:* Yes.
- *Payment for unused annual leave:* Yes.
- *Government-paid move back home:* Yes, but military may limit to original home or home of record.
- *Government-paid storage of household goods:* Yes, for 180 days.

## Back in Civilian Community

- *Unemployment compensation:* Yes, at least twenty-six weeks.
- *Reemployment rights:* Yes, but with many legal subtleties.
- *Obligation toward reserves:* Not unless part of original enlistment or commissioning contract.
- *GI Bill education benefits:* Only if signed up during first weeks on active duty or special sign-up "window."
- *GI Bill home loans:* Yes. Must meet financial qualifications for loan.
- *Life insurance:* Yes, must sign up within 120 days after discharge, pay regular premiums.
- *Preference for government jobs:* Must be a combat vet or disabled.
- *On-base military medical care:* No.
- *VA medical care:* Low priority.
- *Transition health insurance:* Yes, for most vets. Apply within thirty days after discharge, pay premiums. Eighteen-month maximum duration.

- *VA dental care:* Yes, for all vets within 180 days of discharge. Later, restricted eligibility.
- *Visit military commissary, exchange:* No, must qualify as retiree, reservist, or exit bonus veteran.
- *Continuing job-hunting help:* Yes.
- *Small-business loans:* Yes, but limited program with restricted eligibility.
- *VA disability compensation:* Only for medical problems officially recognized as service connected.
- *VA pension:* Only for low-income veterans in poor health.

## Other Veterans Issues

- *Wear military uniform:* At appropriate events.
- *Wear medals:* As appropriate, usually as lapel pin.
- *Replace medals:* Can request at any time.
- *Improve discharge:* Can apply at any time.
- *Correcting military records:* Can apply at any time.
- *Homes for veterans:* Must meet local eligibility rules.
- *Burial in national cemetery:* Yes, for most vets, plus spouses and dependent children.
- *Burial payments:* Yes, for most vets.
- *Burial flags:* For all in national cemetery or receiving burial payments.
- *Last honor guard:* Yes, but not absolute right. Unit must be available.

## Spouse's and Children's Benefits

- *VA pension for widows, widowers:* Not for JPV vet. Must qualify in some other category.
- *Pension for children:* Not for JPV vet. Must qualify in some other category.
- *Educational benefits:* Not for JPV vet. Must qualify in some other category.
- *Appointment to military academy:* Not for JPV vet. Must qualify in some other category.

## EXIT BONUS VETERANS

The reduction in the number of people on active duty after the end of the Cold War created a group of veterans with distinct experiences and unique federal benefits.

They continue to shop in commissaries and to visit military-run clinics for a period after their discharge. Previously, the only group of veterans who enjoyed these privileges were military retirees.

But the Pentagon still decides who can be Exit Bonus veterans. Either the military has tapped these people for involuntary discharges (and, in the process, given them separation pay) or it notified them that they could apply for special, early discharges and receive the Voluntary Separation Incentive (VSI) or Special Separation Benefit (SSB).

A word of caution: The term "Exit Bonus veteran" is used here for convenience. It doesn't show up in any federal law or military regulation. Identifying yourself as an Exit Bonus vet to a VA official, personnel clerk, or veterans counselor isn't going to help them understand your eligibility for any benefits or programs.

Here are the factors that, for our purposes, make a veteran an Exit Bonus veteran:

• Left active duty after October 1, 1990, with separation pay.

• Left active duty after October 1, 1990, with Voluntary Separation Incentive.

• Left active duty after October 1, 1990, with Special Separation Benefit.

It's important to note that the drawdown of the 1990s isn't a new phenomenon for the U.S. military. Periodically in recent decades, the armed forces have accelerated the return of people to the private sector.

Those earlier personnel reductions relied on a number of financial incentives to persuade people to leave, or to offset some of the pain for those selected involuntarily to go. Those

incentives have many names, such as severance pay and relo-
cation pay. They may resemble exit bonuses, but they're not the
same thing. Therefore, veterans who left the military before
October 1, 1990, shouldn't read their rights into any discussion
of benefits for Exit Bonus veterans.

Exit Bonus veterans are entitled to the full range of benefits and programs discussed above for Just-Plain-Veteran veterans. Plus, they qualify for a bit more. Here are some of those
additional benefits:

### Transition Benefits

- *Exit bonus:* Lump-sum bonus or annual payments.
- *Government-paid move back home:* Yes, to any place
selected.
- *Government-paid storage of household goods:* Yes, for
one year.

### Back in Civilian Community

- *Unemployment compensation:* Yes. VSI, SSB, and sepa-
ration pay may affect amount or duration.
- *Obligation toward reserves:* Yes. Length depends on type
of exit bonus.
- *GI Bill education benefits:* Can sign up before discharge.
- *Preference for government jobs:* Priority for non-appro-
priated-fund jobs.
- *On-base military medical care:* Yes, for 60 or 120 days,
depending on exit bonus.
- *VA medical care:* Low priority.
- *Transition health insurance:* Yes. Apply within 30 days
after end of eligibility for on-base medical care.
- *Visit military commissary, exchange:* For two years. Also
for spouse and dependents.

### Spouse's and Children's Benefits

• *Pension for widows, widowers, children:* VSI families continue to receive annual exit bonus payment.

## DISABLED VETERANS

Even during peacetime, the military is a dangerous place to be. The federal government recognizes that, and traditionally has offered special benefits for the men and women who have wounds, illnesses, or medical problems linked to their military service.

The major benefits involve a priority for free treatment in VA medical facilities and a monthly payment called "disability compensation."

Many veterans discover that the eligibility rules have been written generously. A medical problem doesn't have to be *caused* by military service: It's enough if a problem was *aggravated* during your time in uniform.

And there's no distinction between combat-related and non-combat-related problems. Veterans advocates like to point to the case of two veterans with the same chronic knee disorder. One was caused by a bullet in a firefight during active duty, the other by a cleat in a softball game during leave. Both knee injuries qualify as service connected, and that's the only distinction made by VA rules. But having an injury or illness officially certified as service connected requires an official ruling that can take months.

Once medical problems are rated as service connected, the veteran is then assigned a percentage figure ranging from 10 percent to 100 percent that denotes the severity of the problem.

Disabled veterans qualify for the full range of benefits offered to JPV vets. They also get more. Here are some special benefits for disabled veterans who already have rulings for service-connection status and percentage of disability:

## Transition Benefits

• *Exit bonus:* Can't receive this if being discharged with disability.

## Back in Civilian Community

• *Unemployment compensation:* Varies. If disability affects job performance, might not qualify.

• *Obligation toward reserves:* No. Disability prevents reserve service contract.

• *Home grants:* In addition to GI Bill loans, may receive money to adapt home.

• *Life insurance:* Special program for veterans with VA loans to adapt homes.

• *Vehicle allowance:* Grant for veterans with impaired mobility.

• *Clothing allowance:* About $500 annually if using prosthetics or orthopedics.

• *Preference for government jobs:* High priority.

• *On-base military medical care:* Space-available for 100 percent disabled.

• *VA medical care:* Free, high priority.

• *Transition health insurance:* No coverage for service-connected disabilities. May be covered for other medical problems.

• *VA dental care:* Yes, if 100 percent disabled or service-connected disabilities related to dental problems.

• *VA vocational rehabilitation:* Yes.

• *Visit military commissary, exchange:* If 100 percent disabled; privilege extends to spouse and dependent children.

• *VA disability compensation:* Yes.

• *VA pension:* No. Cannot receive pension and disability compensation at same time.

## Other Veterans Issues

• *Burial in national cemetery:* Yes.

• *Burial payments:* Yes.

## Spouse's and Children's Benefits

• *VA pension for widows, widowers:* Yes. Called "Dependency and Indemnity Compensation."

• *Pension for children:* Yes, if (1) unmarried and under eighteen, (2) in school and under twenty-three, or (3) older but medically incapable of self-support.

• *Educational benefits:* Special program for survivors, spouses, and children of disabled vets.

• *Home loans:* One-time benefit for spouse of disabled vets who die from service-connected disability.

• *Appointment to military academy:* Small number of appointments set aside for children of disabled veterans.

## LOW-INCOME VETERANS

Veterans were the beneficiaries of the country's original social safety nets. Going back to the time of the American Revolution, communities did special things to help the people who responded when the call to arms went out.

Then and now, not all of the things done for veterans relate directly to the hardships and health problems of serving in the military. A benefit providing an economic lifeline for thousands of veterans is the system of VA pensions. The pensions don't have anything to do with what you did in the military or what happened to you on active duty. Rather, VA pensions are given to veterans with low incomes. With the pensions goes eligibility for a range of other benefits.

Two pieces of fine print deserve special attention. First, VA pensions aren't welfare. Recipients must be unable to work because of age or a medical problem that doesn't qualify for VA disability compensation. Among the additional benefits that go with VA pensions are educational and vocational programs to get veterans back into the workforce.

Second, VA pensions are the one major veterans benefit that's linked to service during wartime: They are available only to veterans who served on active duty during officially declared periods of hostilities.

As with all veterans, recipients of VA pensions qualify for the basic package of benefits offered to JPV vets. Additionally, they're subject to these changes in that package:

## Back in Civilian Community

- *Obligation toward reserves:* Can't serve while drawing a VA pension.
- *Vocational training:* Special programs.
- *Preference for government jobs:* Yes, if received campaign ribbon.
- *On-base military medical care:* No.
- *VA medical care:* High priority.
- *VA dental care:* Yes.
- *VA disability compensation:* No, can't receive while drawing VA pension.
- *VA pension:* Yes. Monthly payment.

## Spouse's and Children's Benefits

- *VA pension for widows, widowers:* Yes, based on financial need.
- *Pension for children:* Yes, based on financial need for dependent children.
- *Educational benefits:* Special program for widows, widowers, and dependent children.

## "BAD PAPER" VETERANS

Not everyone who leaves the military is eligible for the full range of benefits that's available to the JPV vet.

People who get in trouble while on active duty often receive formal discharges that bar them from most veterans benefits. These are commonly called "adverse" discharges. Veterans advocates often refer to them as "bad paper" discharges. Into this category fall dishonorable discharges, bad conduct discharges, and discharges officially rated as "under conditions other than honorable." Also affected are discharges ordered by a general court-martial, discharges of conscientious objectors who refused military service, and discharges after 180 continuous days of unapproved absence, or AWOL.

The best news for Bad Paper veterans is that they don't have to stay that way for the rest of their lives. The military can review discharges and issue better ones—called "upgrades"—to veterans long after they leave active duty.

Getting an upgrade is your responsibility. Discharges aren't routinely reviewed with that in mind. To get an upgrade, you have to begin the paperwork. The chapter entitled "Tying Up Loose Ends with the Military" later in this book can get you started.

Not all Bad Paper veterans are equal. Many benefits are determined on a case-by-case basis. Still, here's a summary of the major benefits as they apply to most Bad Paper veterans:

## Transition Benefits
- *Exit bonus:* No.
- *Final physical:* Yes.
- *Final dental checkup:* Yes.
- *Time off for job and house hunting:* No.
- *Job-hunting classes, counseling, data banks:* Yes.
- *Payment for unused annual leave:* No.
- *Government-paid move back home:* Yes, but very restricted. Vets may get a bus ticket home.
- *Government-paid storage of household goods:* No.

## Back in Civilian Community
- *Unemployment compensation:* Frequently barred. Case-by-case decision.

- *Reemployment rights:* Frequently, no. Case-by-case decision.
- *Obligation toward reserves:* No, barred from service.
- *GI Bill education benefits:* No. Not even if previously signed up. Bar includes veterans with "general" discharges.
- *GI Bill home loans:* No.
- *Life insurance:* Case-by-case decision.
- *Preference for government jobs:* No.
- *On-base military medical care:* No.
- *VA medical care:* Case-by-case decision for treatment of service-connected problems.
- *Transition health insurance:* Yes.
- *VA dental care:* Case-by-case decision for treatment of service-connected dental problems.
- *Visit military commissary, exchange:* No.
- *Continuing job-hunting help:* Yes, through state-run programs, same as nonveterans.
- *Small business loans:* No.
- *VA disability compensation:* Not for discharge "under dishonorable conditions."
- *VA pension:* Not for discharge "under dishonorable conditions."

## Other Veterans Issues

- *Replace medals:* Can request at any time.
- *Improve discharge:* Can apply at any time.
- *Correcting military records:* Can apply at any time.
- *Homes for veterans:* Must meet local eligibility rules.
- *Burial in national cemetery:* Not if discharged "under dishonorable conditions."
- *Burial payments:* Not if discharged "under dishonorable conditions."
- *Burial flags:* Not if discharged "under dishonorable conditions."

• *Last honor guard:* Decision of local honor guard.

## Spouse's and Children's Benefits
• *VA pension for widows, widowers:* No.
• *Pension for children:* No.
• *Educational benefits:* No.
• *Appointment to military academy:* Applications considered alongside children of nonveterans.

## MILITARY RETIREES
Military service takes a few years from the lives of many Americans. For some, however, it takes much of their careers.

Military retirees have always been special members of the veterans community. They have devoted a large portion of their working lives to the nation's interests, and they have volunteered their families to join in sharing many of those hardships.

Traditionally, one of the hardships has been military pay. Although its purchasing power has increased substantially in recent decades, military pay still lags behind comparable salaries in the private sector, as measured by governmental and independent salary studies.

To offset this disparity, the government has historically offered military retirees a comprehensive package of programs. Civilian critics may argue it's too generous. But many veterans who have spent two or three years in uniform agree that military retirement benefits still don't make up for the hardships of two or three decades on active duty.

For much of this century, military retirement has been based on a minimum of twenty years on active duty. In 1993, as part of the 1990s drawdown, Congress approved full retirement benefits for selected—and that's a key word, *selected*—people who have spent at least fifteen years in uniform.

The fifteen-year retirement is a management tool to trim

down the active-duty force. Pentagon officials have said they intend to ask lawmakers to strike it from the books on October 1, 1999.

Fifteen-year retirees differ from the usual twenty-year retirees only in the size of their monthly retirement checks. All other benefits are equal.

Here's a summary of the major benefits for military retirees:

## Transition Benefits

- *Exit bonus:* No.
- *Final physical:* Yes.
- *Final dental checkup:* Yes.
- *Time off for job and house hunting:* Yes, but limited by service.
- *Job-hunting classes, counseling, data banks:* Yes.
- *Payment for unused annual leave:* Yes.
- *Government-paid move back home:* Yes, to any home selected.
- *Government-paid storage of household goods:* Yes, for one year.

## Back in Civilian Community

- *Unemployment compensation:* Varies by state.
- *Reemployment rights:* Yes, but with many legal subtleties.
- *Obligation toward reserves:* No. Must forfeit retired pay to join reserves.
- *GI Bill education benefits:* Only if signed up during first weeks on active duty or special sign-up "window."
- *GI Bill home loans:* Yes. Must meet financial qualifications for loan.
- *Life insurance:* Yes, must sign up within 120 days after discharge, pay regular premiums.

- *Preference for government jobs:* Must be combat vet or disabled. Must forfeit retired pay for some federal jobs.
- *On-base military medical care:* Lifetime eligibility, subject to space availability. Medicare becomes primary health provider at age sixty-five.
- *VA medical care:* Low priority.
- *Transition health insurance:* No. May purchase for spouse and dependent children. Eighteen-month maximum duration.
- *VA dental care:* Yes, like any vet, within 180 days of discharge.
- *Visit military commissary, exchange:* Lifetime eligibility for self, also for spouse and dependent children.
- *Continuing job-hunting help:* Yes.
- *Small business loans:* Yes, like any vet.
- *VA disability compensation:* Forfeits $1 in retired pay for each $1 in disability compensation.
- *VA pension:* No.


## Other Veterans Issues

- *Wear military uniform:* At appropriate events.
- *Wear medals:* As appropriate, usually as lapel pins.
- *Replace medals:* Can request at any time.
- *Improve discharge:* Can apply at any time.
- *Correcting military records:* Can apply at any time.
- *Homes for veterans:* Must meet local eligibility rules.
- *Burial in national cemetery:* Yes, same as most vets, plus spouses and dependent children.
- *Burial payments:* Yes.
- *Burial flags:* For all in national cemetery or receiving burial payments.
- *Last honor guard:* Yes, but not absolute right. Unit must be available.

### Spouse's and Children's Benefits

- *Pension for widows, widowers:* Only if signed up—and paid—for Survivors Benefit Plan.
- *Pension for children:* Coverage available through retiree-paid Survivors Benefit Plan.
- *Educational benefits:* Must qualify in some other category.
- *Appointment to military academy:* Limited number of appointments.


## SPECIAL VETERANS

Over the years, VA officials and lawmakers have come to realize that certain categories of veterans have special health problems related to their military service. They need VA-supervised medical care, even though they may not qualify for VA disability compensation, which carries with it an increased priority for medical care.

For these special veterans, VA medical facilities offer free "baseline" examinations to determine the general condition of their health. They are later eligible for priority treatment in VA medical facilities for problems suspected as being related to their military service.

The following are "special veterans":

- Former POWs.
- Veterans exposed to Agent Orange.
- "Atomic" veterans.
- Veterans affected by Gulf War syndrome.
- World War I veterans.
- Mexican Border War veterans.

The phrase "atomic veteran" refers to servicemembers exposed to ionizing radiation during atmospheric nuclear tests or during service in Hiroshima or Nagasaki immediately after the end of World War II.

Vietnam veterans exposed to Agent Orange or Gulf War veterans complaining of the illness known as Gulf War syndrome must be seeking care for problems they believe are directly related to those events.

These special veterans are eligible to apply for VA disability compensation. In all other respects, they have the same basic benefits as Just-Plain-Veteran veterans. Some may also be Exit Bonus veterans or even military retirees, qualifying for benefits appropriate for those statuses.

## SPOUSES AND SURVIVORS

Perhaps in a better, more affluent world, the wives and husbands of military veterans would get a little extra from their government. Many of them have had to make sacrifices and share in hardships because they were married to veterans. Every day, many spouses have to cope with a variety of problems related to the military service of their loved ones. But we live in a world of budgetary pressure, and even the federal government cannot pay for everything.

Still, there are some important benefits available for the spouses and survivors of some veterans. Here are some highlights:

• *Health insurance:* For families of disabled vets and vets who die from disabilities. Called "CHAMPVA."

• *Monthly pensions:* For survivors of disabled vets, vets who die from disabilities, and military people who die on active duty. Called Dependency and Indemnity Compensation.

• *Education assistance:* For families of disabled vets, vets who die from disabilities, and POWs.

• *Home loans:* For families of POWs and vets who die from disabilities. One-time benefit.

• *Federal job preference:* For spouses of veterans who die on active duty, spouses of 100 percent disabled veterans, and mothers of some disabled vets.

# THREE

# THE SOON-TO-BE VETERAN

### In This Chapter:

- *Exit Bonuses*
- *Final Paycheck*
- *Final Physical*
- *Health Care*

- *Dental Care*
- *Time Off*
- *Getting Home*
- *Job Search*

- *Unemployment Compensation*
- *Veterans Preference*

All who have ever been in the military carry for the rest of their lives sharp memories of the experiences they had, the emotions they felt, and the lessons they learned during those first fateful days as they made the switch from civilian to soldier.

Those heading in the opposite direction—leaving the military world and reentering the private sector—face a transition that's nearly as great. Granted, they've been civilians before, so the "unknowns" aren't as formidable. Still, taking off the uniform can be difficult for some people precisely because they're so sure they know what to expect on the "outside." Sadly, they're often wrong.

The civilian job market is changing at a dizzying pace. But there are other factors that make a transition difficult. Every upheaval in life is demanding, and people tend to lose their emotional resilience over the years. And everyone succumbs, from time to time, to pleasant fantasies about how effortless life is going to become after they cross some threshold.

Many emotional crises are natural and unavoidable. Some are completely preventable, especially the ones that can be eliminated by having sound plans and reasonable expectations built upon reliable information.

For the military member preparing to walk out the main gate for the last time, the government has provided a wide array of programs and benefits. Used successfully, transition benefits can ease the new veteran's return to the private sector. Used smartly, they can save time, eliminate financial difficulties, and lessen the emotional price that's paid whenever people make major changes in their lives. The key to using these benefits smartly and successfully is to understand them and to incorporate that knowledge into realistic plans.

Some benefits, like exit bonuses, are available only to specific categories of people. Others, like veterans preference and post-discharge health care, have significantly different provisions for different kinds of veterans. Even those benefits available to all veterans have fine print in their rules governing deadlines and application procedures.

A smooth transition is a well-planned transition. And a well-planned transition begins with solid information.

## EXIT BONUSES

For the last half century, one aspect of military life has been fairly constant. People who were planning to leave active duty and return to the civilian sector didn't have to worry about whether they would qualify for a special payment as they were walking out the door.

They didn't worry about that because there were no special end-of-service payments. People who served twenty years qualified for a retirement check, and people who had served less time than that didn't receive any special payments when they came to the end of their stint on active duty or in the reserves.

*E*xit *bonus* is an unofficial term with no precise meaning. Here, it's being used to describe the following:
- Voluntary Separation Incentive (VSI).
- Special Separation Benefit (SSB).
- Separation pay.
- Fifteen-year retirement.

Of course, there have been exceptions to this rule—principally, for servicemembers who became disabled and for people formally selected for discharge through proceedings that make them eligible for separation pay—but the vast majority of new dischargees didn't receive any sort of "walking money."

The personnel reductions that began in the early 1990s were a new experience for the U.S. military. For the first time since before World War II, the active-duty force was composed exclusively of people who wanted to be there. And they wanted to stay in uniform.

Congress and the Pentagon created new bonuses to entice some people to leave voluntarily and to soften the financial blow to others who were tapped for an involuntary departure. Rules for at least two venerable military institutions—retired pay and separation pay—were altered to fit changing circumstances.

This section on exit bonuses will discuss four financial tools that the military is handing to some soon-to-be veterans. They are the Special Separation Benefit (SSB), Voluntary Separation Incentive (VSI), separation pay, and fifteen-year retirement.

Like the drawdown itself, these exit bonuses won't go on forever. As of press time, Congress had planned to take away the military's legal authority to offer most of these exit bonuses on October 1, 1999.

If Congress goes ahead with that plan and the exit bonuses end, veterans who had already agreed to accept VSI or the fifteen-year retirement—two plans that provide yearly or monthly checks well into the twenty-first century—would continue to get their money on schedule.

## Eligibility

All of the exit bonuses have their own detailed eligibility rules. One rule, however, is shared by all four and stands out above all the fine print on qualification: If you're eligible for one of the exit bonuses, you'll be officially notified.

Keep in mind that the exit bonuses are a management tool that the military is using to thin the ranks. The goal is to have highly selective cuts. People with skills that are declining in usefulness will be offered exit bonuses. At the same time, others with needed skills are being held to serve out their entire enlistments or periods of obligation.

Skills aren't the only factor that determines who may be offered an exit bonus. Rank and branch of service also come into play. A final factor is time. As more—or fewer—people voluntarily leave the military from a group targeted for exit bonuses, the services will change the list of skills and ranks that qualify for exit bonuses.

## Common Traits

Each exit bonus also has its own rules and its own formulas for calculating benefits for eligible veterans. The bonuses have a few traits in common, one of which is very significant, especially around April 15 of each year: All of them are fully taxable.

Even though SSB, VSI, and separation pay may resemble pensions, and federal law has provisions protecting pension funds from taxes when they're being transferred from one financial account to another without passing through a retiree's hands, these exit bonuses are still treated as regular income by the Internal Revenue Service and state tax agencies.

Another common trait is that not everyone on active duty is equally eligible for the exit bonuses. The armed forces open up these programs from time to time to clearly defined groups of servicemembers.

Yet another trait that many—but not all—of them share is a fixed end. Congress has written into law the date of September 30, 1999, as the end for SSB, VSI, and the fifteen-year retirement. That end date may be extended or dropped entirely, so servicemembers anticipating a discharge near or after September 30, 1999, should check with a military personnel office to make sure that they have the latest information about those exit bonuses.

Separation pay will continue to be on the books. In fact, it was around long before the other exit bonuses. Its primary purpose has been to provide a financial cushion for a small number of senior people who are involuntarily discharged for reasons unrelated to the drawdown of the 1990s.

A final trait that all these special payments share is that their amounts are determined by using formulas that rely on "basic pay," the portion of every military paycheck that's based strictly on rank and number of years in uniform. Those formulas don't include such things as housing allowances, reenlistment bonuses, and hazardous duty pay.

## Special Separation Benefit

SSB is a onetime, lump-sum payment made on a person's last day in the military. To determine how much the servicemember will receive, the amount of basic pay that was paid for a person's last year on active duty is multiplied by 15 percent. That figure, in turn, is multiplied by the number of years on active duty.

SSB recipients must agree to spend at least three years in the Ready Reserve. Later, if they qualify for military retirement as reservists, they must repay the government for the full amount of the SSB.

If they later qualify for a retirement as federal civilians and use their military time to compute the amount of their civil service retirement checks, then they must pay a portion of their SSB into the civil service retirement fund.

## Voluntary Separation Incentive

VSI is a payment made first on the servicemember's last day of active duty and then annually on the anniversary of that date. Veterans receive VSI payments each year for twice the number of years that they spent on active duty.

Like the other exit bonuses, the VSI formula begins with the amount of basic pay that the veteran earned during his or her last year on active duty. That figure is multiplied by 2.5 percent. The figure derived from that calculation is then multiplied by the number of years the person spent on active duty.

VSI recipients must agree to serve in the Ready Reserve for as long as they receive the exit bonus. The pay they receive from the military for drill periods and two-week annual stints on active duty is unaffected by their VSI.

If these former servicemembers qualify for military retirement as reservists, their obligation to serve in the reserves ends without affecting their annual VSI payments. Some money will be withheld every month from their reserve retired pay, however, until they've paid back the entire VSI amount.

VSI recipients who qualify for retirement as federal civilians don't have to pay a portion of the VSI they have received into the civil service retirement fund, as happens with SSB recipients. If a VSI recipient dies before receiving the full amount of the exit bonus, annual payments will continue to his or her survivors.

## Separation Pay

Separation pay is a onetime, lump-sum bonus paid to some people who are forced out of the military involuntarily. To calculate the payment, the amount of basic pay earned by the veteran during the last year on active duty is multiplied by 10 percent. The product of that calculation is then multiplied by the number of years the person spent on active duty.

Separation pay recipients must spend at least three years in the Ready Reserve.

Unlike the other exit bonuses, separation pay comes in two distinct varieties—full separation pay and half separation pay.

Those with half separation pay, as the name implies, receive half the bonus determined by the usual formula for separation pay. It goes to specific categories of veterans who have blotches upon their military records but who still receive discharges that are graded as honorable or general.

Usually, full separation pay goes to people with good military records who are prevented from continuing in uniform, usually because too many people in the service possess the same skills. To be eligible for separation pay, servicemembers must have at least six years of total time on active duty, at least five years of continuous active duty, and less than twenty years in uniform.

Ineligible for either full separation pay or half separation pay are veterans who can receive military retirement pay, servicemembers who have spent only their initial obligated periods or initial enlistments on active duty, and people receiving dishonorable discharges, bad conduct discharges, or discharges rated as "other than honorable."

Separation pay is the oldest exit bonus. Started long before the post–Cold War drawdown, it was once restricted to officers and capped at $30,000.

The rules for separation pay have undergone a major overhaul to make it solve some of the problems of the current reduction in military forces. Enlisted members and warrant officers are now eligible, without any limits on maximum payments.

## Fifteen-Year Retirements

Since 1993, military people have been able to retire after periods in uniform that are at least fifteen years but less than twenty years.

Until the fifteen-year retirement took effect, twenty years was the magic milestone for retirees. Anyone with less than twenty years' service was ineligible for any kind of annuity from the military.

Although fifteen-year retirees are every bit as much military retirees as the twenty-year people, there are some differences. The major one involves eligibility for the fifteen-year retirement. Like the other exit bonuses, the fifteen-year retirement isn't something that military people volunteer for: They're selected. The selection relies on the manpower needs of the armed forces, based on skills, rank, and other factors.

Although it's commonly called the "fifteen-year retirement," this program applies to those with between fifteen and twenty years of service.

Like the other exit bonuses, the computation of the monthly payment to fifteen-year retirees begins with the person's basic pay and does not consider such military income as housing allowances, reenlistment bonuses, and hazardous duty pay. As with the twenty-year retirement system, that starting amount of basic pay is an average of the amount received during the servicemember's last thirty-six months on active duty. This is commonly called the "High-Three" system, meaning the peak earning of basic pay for the last three years. That average basic pay is multiplied by 2.5 percent for each year the person spent on active duty.

But here's where the formula for fifteen-year retirements gets tricky. Once a figure is achieved by multiplying years of service by 2.5 percent, that figure, in turn, is reduced by one-twelfth of a percentage point for each month that a person's active-duty service falls short of the twenty-year mark.

When it comes to military benefits, fifteen-year retirees are treated in the same way as twenty-year retirees. They have lifetime access to commissaries and base exchanges. They have access, on a space-available basis, to on-base clinics and hospitals, and until they qualify for Medicare, they can rely on CHAMPUS or Tricare, the military's health insurance programs.

Spouses, dependent children, and some other dependents qualify for many of the same benefits. And fifteen-year retirees can also sign up for the Survivors Benefit Plan, which guarantees a regular monthly check for family members if a military retiree dies.

Like the more traditional twenty-year retirees, those with at least fifteen years' service are technically subject to recall to active duty during emergencies but are ineligible to serve in the reserves or National Guard while drawing retirement pay.

And if they later qualify for retirement as federal civilians, they may have to repay the government some of their military retired pay if they include their years on active duty in computing their civil service retirements.

## Fine Points

Although the military labels some exit bonuses as voluntary and others as involuntary, the overriding goal of those programs is to reduce the number of people on active duty.

As the rules have been written, if someone is going to leave the military anyway, like a retiree or a new servicemember nearing the end of the first enlistment, there's no reason to pay him extra to leave. Consequently, the military doesn't.

Some servicemembers have painted themselves into an unpleasant corner by formally beginning the string of paperwork that leads to a discharge, confident that they'll receive an exit bonus, only to discover later that the military won't give them extra money to leave because they've already volunteered—in writing—to separate without a bonus.

Be slow and deliberate in all decisions involving your discharge from active duty. If you want an exit bonus, make sure the military has decided that you're eligible for one before signing any agreements to separate from service.

## FINAL PAYCHECK

The last check that most veterans receive from the military is a pleasant surprise. If they have accumulated leave time that hasn't been used, those days are converted into dollars and added to the check. For some, however, the final paycheck is an unpleasant surprise, when they discover the government is balancing the books for debts owed.

> The worst day to settle pay problems is your last day. Count on the government to remember—and settle—all debts you owe them. Plan as if they'll overlook all money they owe you.

Far more new veterans leave the military confused about their paychecks. On discharge day, the government gives everyone paperwork showing what's been done to the final paycheck, but the paperwork isn't always clear. This section outlines some important information you should know about the final paycheck.

### Method of Payment

More and more servicemembers are choosing the direct deposit option for their regular paychecks. That's the system in which the government electronically sends their paychecks to a bank or other financial institution. The last paycheck, however, isn't a part of the direct deposit scheme. In fact, it usually cannot be made by electronic deposit. If you do nothing, the government will give you a check during your last day on active duty for all the money the government owes you.

You may be able to receive all—or some—of your final payment in cash. That depends on your local installation. If you want cash, find out well in advance of your final day what the local rules are. You'll have to submit a formal request for a cash payment.

Cash payments cannot be picked up by anyone other than the person leaving active duty, even if that person has power of attorney. When the final pay is issued in the form of a check, servicemembers can have someone else pick it up. Usually, this requires a formal power of attorney that specifically empowers a person to perform such functions. Again, don't wait until the last day to find out what the local rules are.

### Leave

Everyone in the military gets thirty days off each year. For most people, any leave that has not been used by the last day of service will be automatically "cashed in" in the final paycheck.

For each day of unused leave, veterans receive one-thirtieth of their basic pay. Sixty days' leave is the most a servicemember can cash in.

Subtractions for leave can be made from the final paycheck if the servicemember was absent without leave or exceeded time-off limits for such transition-related items as house hunting or job hunting. For all subtractions from the final paycheck, finance offices again use the formula of one-thirtieth of the monthly basic pay for each day of unauthorized absence.

Not everyone is eligible to cash in unused leave. Cash-in privileges are denied to veterans with dishonorable discharges, bad conduct discharges, and discharges that are officially labeled as "under other than honorable conditions."

## Debts

Death and taxes are supposed to be the two certainties in life. Military people approaching the end of their active-duty stints can add a third: The government won't forget to collect for any debts.

Outstanding bills for damaged or missing equipment come due on discharge day if servicemembers haven't resolved the issue beforehand.

Reenlistment bonuses and some special education that carried an obligation for specific periods of additional active duty can also result in deductions if the servicemember hasn't given the government all the time for which he or she was paid.

## Exit Bonuses

Recipients of SSB and separation pay can expect to receive bonus checks on their last day on active duty.

VSI recipients will receive their first year's payment on discharge day. Additional payments will follow on the anniversary of that date.

Fifteen-year retirees will receive monthly retirement checks for the rest of their lives, usually beginning a month after leaving the service.

## Taxes

Taxes are still a certainty for everyone taking off the uniform. You can count on the finance office to deduct federal and state income taxes, plus Social Security taxes, from the final paycheck, including exit bonuses. The amount of the withholding is determined by standard tax tables.

If a servicemember had no state tax withheld from the regular paychecks because he or she claimed residence in a state that doesn't have an income tax, then no state tax will be withheld from the final paycheck.

Veterans should be forewarned, however. Moving after discharge to a state that imposes a state income tax may put you in a position in which you owe state income tax on portions of the final paycheck.

### Health Insurance

Except for retirees, everyone leaving active duty can apply for a transitional health insurance plan. As with civilian health insurance, participants must pay premiums for the coverage. The first premium is due on the day of discharge. People who want the coverage can pay the premium by subtracting it from the final paycheck.

If a paycheck is smaller than a premium, which happens only for folks with unusually large families or sizable debts to the government, then the servicemember must write a check on the spot to the government for the balance.

### FINAL PHYSICAL

You were in top-notch physical condition when you entered the military. Otherwise, they wouldn't have taken you.

If your military service created or aggravated medical problems, you're entitled to compensation and treatment from the Department of Veterans Affairs.

> Insist on a final physical exam. Decades from now, your family's financial future may depend on VA benefits based on that physical.

VA compensation and care can begin years after your discharge. You don't have to be among the "walking wounded" limping out the main gate to qualify—eventually—for treatment for a service-connected medical problem.

What is a minor ailment at age twenty-three, for example,

an occasionally painful back injury incurred on active duty, can become a disability that prevents you from earning an income when you're fifty-three.

VA offices routinely grant benefits to veterans decades after their original injuries, wounds, or illnesses in the military, but establishing the connection between those medical conditions and military service becomes more difficult for veterans who didn't receive a comprehensive physical examination when they left active duty.

Everyone has a legal right to a final physical. Transition counselors and veterans advocates urge that everyone leaving the military insist upon getting one.

Be sure to mention any injuries or serious illnesses that occurred on active duty, even ones that don't seem to have left any major aftereffects. Some ailments have a tendency to worsen over time.

And while you're at it, transition counselors recommend applying for VA disability compensation as part of the discharge process. A small legal subtlety becomes very important here. You don't need to have a disability in order to apply for disability compensation. You can even shout at the top of your lungs as you're signing the application form that you're a remarkable physical specimen.

Filing the application is a tactical move. By applying for VA disability compensation, you transfer a copy of your military medical files into the VA system and open up a file with the VA. Any later dealings with a VA office, even decades after your discharge, will be easier if those steps have already been taken.

And let's not forget a more immediate and traditional reason for getting a physical examination. Some folks have medical problems that haven't displayed major symptoms yet. The predischarge physical will be the last time for years that many soon-to-be veterans will see a doctor.

## HEALTH CARE

The medical bills of many people in the United States are paid by health insurance plans offered by their employers, but until recently, new veterans looking for civilian jobs often found themselves having to decide between two unfavorable options: They could gamble that they would stay healthy until they got a job with employer-provided coverage, or they could pay from their own pockets the exorbitant premiums demanded by many private health insurance plans.

Since the start of the drawdown in the early 1990s, however, Congress and the Pentagon have rewritten the traditional rules about health care for veterans. The result is two major services—a government-sponsored health insurance plan and continued access to on-base medical facilities—that are available to new veterans and their families.

### Health Insurance

Nearly everyone leaving the military is able to purchase coverage from a special transitional health insurance plan, which offers veterans the low rates usually available only from group plans.

Health-care rules are constantly changing. Make sure your medical plans are based on the latest, most detailed information.

The longest for which coverage can be purchased is eighteen months; the shortest is three months. The coverage can be purchased only in three-month blocks, and the first payment is due on the date of discharge. Premiums for three months' coverage in 1997 were $993 for an individual and $1,996 for a family.

Generally, participants pay the first $500 in yearly medical expenses, and the plan picks up 80 percent of the rest. These figures are only approximations.

Lawmakers designed this health insurance plan to make it available to the widest possible group of veterans. Even those with dishonorable discharges, bad conduct discharges, or discharges that are officially rated as "under other than honorable conditions" can obtain this insurance.

Coverage can also be provided under the plan for spouses and dependent children. Servicemembers don't have to take the insurance for themselves in order to purchase it for their families.

Generally, military retirees and those leaving active duty with an officially rated disability are ineligible for this health insurance, although those veterans can purchase coverage for their spouses and dependent children.

Booklets with detailed information about these plans, including covered services and current rates, are available from transition offices and family support centers.

## Transition Health Care

Until the 1990s drawdown, the only veterans with access to the military's on-base hospitals and clinics were military retirees. Everyone else had to go to a VA medical center, even to deal with complications that resulted directly from treatments on active duty.

That's changed, at least for recipients of SSB, VSI, and separation pay, both at the full rate and at the half rate. For them, it's possible to continue using an on-base military medical facility for a few months after discharge. Coverage includes the family members of eligible veterans.

Open to these veterans are military hospitals, outpatient clinics, dental facilities, and rehabilitation facilities. The benefit also includes coverage under CHAMPUS and Tricare, the military's health insurance programs.

Participants receive the same priority on the waiting list as the dependents of active-duty people. There is no charge for on-base medical care; veterans pay the same CHAMPUS and Tricare rates as everyone else.

This on-base health care is not available to first-termers or officers completing their initial obligated tours. Military retirees, including fifteen-year retirees, and veterans receiving VA disability compensation are covered by other medical programs.

This is one benefit with two crisp deadlines. The deadline that applies to you depends on your time in uniform. The coverage lasts 60 days for people with less than six years on active duty and 120 days for people with six or more years on active duty.

While most veterans must purchase government-backed health insurance on discharge day and only have eighteen months' coverage, those eligible for transitional health care don't have to sign up for this special health insurance until the end of their 60-day or 120-day periods of on-base care.

Like everyone else, they can purchase health insurance for only eighteen months. But the "clock" on that one-year period doesn't begin until they've ended their 60-day or 120-day stretches of free, on-base medical care.

## DENTAL CARE

Routine dental checkups shouldn't be put off until the last minute by military folks approaching their discharges. Under the best of circumstances, appointments are hard to get. And under the worst, if a checkup detects a problem that requires additional stretches in the dental chair, there may not be enough time left on active duty to schedule follow-up appointments.

The special transition health insurance plan doesn't cover routine dental checkups or most dental services.

Recipients of exit bonuses who are in their special postdischarge periods of 60 or 120 days of continued access to on-base military facilities are eligible for dental care. They don't receive an extra priority when it comes to scheduling appointments, however.

Because of the difficulties many military members experience in getting dental care before their discharges, the government has created a unique benefit for new veterans: Most veterans are eligible for a onetime dental examination and treatment in any VA dental facility, without going through the normal hassles of filing for VA benefits.

To receive this onetime VA dental care, veterans must apply for it at a VA medical facility within 90 days of discharge. In most cases, the treatment must be completed within 180 days of discharge. This VA care will be denied to veterans who saw a military dentist within 90 days of discharge. Exceptions can be made for veterans whose treatments in active-duty dental facilities were incomplete at the time of discharge.

## TIME OFF

A successful transition from active duty to civilian life takes planning. And some plans require your physical presence to find facts, discuss arrangements, and make deals. In fact, it's nearly impossible to find a home or a job by long distance. You need to be there. And that will require time away from the military before you're discharged.

Several different programs are on the books that make it easier for active-duty people to get away from their military duties during the last months in uniform. They all share one major trait: They're not absolute rights. Unit commanders have the final say in whether people get time away from their official duties.

### Excess Leave

Commanders can grant up to an extra thirty days' leave (beyond the thirty days' leave everyone in the military receives) for people approaching the end of their military careers. This is called excess leave.

First, let's put excess leave in perspective. Everyone in full-time military service, regardless of rank or the time they've spent in uniform, receives 2.5 days of leave every month.

Excess leave is permission to use leave time that hasn't been earned yet but that will be earned by the time the person is discharged. Say you're scheduled to leave the military in December and your commander grants excess leave in August, knowing you'll be credited with at least seven more days of leave by your discharge date.

In this example, if you suddenly leave the military in September, which is after you've taken the extra days away from work but before you've been credited with enough leave to fill the gap, then you would have to repay the government for the excess leave. In that case, you would see your final military paycheck shrink by one-thirtieth of your basic pay for each day of excess leave.

## Permissive Temporary Duty

Time away from work that isn't charged against annual leave is called permissive temporary duty. Sometimes, commanders give people in their units permission not to report for work. Instead, they're supposed to use that time for specific, approved activities. House hunting and job hunting can fall into this category.

This time doesn't affect annual leave: Servicemembers won't see their final paychecks reduced because they've taken it.

For transition-related activities, Congress has placed a limit of ten days' permissive temporary duty for everyone in uniform. Keep in mind that the ten-day limit isn't the same as a right to ten days. The individual services can impose ser-vicewide limits of less than ten days, as can major commands and specific units and offices.

### Terminal Leave

When you spend your last active-duty days on leave, you're said to be on terminal leave.

Many veterans find it convenient to take official leave time from their military jobs in the weeks before discharge. Then, instead of returning for a few days when their discharge date approaches, they go directly from "leave status" to civilian status.

Like so much in the military, terminal leave is subject to a swarm of restrictions. The first major hurdle is getting the approval of one's unit commander. Other restrictions may apply to veterans leaving active duty with exit bonuses.

Still more complications can arise for people who use terminal leave for vacations or to travel to their new homes. These folks are still on active duty and drawing regular military pay, but the government won't pay extra mileage or per diem for vacations or extra travel. If you're traveling or vacationing while on terminal leave, make sure you've clearly discussed your plans with people from the local personnel office. Make sure you—and they—understand the portions of your trip that should be covered by government benefits and the portions that must be paid from your own pocket. This can prevent a rude surprise when you open your final paycheck. Odds are, the government will resolve any discrepancies in its favor.

### GETTING HOME

When you came on active duty, the military paid to move you away from home. At the end of your stint in uniform, the military will pay to send you back home.

That's the good news. The bad news is that the who-gets-what-and-how-much-of-it rules governing household moves in the military are complex. And they're not any simpler for the last move back to the civilian world.

In a nutshell, most of the same allowances and limitations that affect regular active-duty moves—what the services call permanent-change-of-station, or PCS, moves—are in force for the final move.

## Where's Home?

Generally, the military will pay to send newly discharged servicemembers, their families, and their worldly possessions back to their official homes—called the "homes of record"—or to the places they entered active duty.

Many veterans, however, don't want to go there when they walk out the main gate for the last time. They go to other parts of the country.

Free booklets for a low-hassle last move are available from military transportation offices.

In those instances, the military figures out what your benefits would be if they sent you back to your home of record or the place you entered active duty. That calculation becomes a maximum payment. You can't get more by moving to a more distant part of the country.

If the place you actually settle is closer to your last assignment than your home of record, however, then your allowances and payments are based on the actual distance to your new home.

Those are the rules for most veterans. A more generous definition of "home" applies to others. They can have their household goods moved to anywhere in the country. Eligible for this expanded benefit are military retirees (including fifteen-year retirees) and recipients of VSI, SSB, and separation pay.

Even for this group, however, there can be a hitch getting the military to pick up the bills to move to Hawaii or Alaska.

If a veteran entered the military from either of those states or lists one as the official home of record, there should be no problem. Other retirees or exit bonus recipients dreaming of a government-paid move to the Yukon or Waikiki should check the fine print in the rules at the nearest military transportation office.

Veterans with "bad paper," that is, with discharges that are officially rated as "under other than honorable conditions," typically get a bus ticket—or enough money to purchase one—returning them to their civilian homes.

## Household Goods

The government promises to do more than put discharged veterans on an airplane. It will also make the necessary arrangements and pay the bills for the shipment of all the stuff in their homes.

Generally, personal property and household goods are treated in the last government-paid move under the same rules and benefits that apply to government-ordered moves while people are still on active duty.

The nearest military transportation office will make most of the arrangements with trucking companies to pick up your household goods and to deliver them.

As with normal PCS moves, folks returning home from active duty must keep an eye on the household goods weight table, the chart that specifies how many pounds of stuff the government will pay to move. Each rank has its own weight allowance, and there are different rates within each rank for single people and those with families. Trucking companies send their bills for those moves directly to the government. If discharged veterans go over their weight allowances, they must pay for the excess.

## WEIGHT ALLOWANCES
### (Limits in Pounds for Government-Paid Moving and Storage)

| Rank | With Dependents | Without Dependents |
|------|-----------------|--------------------|
| 0-6 to 0-10 | 18,000 | 18,000 |
| 0-5, W-5 | 17,500 | 16,000 |
| 0-4, W-4 | 17,000 | 14,000 |
| 0-3, W-3 | 14,500 | 13,000 |
| 0-2, W-2 | 13,500 | 12,500 |
| 0-1, W-1 | 12,000 | 10,000 |
| E-9 | 14,500 | 12,000 |
| E-8 | 13,500 | 11,000 |
| E-7 | 12,500 | 10,500 |
| E-6 | 11,000 | 8,000 |
| E-5 | 9,000 | 7,000 |
| E-4>2Years | 8,000 | 7,000 |
| E-4<2Years | 7,000 | 3,500 |
| E-3 | 5,000 | 2,000 |
| E-2 | 5,000 | 1,500 |
| E-1 | 5,000 | 1,500 |

## Payments

The government will also pay to get you and your family members back home. At one time, that government obligation could be met by handing soon-to-be-discharged people a bus ticket. Later that was upgraded to an airplane ticket. In fact, a government-paid airline ticket is what single veterans who don't own a car will receive.

Usually, for family members to qualify for a government-paid move, they must meet all the official criteria for being "dependents." The general rule is that if the military will give them ID cards, it will pay to move them.

Most veterans driving their personal cars to postdischarge homes qualify for two separate payments: MALT and per diem.

***MALT:*** MALT (which stands for mileage allowance in lieu of transportation) is a payment to cover the expenses of operating the car. It's calculated at so many cents per mile—fifteen cents per mile in 1997. The rate increases if dependents are in the car. In 1997, the top payment was twenty cents per mile. Two-car families can get those rates for each car.

***Per Diem:*** This per diem (which means "by the day") is an allowance paid by the government for food and lodging expenses during a move. In 1997, the rate was $50 daily for the veteran, plus $37.50 for a spouse, $37.50 for another dependent over twelve, and $25 for a dependent under twelve.

If travelers pay less for food and shelter than they receive in their per diems, they can pocket the savings. If they pay more, the government won't give them extra money.

Normally, the people receiving this per diem are the ones driving home after leaving the military. Partial payments may be offered to people using airplanes, buses, or trains.

The military has several different things that are called "per diem." Perhaps the most widely known one, which can range up to several hundred dollars daily, goes to people on official duty for short periods of time in high-cost areas.

The per diem offered to discharged veterans has a single rate. It doesn't increase for people passing through expensive cities on their way home.

## Storage

Quite often, home isn't ready when newly discharged veterans arrive there. Despite the best planning and precious days of annual leave spent in the new community long before discharge, many veterans still aren't able to occupy their new homes after the moving van pulls up at the curb. For them, the government will put property into storage at government expense. The usual limit is 180 days of storage, and most often, the government picks the storage facility. The government also pays to have the goods moved from storage and into the new home.

The time limit on government-paid storage is considerably longer for some veterans. Included in this group are retirees, SSB recipients, and VSI recipients. They are entitled to one year's storage at government expense.

Stored goods also figure into the official weight table for household goods. The material put in storage, *plus* the goods moved directly into the home, must total fewer pounds than the amount listed on the table. Veterans must pay for any excess.

### Calculating Days and Miles

The military has its own version of practically everything, including its own way of measuring time and distance. Veterans planning for their final government-paid move shouldn't assume that the military relies on the standard way of reading a map or the calendar.

Transportation offices have their own charts that give the official distance between two points. For computing the mileage used in the MALT formula, for example, officials will rely on the distance cited in those charts. A veteran's actual experience on the road doesn't carry any weight.

When it comes to per diem, which is based on the number of days a veteran spends on the road, the military also has its own calendar. Generally, for people traveling by car, per diem is computed on the basis that folks will travel 350 miles in one day. Put another way, one day equals 350 miles.

If you can cover more ground and consequently spend less time on the road, you can keep the extra per diem money. If you travel at a slower rate than 350 miles per day, you can't get extra per diem for the additional time.

## The Bottom Line

In many ways, your discharge from active duty is the end of your relationship with the U.S. military. In one sense—the financial sense—the military wants to make your last day in uniform the end of its dealings with you.

The military wants to give you all the money you're owed, including all the travel-related payments for moving back home, on your last day on active duty.

Don't wait till the last minute to understand what your travel benefits should be. And if you don't understand—or don't agree with what's offered—don't assume you can straighten it out after discharge.

Problems with pay and allowances get tougher to solve the closer you get to walking out the main gate for the last time.

## JOB SEARCH

Leaving the military, for most people, is the second major problem confronting them as the day of their discharge approaches. The number one priority is finding a civilian job.

> Don't wait for an invitation to use transition programs. Invite yourself. Learn about the job-hunting tools that the military offers.

Military veterans return to the private sector with experiences, skills, and formal training they didn't possess when they first marched off to active duty. Many employers need people with the skills and knowledge acquired only during years of service in the military. Supervisors value the personal traits—the reliability, trainability, maturity, and drug-free status—of people who have put in a few years in uniform. For these reasons, many jobs go to veterans instead of equally qualified—or perhaps even slightly better qualified—civilian competitors.

Still, the first job search after taking off the uniform is a painful, perplexing time for many veterans. Too often, they don't have a realistic sense of their own value to employers. Few have much experience "selling" themselves to a potential boss, and most are hard-pressed to translate their military skills, experiences, and training into terms meaningful to a nonveteran.

Fortunately, there are a variety of resources available to help veterans find private-sector jobs that are tailored to their interests, skills, and financial obligations.

## State Employment Agencies

Perhaps the most valuable and underused resource for returning veterans is the employment agencies operated by every state. These offices charge no fees, and they're professionally staffed. They offer free, one-on-one counseling for job seekers. They hold their own free seminars on job search skills and resume writing. They serve as clearinghouses for other private and governmental agencies with information of use to people seeking employment.

The staffs include people who work largely with veterans. Disabled veterans are a special priority, and everyone with an officially rated disability should make sure that his or her counselors at the state employment agency are aware of that. Often, it can make the difference at hiring time.

Of course, the most valuable tool at these agencies is the listing of available jobs. Many firms get most of their new employees through these state agencies.

Although each agency has slightly different procedures, at all offices job seekers are able to browse through the list of vacancies and see what jobs are open, which employers are hiring, and what skills are demanded for specific vacancies.

As the country becomes increasingly computerized, more state offices are linking themselves to a computer network only available to state employment agencies. This computer network has up-to-the-minute listings for jobs across the entire country, making it possible for servicemembers in the last months of active duty to find out about openings in their hometowns.

### Defense Outreach Referral Service

One of the best employment tools for veterans is used strictly by employers. The Defense Outreach Referral Service, or DORS, is a computerized system for distributing mini resumes.

Participating employers tap into this computer network when searching for new employees. It permits them to scan rapidly through a large number of mini resumes and identify veterans with specific training or on-the-job experience.

If employers see a computerized mini resume that looks promising, they will contact the servicemember and ask for a more detailed, traditional resume. Or they may even summon the veteran for an interview.

DORS is free and voluntary for military people during their last months on active duty. Different services and installations have their own guidelines for when folks may submit their mini resumes to DORS, but usually it's within the last six months on active duty.

Servicemembers must take the initiative to ensure that their names and backgrounds are entered into DORS. To start, military folks first must get a standardized DORS application. These are usually obtained at the transition centers, although at some installations they may also be available at personnel offices or family support centers.

After filling out the form and returning it to the proper office, military people will have that information entered into the computer system, usually by a personnel clerk, although computer-literate folks may be asked to enter the information themselves.

The mini resumes are automatically erased after a certain interval, usually about ninety days. Military members can resubmit their applications, even after discharge, although individual services and installations set their own deadlines. You must take the initiative. Find out when your initial mini resume will be purged from the system. Then hand in another application at the correct date.

## Transition Bulletin Board

Although employers are the only ones who can call up information from DORS on a computer screen, there is at least one computer network that's used directly by servicemembers and veterans. Called the Transition Bulletin Board, it's a way for people approaching their discharge dates to get information that will help them return successfully to the private sector.

Job fairs, regional updates on the employment picture, and names and addresses of organizations interested in helping newly discharged veterans are posted on the Transition Bulletin Board.

Like DORS, this computerized service is free. Terminals connected to the network are located in transition assistance centers, personnel offices, or family support centers. Also like DORS, it's a tool with a specific purpose. It can't take the place of other efforts, like checking the vacancies at a state employment agency, reading the want ads in a newspaper, or networking with potential employers.

## Veterans Associations

Some of the best networking tools for new veterans, especially those who settle in a strange community after their discharge, are the veterans associations.

For the 1990s drawdown, many of these organizations have created programs to help recently discharged job seekers. Most of the formal programs are free, available to nonmembers, and even open to folks not eligible for membership. Local chapters of the groups are usually listed in the telephone book. The Appendix of *Veteran's Guide* contains addresses and telephone numbers for national offices.

The Non Commissioned Officers Association (NCOA) is a major sponsor of job fairs for all veterans, even officers. The Retired Officers Association and Air Force Association offer one-on-one counseling and resume critiques.

Broad-membership veterans groups like the American Legion and the Veterans of Foreign Wars have their own job-search programs. Disabled American Veterans and Paralyzed American Veterans have specialized programs for people who leave active duty with lingering physical problems.

The major veterans groups have chapters in every community, with membership drawn from across the full spectrum of industries, occupations, and skill levels. By joining one of them and taking an active role in its local activities, you begin the process of meeting people who can pass along information about good places to work, places to avoid, and job openings that haven't been publicized.

## UNEMPLOYMENT COMPENSATION

Not everyone lands a job immediately after leaving active duty. Many new veterans spend their first weeks back in the private sector looking for work. Most of them are eligible for the same unemployment compensation paid to civilian workers who lose their jobs through layoffs and plant closings.

Although unemployment compensation is a nationwide program, each state administers it. States write their own rules within broad guidelines issued by the federal government. For many years, the states wrote those rules quite differently when it came to ex-military people. Veterans applying for unemployment compensation immediately after leaving active duty were treated differently than civilians. Typically, the first month of postdischarge unemployment wasn't covered by unemployment compensation. Veterans were often eligible to receive the weekly financial help for only about half as long as civilians.

That changed in 1991, when Congress passed a federal law equalizing the benefits for veterans and civilians.

While the same rules must apply within each state for veterans and civilians, there still are differences in the rules from one state to another, and veterans shouldn't assume that some fact about unemployment compensation in one state will hold true in another. Ask direct questions to learn about the details in the state in which you plan to settle after taking off the uniform.

### Eligibility

Most people leaving active duty are eligible for unemployment compensation. A few specific categories of people aren't eligible.

An unexpectedly pleasant rule for many veterans is the fact that there are no residency requirements for unemployment compensation. You can file for unemployment compensation in any state. It doesn't have to be your home state. It doesn't have to be the most recent state in which you've lived. It doesn't even have to be a state where you've ever lived. The only residency requirement is that you file for unemployment compensation from the state where you live after leaving active duty.

While most veterans are eligible for unemployment compensation, a few groups may run into trouble. Here's the breakdown for those groups:

- *Retirees:* Usually ineligible.
- *Bad Paper veterans:* Frequently ineligible. Depends on specific discharge and the state.
- *Disabled veterans:* Not eligible if disability prevents veteran from holding a job.

- *Early outs:* May have trouble in a few states.
- *Exit Bonus veterans:* May find their eligibility delayed.

## Leaves and Government Checks

The basic idea behind unemployment compensation is to use taxpayer money to help folks without an income while they're looking for work. If people have an income—or something that looks like an income—then state officials become reluctant to approve them for the program.

To most states, "cashing in" leave time looks like income. Typically, if you cashed in twenty-one days of unused leave when you left the military, state officials will say you're ineligible for unemployment compensation for the first twenty-one days after discharge.

Something similar happens in many states to recipients of exit bonuses. They will treat an exit bonus as if it is an advance salary payment, then refuse to give the veteran unemployment compensation until after the "salary" runs out.

For example, let's consider the case of someone whose basic pay on active duty was $3,000 per month and who receives an exit bonus of $30,000. In most states, the $30,000 will be treated as if it's ten months' salary for this veteran, and the veteran won't be eligible for unemployment compensation until the start of the eleventh month after leaving the military.

In a slightly different way, the same philosophy affects military retirees and those receiving some sort of disability pay. If the state law permits unemployment compensation for retirees and the disabled—and that's a big "if"—then the state may reduce unemployment compensation by one dollar for each dollar of retired pay or disability pay.

## Details of the Program

Each state has its own rate for unemployment compensation. Amounts vary widely across the country. Rates for each person are determined by the individual's salary at the last job. In every state, unemployment compensation is less than half of a person's last weekly salary, and in most, it's significantly less than half.

States also have limits on the length of time that unemployment compensation will be paid. In most states, it's capped at twenty-six weeks. That has been increased by Congress during times of high unemployment, usually by the addition of another thirteen weeks per person.

Unemployment compensation comes with some strings. Recipients must be actively looking for work while receiving unemployment compensation. Most states require recipients to document their job-search efforts. Usually, that involves filling out a form that lists the specific places where someone has looked for work. Typically, those forms have blanks for the names, titles, and phone numbers of people talked to. Folks who falsify those forms, or who don't make the effort to find work, can lose their unemployment compensation.

### Application

Unemployment compensation is administered by the same state employment agencies that maintain listings of job vacancies. Everyone—veterans, too—must apply in person for unemployment compensation. Former servicemembers should bring extra copies of their formal discharge papers, DD Form 214.

### VETERANS PREFERENCE

Veterans should get a break when the federal government is hiring. That seems fair. And that's the way the federal civil service has been operating for a long time.

For just as long, it's been misunderstood. Military service doesn't guarantee anyone a spot on the federal payroll. Your status as a veteran won't get you hired for a job for which you're not qualified.

What their time in the military gives veterans when hiring time arrives at a civil service office is an edge, an advantage, a slight nudge toward the front of the pack. It's called the "veterans preference," not the "veterans *guarantee*." Here are some of the basics:

## Regular Preference

Qualified veterans receive an extra five points for any competitive examinations when they have honorable discharges and meet at least one of the following criteria:

- Earned a campaign ribbon.
- Started active duty after September 7, 1980, and spent two years on active duty.
- Spent more than 180 days on active duty between January 31, 1955, and October 14, 1976.
- Spent any time on active duty between December 7, 1941, and July 1, 1955.

Ten extra points are added to examination results if the veteran was discharged with a disability or has a Purple Heart. Ten points can also be awarded, under certain circumstances, to the spouses and survivors of disabled veterans and people who died on active duty.

Not eligible for any veterans preference are former servicemembers who don't have disabilities and who retired in the rank of major or lieutenant commander (or higher).

## VRA Preference

A special provision on the books of the U.S. civil service, called the "Veterans Readjustment Appointment," or VRA, permits veterans to be hired directly, without taking a competitive examination.

The VRA system has created an unusual amount of confusion and bad feelings. The first step in the process occurs when a federal manager decides to fill a vacancy using VRA. The manager doesn't have to use VRA. If he wants to use the usual civil service selection process, that's how it's done. There's no way to force a manager to use VRA.

Each major federal agency has its own guidelines for designating vacancies to be filled using VRA authority.

Generally, the program is open to veterans who have spent at least 1 day on active duty since August 4, 1964, have a total of 180 days on active duty, and have something other than a dishonorable discharge. The requirement for 180 days' active-duty service is waived for veterans with a campaign ribbon or people discharged with a service-connected disability.

## Other Preferences

State, county, and municipal civil service systems frequently have their own versions of the veterans preference program. For details, check with the appropriate personnel office.

# FOUR

# Health Care

When veterans take off their uniforms for the last time, many are unable to leave behind all of the consequences of military service.

Untold thousands have battlefield injuries that require life-long care. Many more have lingering health problems that didn't directly arise from combat but that can be traced to injuries and illnesses that began on active duty.

Helping these veterans is the central mission of the extensive medical system—the largest in the country—that's run by the Department of Veterans Affairs, or VA. More than 170 VA medical centers are in operation, providing unsurpassed care with up-to-date medical technology and a cadre of trained professionals.

These centers are located in every state in the union, plus a few other places. VA officials try to treat veterans in the facilities closest to their homes, but eligible veterans can be treated at any VA medical center. In fact, veterans are routinely sent to facilities away from home if those places have the medical hardware or the specialists best suited for treatment. And if the VA doesn't have the needed resources for an eligible veteran, the veterans agency will pay for treatment in a hospital run by the military, the Public Health Service, or even the private sector.

Historically, the VA medical system has concentrated on helping the sickest veterans. Its resources in many communities are still focused on inpatient care. That means getting treated as an outpatient is difficult in many places. Partially picking up this slack is the VA's nursing home system. A VA nursing home is not a geriatric facility: It treats patients who don't require hospitalization and who might be outpatients in the private sector.

It may come as a surprise to some veterans that care in a VA medical center is not free to all veterans. Limited resources have forced VA officials to put priorities on treatment for different categories of veterans. Some veterans have to be admitted—the so-called "mandatory" category. Others—called the "discretionary" category—can be admitted if there's room. And some middle- to high-income veterans in the discretionary category must pay the government for any treatment they receive from a VA medical facility.

Veterans and family members curious about the eligibility rules for VA medical care must ensure that they're basing their health-care decisions on the latest information.

The nationwide effort that began in the early 1990s to reform the nation's health-care system will affect the VA medical system. It's impossible to predict exactly what that effect will be.

There's no shortage of sources for the latest information. The best place to start is at a nearby VA medical center, where people known as "veterans benefits counselors" can explain recent changes in the rules. Regional VA offices and the major veterans organizations also are invaluable resources.

## VA INPATIENT CARE

If there's one segment of the federal government suffering from an unjustified image problem, it's the network of 172 hospitals operated by the Department of Veterans Affairs.

Some media accounts have depicted VA facilities as antiquated and their staffs as uncaring, but patients, staffers, and other members of the medical community have personal experiences and hard statistics that prove that the care in VA facilities is among the best in the nation.

More than one-quarter of all physicians in the United States undergo some part of their training at a VA medical facility. For years, the professional commission that evaluates hospitals has given the average VA hospital a higher grade than the average private-sector hospital.

In many communities, even in some of the largest cities, the local VA medical center has state-of-the-art diagnostic and treatment hardware. Those VA facilities are made available to private-sector hospitals.

Even students in medical colleges routinely go to VA medical centers to study the most advanced tools in the profession. VA hospitals have been the home for basic research that is advancing medical understanding in fields ranging from prosthetics to AIDS.

The full range of services from this medical powerhouse can be brought to bear in the diagnosis, treatment, and rehabilitation of that select group of people with the proud title of "Veteran."

There is a downside, however. The doors of VA medical centers would be jammed if every veteran had an identical right to treatment. For several years, the system has given priority to two special groups of former servicemembers—those with health problems directly related to their military service and those without the financial means to obtain care elsewhere. These people, along with a few other narrowly defined groups of veterans, receive their care without any charge.

Veterans who don't fit into one of these high-priority groups may be billed for their treatment. Generally, those expenses are lower than rates in private-sector hospitals. But even for the paying customers, no one gets treated unless there's room.

The trend for more than a decade in the VA medical system has been a constant tinkering with the eligibility rules to make a shrinking budget fit the categories of veterans with an absolute right to care.

The national drive toward health-care reform also has an effect on VA medical centers. Make sure you have the latest information.

## Eligibility

More than any other veterans program, the VA medical system is governed by a balance between eligibility and access. "Eligibility" says whether you have a legal right to treatment. "Access" says whether there's a vacant bed in which to put you.

Every veteran who has a discharge that's officially rated as "under conditions other than dishonorable" is eligible for care in a VA facility.

In 1997, admission rules for VA medical centers gave top priority for inpatient treatment to veterans with one of these factors in their files:

- Service-connected disabilities.
- VA pension.
- Eligibility for Medicaid.
- Former POW status.
- Agent Orange exposure.

- "Atomic" veteran status.
- Gulf War syndrome.
- World War I service.
- Mexican Border Wars service.

As previously noted, the phrase "atomic veteran" refers to servicemembers exposed to ionizing radiation during atmospheric nuclear tests or during service in Hiroshima or Nagasaki immediately after the end of World War II. Vietnam veterans exposed to Agent Orange or Gulf War veterans complaining of the illness known as the "Gulf War syndrome" must be seeking care for problems they believe are directly related to these events and must have entered their names on the appropriate list—known as a "registry"—maintained by the Department of Veterans Affairs to keep track of these former servicemembers.

While the veterans listed above had top priority for admission to VA medical centers under the rules in effect in 1997, other veterans can be admitted if space is available and no higher-priority veterans are on a waiting list.

Veterans with low incomes can receive free treatment if their incomes fall below certain limits. VA rules spell out the income restrictions based on family size. Those income statistics change every year. In 1997, this category of veterans included people without immediate families with incomes less than about $21,000, and veterans with a spouse and an income less than about $25,000.

Once the top-priority veterans and the low-income veterans have been taken care of, all other veterans may be admitted.

### Service-Connected Problems

Top priority for care in VA medical centers goes to veterans with disabilities that are officially rated as "service connected."

Getting that official ruling can take months, even longer

than a year. One of the best ways to ensure access to a VA hospital in the future is to do the work now to get a service-connected rating. That comes from applying for disability compensation, which is discussed in the chapter entitled "Disability Pay."

A service-connected medical problem is one that was caused by military service, that developed during military service, or that was aggravated by military service. Those lingering medical problems are officially known as "disabilities." Don't be put off by the term. Many veterans with VA disabilities aren't suffering from obvious handicaps. That's just the official label attached to their problems.

Veterans with service-connected medical problems also have ailments that aren't service connected. Expect different admission and reimbursement rules for non-service-connected ailments.

The severity of a disability is usually expressed as a percentage figure, ranging from 10 percent to 100 percent. Complex rules govern these ratings. For example, implantation of an artificial shoulder qualifies as a 100 percent disability immediately after the operation. Later the disability rating drops to 30 percent if there are no complications, or to 60 percent if pain and weakness in the arm continue.

Veterans who are concerned about getting access to inpatient VA services should keep their eyes on something called a "zero compensable disability." That arises when the official VA review of their medical files determines that, in fact, they do have a medical problem that is service connected, but this problem is not severe enough to justify the minimum monthly payment for VA disability compensation, which requires a 10 percent disability.

Veterans with "zero compensable disabilities" don't receive

monthly disability checks, but their records do note that they have a disability that meets the official definition of being service connected, which makes them eligible for free care in a VA hospital.

Be warned, though, that sometimes veterans with service-connected medical problems can get care in VA medical centers only for those specific ailments. For example, if chronic foot problems have been officially rated as service connected, a VA hospital might not treat you for a cardiac problem that hasn't been rated as service connected.

### Waivers

What if you haven't planned well and you need medical care now? You are sure that your ailment will qualify as service connected, but you haven't received—or even applied for—an official ruling from VA officials.

The rules governing eligibility for inpatient care permit the immediate admission of some veterans when VA officials, in their considered opinions, decide it's likely the veterans will have their medical problems officially rated as service connected.

This special waiver, however, can be used only if the applicant has a medical emergency or has been recently discharged and filed for a service-connected ruling within six months of discharge.

### Costs

VA medical facilities don't charge anyone for treatment of an ailment that's officially rated as service connected, but, in order to hold down costs, officials will try to get reimbursed for treatments that aren't for problems directly related to military service. Veterans with service-connected disabilities shouldn't expect free care for non-service-connected medical problems.

Insurance companies and the government's Medicare

program may be billed by the Department of Veterans Affairs for treating a veteran for illnesses or injuries not related to military service.

## Admission

The VA medical system has its own identification card, called a "VA Patient Data Card," for singling out veterans who are entitled to medical care. You'll get one if you're approved for VA disability compensation or receive a percentage rating for a disability.

Patients who don't have the card should bring some other documentation that proves they have a service-connected disability or that they've applied for a disability rating. The same holds true for veterans receiving VA pensions who seek inpatient care.

For your first visit to a VA medical center, it's a good idea to bring along a copy of your DD Form 214, your discharge papers.

## Locations

An appendix at the back of this book has a state-by-state listing of VA medical facilities, which includes a summary of major services and specialties.

## VA-PAID HOSPITAL CARE

Not all health problems can be treated in VA medical facilities. Sometimes veterans can receive more specialized care in a hospital operated by the Department of Defense, another public agency, or even a private corporation.

The rule is that veterans must be specifically approved to use another medical facility if they expect the VA to pick up the bill.

Approvals are normally restricted to the following:

- Service-connected disabilities.
- Disabilities that caused a veteran's discharge from active duty.
- Disabilities associated with another, service-connected disability.
- Disabilities of veterans in rehabilitation programs.

If veterans who are regular patients at a VA medical center require emergency treatment and they go to another, non-VA facility, they must notify their "home" VA center within seventy-two hours after admission. Failure to meet the seventy-two-hour limit can result in the veteran having to pay the bill, even if it's one that VA officials would otherwise pay.

## VA OUTPATIENT CARE

One quirk of the VA medical system is that it's often easier to get treatment as an inpatient who spends the night in a facility than as an outpatient who takes only a few minutes of a doctor's time. This is the result of efforts of VA officials to devote the full power of their slim resources and overworked staffs to the veterans in most desperate need of medical attention.

### Eligibility

When it comes to outpatient care in a VA hospital or clinic, the top priority goes to three groups of veterans:

1. Those with disability ratings of 50 percent or higher.
2. Those needing care for service-connected disabilities.
3. Those needing care for injuries resulting from VA hospitalization.

Note the wording of the second and third kinds of veterans: They don't get outpatient care *if* they have a disability or VA-caused injury; rather, they get care *for* that disability or injury. A veteran with a service-connected arm disability is entitled to the highest priority for outpatient care to treat that arm, but not to treat a foot.

Next in line for priority are veterans who need outpatient care to prevent later hospitalization, or to complete care that was begun as an inpatient. This second priority goes only to veterans who have disabilities rated between 30 and 40 percent or who have low incomes.

The third level of priority for outpatient care falls to veterans who are enrolled in vocational rehabilitation, are former POWs, are World War I or Mexican Border War veterans, or who receive VA pensions and are unable to care for themselves.

The last priority goes to all other veterans.

## VA NURSING HOMES

Nursing homes are an integral part of the medical system operated by the Department of Veterans Affairs. With only a few exceptions, they're located on the grounds of VA medical centers.

VA nursing homes provide skilled nursing care, related medical services, and psychiatric treatment for veterans who don't need to be hospitalized but who do need institututional care.

Most residents of VA nursing homes come directly from hospitals. Some stay long enough to regain their health and return home, while others remain in the facilities for extended periods. In short, VA nursing homes service both long-term and short-stay patients.

### Eligibility

Traditionally, the eligibility rules for VA nursing homes are identical to the rules for inpatient VA medical care. If you qualify for one, you qualify for the other.

Three general rules are paramount. First, even more than VA hospitals, nursing homes must make decisions based on the availability of space. If the nursing home doesn't have an empty bed, it cannot accept you.

Second, no one has an absolute right to admission to a VA nursing home. In VA medical centers, certain categories of veterans are eligible for "mandatory" treatment as inpatients. But for care in VA nursing homes, they're given an edge at admission time, not a guarantee.

Third, VA nursing homes are principally medical facilities, not residential facilities. As with other medical resources, their operations have become uncertain during the drive for nationwide health-care reform.

In 1997, admission rules for VA nursing homes gave top priority to veterans with one of these factors in their files:

- Service-connected disabilities.
- VA pension.
- Eligibility for Medicaid.
- Former POW status.
- Agent Orange exposure.
- "Atomic" veteran status.
- Gulf War syndrome.
- Service in World War I.
- Service in the Mexican Border Wars.

While the veterans listed above had top priority for admission to VA nursing homes under the rules in effect in 1997, other veterans could be admitted if space was available and no high-priority veterans were on a waiting list.

Veterans with low incomes can receive free treatment in a VA nursing home, again assuming that space is available. VA rules spell out the income restrictions based on family size. Those income statistics change every year. In 1997, this category of veterans included people without immediate families with incomes less than about $21,000, and veterans with a spouse and incomes less than about $25,000.

Once the top-priority veterans and the low-income veterans have been taken care of, then all other veterans may be admitted to the home.

## Costs

Disabled, low-income, and other groups of veterans entitled to priority admission to VA nursing homes will have the government pick up the full costs for the stay, including all charges for medical services, rehabilitation, and even food.

Recipients of VA pensions, however, will have their monthly pensions reduced. The amount of the reduction varies, depending on the specific kind of VA pension received by the veteran, as does the effective date of the reduction. Those reductions leave recipients of VA pensions in nursing homes with between $30 and $90 per month.

Special rules go into play if the recipient of a VA pension has a spouse or another dependent. When those veterans are admitted to VA nursing homes, other family members can receive the rest of the VA pension.

But this doesn't happen automatically. The family member must take the initiative. Contact the veterans benefits counselor or some other official at the VA nursing home to start the paperwork.

If a veteran receiving VA disability compensation is admitted to a VA nursing home, there is no reduction in the amount of that monthly check.

Any veteran admitted to a nursing home who doesn't fall into one of the categories for priority care must pay for his or her treatment. Typically, those bills are lower than the costs in nongovernmental facilities.

Veterans not entitled to priority admission can use their private health insurance plans or the government's Medicare insurance to pay for care. In 1997, for these nonpriority cases, there was a charge of $5 daily, plus an out-of-pocket payment of about $800 equal to the Medicare deductible for each ninety days of care.

## Details of the Facilities

VA nursing homes provide skilled nursing care and related health services to patients needing long-term nursing care and rehabilitation services. Since most VA nursing homes are located on the grounds of VA medical centers, the health-care system's full resources are available for nursing home residents, including rehabilitative services.

## Fine Print

The VA's nursing homes are often referred to as "NHCUs," a sort of verbal shorthand for "Nursing Home Care Units."

## Locations

An appendix at the back of this book has a state-by-state listing of VA medical facilities. If a hospital or clinic has a VA nursing home, it is mentioned there.

## VA-PAID NURSING HOMES

As veterans from the World War II era have grown older and encountered more health problems, the Department of Veterans Affairs has often found itself without enough of its own facilities to take care of their needs.

Fortunately, rules are on the books that authorize VA officials to subsidize the care of veterans in privately owned nursing homes. Called "community nursing homes," they are more convenient for some patients—and easier on families and friends—than VA-run facilities that are a long commute away from home. VA money pays for some of the services offered to veterans who become patients under this program. If there's a gap between actual costs and VA reimbursement, however, the veteran is responsible for paying the difference. Patients can use private health insurance or Medicare.

The VA's community nursing home program isn't strictly for older veterans. It's for any qualified veteran with health problems who requires close medical supervision but who doesn't need to be hospitalized.

## Eligibility

The VA's community nursing home program is open to a broad range of veterans. Here are some eligibility rules:

• Everyone eligible for treatment in a VA hospital, VA nursing home, or VA domiciliary is eligible for the community nursing home program.

• Active-duty military personnel and reservists being treated in a military hospital can use the community nursing home program for long-term convalescence.

• Veterans needing extended treatment for disabilities that are officially rated as service connected qualify.

• VA officials have the authority to permit treatment, on a case-by-case basis, for low-income veterans receiving VA pensions and other veterans with disabilities.

## Costs

Community nursing homes, unlike VA nursing homes and VA domiciliaries, may charge their patients for some services. Private health insurance plans may pick up those costs. Medicare and Medicaid are also used by many veterans to reduce their out-of-pocket expenses. Because of the VA's financial support to these institutions, however, costs tend to be lower than in other private-sector facilities.

Veterans admitted to community nursing homes aren't subject to any automatic reductions in VA disability compensation, VA pensions, or military retired pay, but veterans whose VA pensions normally include a special payment called "Aid and Attendance" will lose that extra money while in the community nursing home.

## Admission

Many veterans go directly into community nursing homes from VA facilities or military hospitals. For them, the government will take care of most of the paperwork and help family members prepare the rest.

But when veterans are going directly from their homes or private-sector hospitals into nursing homes, veterans advocates recommend that they get VA approval in advance. This may require a physical examination in a VA medical facility. However, civilian doctors under VA contract can also provide those examinations.

## Time Limits

Just as VA nursing homes are generally for patients requiring less than six months' care, the six-month rule also applies to most patients under the community nursing home program.

If veterans require longer care, they are moved to other facilities. Frequently, Medicare or Medicaid will pick up the bills for that later care. If veterans needing longer care are able to look after most of their daily needs, they may be eligible for admission to a VA domiciliary.

A major exception to the six-month rule involves veterans with disabilities that are officially rated as service connected. They can stay as long as they need the care.

A more narrow exception involves veterans who are at the end of their six-month periods and have encountered glitches in their arrangements to transfer to another facility. VA officials can extend their stays in the community nursing homes for forty-five days to work out the problems.

Terminally ill veterans at the end of their six-month periods who have a life expectancy of less than six months can remain in the facilities. If the official diagnosis says they should live longer than six additional months, however, they can be transferred from the community nursing homes.

## CARE FOR FAMILY MEMBERS

Veterans aren't the only ones with medical bills. Spouses and children have health-care needs, too.

The federal government isn't able to pick up all the bills for their medical care, but it will share the expense.

For a select group of spouses and children of veterans, the government offers a health insurance program called "CHAMPVA." As with any other health insurance plan, CHAMPVA participants pay monthly premiums. When they need medical care, they are expected to pay a small portion of the bill, but the health insurance plan picks up the lion's share. Because it has government backing, CHAMPVA costs less than most commercial health insurance plans.

CHAMPVA shouldn't be confused with the more widely known CHAMPUS plan, which provides health insurance protection for the families of active-duty people. They're two different programs with similar names.

### Sponsors

Like many benefits for active-duty families, the most important eligibility rules for CHAMPVA don't involve the family members, but the veteran.

In this case, this government-backed health insurance can be purchased by the spouse or dependent child of the following kinds of veterans:

• Those officially rated by VA officials as having a "permanent and total" disability that's service connected.

• Deceased veterans rated at the time of their death by VA officials as having a "permanent and total" disability that was service connected.

• Veterans who died as the result of a service-connected disability.

• People who died on active duty.

## Spouses

Spouses of deceased veterans and the spouses of people who died on active duty lose their right to CHAMPVA if they remarry. They may be able to regain their CHAMPVA benefits if that new marriage ends, however. This is decided on a case-by-case basis.

## Children

As commonly happens in defining "child" for the sake of determining eligibility for VA benefits, the term covers people who are unmarried and who meet one of the following criteria:

* Are under the age of eighteen.
* Are older than eighteen but became permanently incapable of self-support before reaching age eighteen.
* Are older than eighteen but less than twenty-three and enrolled in a full-time educational program approved by VA officials.

They can be natural children, legally adopted children (including those adopted less than two years after the adoptive parent's death), stepchildren residing at home, or illegitimate children officially recognized.

## Medicare

CHAMPVA participants who become eligible for Medicare, CHAMPUS, or Tricare lose CHAMPVA, but if they later lose eligibility for Medicare, CHAMPUS, or Tricare, they can resume CHAMPVA.

## Application

The latest information about CHAMPVA is available at VA regional centers or from benefits counselors at VA medical centers.

Interested people can also contact the CHAMPVA center directly: CHAMPVA Center, P.O. Box 65023, Denver, CO 80206.

# FIVE

# CARE FOR CHRONICALLY ILL OR ELDERLY VETERANS

---

**In This Chapter:**

- *VA Domiciliaries*
- *State Veterans Homes*
- *Adult Day Care*

- *U.S. Retirement Homes*
- *For Spouses*

---

For a young country, the United States has many traditions. One custom that goes back to colonial days involves special homes provided by communities for veterans who are unable to care for themselves, either because of their war wounds or because of simple old age.

In those settings, the men—and now increasingly, the women, too—who have served their country in uniform are given an extra measure of protection and care.

Those facilities have come under conflicting pressures in recent years. The nation's World War II veterans have, as a group, passed into retirement, and the "Old Soldiers' Homes" are receiving unprecedented numbers of applications.

At the same time, governments and charitable organizations are finding themselves squeezed financially. Revenues aren't increasing fast enough to keep up with responsibilities.

Into the competing pull of needs and resources comes a continuing interest in the broad shape of the national health-care system. Efforts to overhaul the nation's medical system are bound to have an impact on the ways we care for our veterans.

As with any discussion touching on health care, former servicemembers should be aware that rules and services for veterans homes and other facilities treating ill or elderly veterans are likely to change as these traditional facilities are fitted into the nation's reshaped medical system.

## VA DOMICILIARIES

Under the medical system operated by the Department of Veterans Affairs, a special kind of facility is available for people who need long-term care but who have some ability to take care of themselves.

Called "domiciliaries," these VA facilities offer rehabilitation, long-term residency, and so-called maintenance care for many former servicemembers. They are, in short, the veterans' homes.

Like VA nursing homes (see chapter 4), VA domiciliaries are part of the overall medical system operated by the Department of Veterans Affairs.

Any tinkering with VA medical systems that's done as a part of the nationwide health-reform effort will also have an effect on VA domiciliaries. Make sure you have the latest rules.

### Eligibility

Perhaps the most important rule for VA domiciliaries involves the availability of space. No one is admitted to a VA domiciliary unless it has the room for one more resident. And like many other facilities catering to the nation's aging population, the domiciliaries are finding their resources put under great pressure as their waiting lists expand.

The eligibility rules are broadly written and depend on a number of factors.

*Military Service:* Everyone admitted to a VA domiciliary must have served in the military, either on active duty or in the reserves. They don't have to have served in wartime or to have served for any specific period of time.

*Discharge Status:* Only a narrow range of discharges make a veteran ineligible for admission to a VA domiciliary. Those are discharges officially rated as "under other than honorable conditions." These discharges shouldn't be confused with dishonorable discharges. They're two different things.

*Income:* In most cases, to be eligible a veteran must also meet a very specific income standard: The veteran's annual income must be less than the rate set up for people receiving a VA pension, plus the additional VA payment known as "Aid and Attendance."

The figure for VA pensions plus "Aid and Attendance" changes annually. For 1997, it was about $13,000 for people without any dependents, slightly higher for those with families.

*Special Cases:* Federal law gives the secretary of the Department of Veterans Affairs broad authority to admit people to domiciliaries when they have "no adequate means of support." Usually, this applies to veterans who exceed the income limitation by relatively small amounts.

Nevertheless, veterans admitted under this special-case rule must be able to take care of themselves. That means they must be able to feed themselves, dress with minimal assistance, and bathe without help.

Those special-case veterans also must be able to make "competent and rational decisions," especially concerning their admission to the domiciliary. VA domiciliaries are not for the long-term care of mental patients.

*Spouses:* Some long-term care facilities in the private sector permit spouses to live in the facilities with patients. Under VA rules, however, only veterans can be admitted.

## Costs

Low-income veterans are entitled to have the government pay all the bills for their stays in VA domiciliaries. By "low-income," we mean people who earn less than the amounts detailed in the "Eligibility" section above.

Nevertheless, recipients of VA pensions will have their monthly pensions reduced if they're admitted to VA domiciliaries. The amount of the reduction varies, depending on the specific kind of VA pension received by the veteran, as does the effective date of the reduction. Those reductions leave recipients of VA pensions in domiciliaries with between $30 and $90 per month.

Special rules apply if the recipient of a VA pension has a spouse or another dependent. When those veterans are admitted to VA domiciliaries, other family members can receive the rest of the VA pension.

But this doesn't happen automatically. The family member must take the initiative. Contact the veterans benefits counselor or some other official at the VA domiciliary, who can start the paperwork.

If a veteran receiving VA disability compensation is admitted to a VA domiciliary, there is no reduction in the amount of that monthly check.

Veterans who earn more than the income limit can still be admitted to VA domiciliaries, but they will be billed for their care. Typically, those bills are lower than the costs in nongovernmental facilities.

Veterans not entitled to priority admission can use their private health insurance plans or the government's Medicare insurance to pay for care.

## Details of the Facilities

For many of the nation's veterans, VA domiciliaries are—in a word—home. They are places where veterans live and pursue

PRAIRIE CREEK PUBLIC LIBRARY DISTRICT
501 Carriage House Lane
Dwight, IL

their own interests, with many of the day-to-day responsibilities of running a household left to others.

Domiciliaries provide their residents not only with food and shelter, but also, if needed, with clothing and toiletry items.

Medical care by VA professionals is another service offered to the residents of VA domiciliaries. In fact, most of those facilities are located on the grounds of VA medical centers.

Many of the ingredients for a useful, interesting life are offered on the grounds of the facilities, from recreational and social events to a safe, secure place to meet with family and friends.

To the extent permitted by any health problems, residents are expected to help the staff by performing light housekeeping chores.

Unlike VA nursing homes, which generally limit stays to six months, there is no time limit for residency in a VA domiciliary.

Again, domiciliary residents have to be able to take care of many of their own needs. The facilities simply don't have the staffs to meet all of the needs for all of their residents. Residents of a VA domiciliary who become unable to care for themselves may be transferred to a private or state-run facility that provides the needed level of care.

### Locations

A state-by-state listing of VA medical facilities appears at the back of this book. If a hospital or clinic has a VA domiciliary, it is mentioned there.

### STATE VETERANS HOMES

Not all the nursing homes and domiciliaries for veterans are operated by the Department of Veterans Affairs. Many states have their own facilities.

Although they go by many names, they're generally known

as "state veterans homes." In the late 1990s, about fifteen thousand veterans were receiving care in these facilities every day.

State veterans homes are operated by the various state governments under a special, close arrangement with the VA system. They receive some VA funds for operation, follow VA admissions rules, pass periodic VA inspections, and receive VA money for construction.

Many residents of state veterans homes have come directly from VA nursing homes. Unlike VA nursing homes, the state facilities rarely have a time limit on stays.

> Consumer tip: A nursing home can call itself anything it wants. Ask if it "has VA recognition." If it does, you know it meets VA standards.

Some of these state facilities are allied with state-run hospitals for veterans. Like the VA system, states operate both domiciliaries and nursing homes. Domiciliaries tend to be for people who can take care of most—if not all—of their needs. State nursing homes are for patients who require long-term care but who don't need the full services of a hospital.

It's not always clear from the name of a state veterans home whether it's a domiciliary or a nursing home. But to receive VA financial support, it must be one or the other or both.

### Eligibility

Each state has its own detailed eligibility rules for its state veterans home.

As with VA facilities, sometimes the most important rule is that no one will be admitted unless there is room. Waiting lists for state veterans homes are common.

The federal government has set down broad rules for domiciliaries and nursing homes, within which the states must operate if they want to keep their federal funding. Remember, these are minimum requirements. States can open their facilities to other categories of veterans, but they may have to pay more for their care.

*Domiciliaries:* Eligibility rules are the same as for VA domiciliaries.

*Nursing Homes:* Residents must fall into one of the following categories:

- Service-connected disability.
- Disabled by a condition not related to military service and unable to pay for private nursing.
- Discharged with a disability.
- Receiving VA disability compensation.
- Eligible for VA disability compensation but receiving military retired pay instead.

## Costs

Unlike VA nursing homes and domiciliaries, state veterans homes don't provide free care to their patients. There is a cost for their services.

Those costs tend to be lower than at private-sector facilities, however, because the Department of Veterans Affairs is subsidizing the facilities for some expenses.

There are no automatic reductions in VA Disability Compensation or VA pensions following admission to a state veterans home.

## Details of the Facilities

State veterans homes provide a complete array of services for the long-term resident, ranging from medical and rehabilitative care to recreational facilities and social events.

A few state veterans homes are located on the grounds of state-owned hospitals, assuring quick access to a full range of medical services.

Some state veterans homes are actually part of larger facilities, but VA rules require them to house veterans in areas set apart from civilian patients.

## Locations

An appendix at the back of this book has a state-by-state listing of state veterans homes. The list includes state veterans hospitals.

## ADULT DAY CARE

As the average age of the nation's veterans gets older, new ways are being found to take care of their needs. A program that entered the VA system in the 1980s is called Adult Day Care. As the name implies, it is similiar to day-care programs that have been around for many years for children.

Veterans taking part in Adult Day Care may live in their own homes, with their children, or in a group setting, but they spend many of the daylight hours in an Adult Day Care center.

Increasingly, Adult Day Care programs are opening up in VA medical centers, but not all the care is provided within these facilities. There's a separate, but related, program that uses VA money to subsidize the treatment of veterans in Adult Day Care programs run by the private sector.

### Eligibility

The two versions of the program—in VA facilities and in private facilities—are governed by the same eligibility rules.

Admission is limited. Not everyone eligible for care in a VA domiciliary, for example, qualifies for admission to the Adult Day Care program. Generally, eligibility for both the VA-run and private-sector programs is limited to the following:

• Veterans with disabilities that are officially rated as service connected and at least 50 percent.

• Veterans who are released from VA medical centers

VA officials will help families find facilities offering long-term care in the private sector. That's a service they offer all veterans. Family members shouldn't hesitate to ask for help.

whose doctors say they require the continued care available in Adult Day Care centers.

• Active-duty personnel who are released from military hospitals whose doctors say they need Adult Day Care.

## Costs

Adult Day Care in a VA facility is free. It doesn't affect a veteran's Disability Compensation, VA pension, or military retired pay.

Private-sector facilities charge for their services, and the individual veteran is responsible for paying those bills. Programs such as Medicare and Medicaid can reimburse veterans for some—perhaps, even all—of those expenses.

## Details of Facilities

A proper Adult Day Care facility does more than provide food and shelter for part of each day. It offers medical care, some physical therapy, limited rehabilitative services, recreational outlets, and reliable nutrition.

Whether run by the VA or the private sector, each facility is under the overall supervision of a physician and provides assistance with eating, bathing, and toileting. Records are kept on each patient.

The private-sector facilities must meet certain minimum standards laid down by the Department of Veterans Affairs.

## Locations

An appendix at the back of this book has a state-by-state listing of VA medical facilities. If a hospital or clinic has an on-site Adult Day Care center, it is mentioned there.

## U.S. RETIREMENT HOMES

For more than a century, two places have offered special care and attention for older veterans. The U.S. Soldiers' and Airmen's Home in Washington, D.C., and the U.S. Naval Home in Gulfport, Mississippi, provide long-term care for men and women who once served their country in uniform and who are now in their retirement years.

Residents have the best that a grateful nation can offer to its older veterans—from a full range of up-to-date medical facilities in a secure environment to every imaginable recreational opportunity and the companionship of fellow veterans.

Veterans come in two basic varieties—male and female—and these two U.S. veterans homes have long accepted women veterans as residents.

Despite their names, both facilities accept people who have served in every branch of the military.

### Eligibility

For most of their histories, the two homes operated independently, with their own eligibility rules. Now they have identical admissions procedures.

One major rule weeds out most officers. To be accepted in the homes, veterans must have been enlisted personnel or warrant officers during their entire time on active duty, or they must have been officers who spent at least 50 percent of their active-duty time as enlisted people or warrant officers.

Once veterans meet that basic requirement, they must also fit into one of these four categories:

1. Retired with twenty years on active duty and at least sixty years old.

2. Unable to earn a livelihood because of a disability that's officially considered service connected.

3. Have served in an official theater of war and unable to earn a livelihood because of a disability not connected to military service.

4. Have once received hostile fire pay or combat pay and now unable to earn a livelihood because of a disability not connected to military service.

Coast Guard veterans can qualify for admission, if they meet the admission rules above and if at least some of their active-duty service was during wartime when the Coast Guard operated under the control of the Department of the Navy.

## Costs

Many of the basic necessities of life—food, shelter, and medical care—are part of the services offered to the residents of the U.S. veterans homes. But they're not completely free. Residents give up 25 percent of any federal annuities they receive. That includes military retired pay, VA Disability Compensation, and Social Security.

No additional charges are imposed on residents based on other sources of income.

## Details of Facilities

With renovations steadily in progress, the U.S. veterans homes are on their way to offering private rooms and baths to all residents.

Everyone on active duty automatically contributes one dollar each month for the U.S. veterans homes. The facilities also receive all fines imposed by courts-martial.

Virtual cities-within-cities, they offer a wide array of arts and crafts, hobby shops, libraries, social events, indoor recreation facilities, and outdoor exercise areas.

Extensive medical services are part of the leases. At no cost, residents are eligible for hospital care, assisted living arrangements, specialized medical care, and rehabilitation and physical therapy.

## More Information

More information can be obtained by writing to the U.S. Soldiers' and Airmen's Home, 3700 N. Capitol Street, N.W., Washington, DC 20317, or U.S. Naval Home, 1800 Beach Drive, Gulfport, MS 39507.

## FOR SPOUSES

The "Old Soldiers' Homes" discussed earlier in this chapter are for veterans. Unlike some private-sector facilities for the elderly, which admit the spouses of the people needing care, these homes don't have the room to permit spouses to stay, too.

But some special facilities, sponsored and financially supported by veterans groups, keep families together when one spouse needs special care. In most cases, they're also open to the widows and widowers of veterans.

## Knollwood

Formerly known as the Army Distaff Hall, Knollwood is located in Washington, D.C., and is open to retired Army officers and their female relatives, including spouses, widows, mothers, daughters, sisters, and mothers-in-law. Retired Army Reserve officers are also eligible for admission, along with their female relatives.

For more information, write to the Army Distaff Foundation, 6200 Oregon Avenue, N.W., Washington, DC 20015.

## Vinson Hall

Located in McLean, Virginia, Vinson Hall was founded by the Navy-Marine-Coast Guard Residence Foundation and is open to retired officers of all services and their spouses, widows, and parents, as well as other relatives of retired officers on a case-by-case basis.

For more information, write to Vinson Hall Corp., 6251 Old Dominion Drive, McLean, VA 22101.

## Air Force Village

Retired officers from all services and their widows or widowers are eligible for residency at the Air Force Village in San Antonio, Texas. The home is also open to young widows and children of Air Force officers for one year. Widowers are ineligible.

For more information, write to Air Force Village Foundation, 5100 John D. Ryan Boulevard, San Antonio, TX 78245.

## Air Force Enlisted Men's Widows and Dependents Home

The Air Force Enlisted Men's Widows and Dependents Home in Shalimar, Florida, is open to widows and widowers of enlisted personnel who had retired from the Air Force, Air Force Reserve, or Air National Guard, as well as to a limited number of retired couples and younger widows. Young widowers are ineligible.

For more information, write to Air Force Enlisted Men's Widows and Dependents Home Foundation, 92 Sunset Lane, Shalimar, FL 32579.

# SIX

# DISABILITY PAY

Military service is dangerous, even during peacetime. Veterans are eligible for some sort of financial payment from their government for injuries and illnesses that resulted from time in uniform, or for medical problems that were aggravated by military service.

The people at the heart of the government's system of disability pay lost limbs or were permanently crippled while serving their country. But most recipients of disability pay—especially the VA's disability compensation—aren't in that category. They are former servicemembers with physical ailments incurred during active duty or reserve service.

Both the military and the Department of Veterans Affairs provide monthly checks to veterans who can pass through all the legal hoops necessary to qualify for disability payments.

It's possible to receive disability pay from both the military and the VA, but as the rules discussed in this chapter reveal, for every dollar in disability pay you receive from one federal agency, you will lose another dollar from the other agency.

For most veterans, it's not important to understand the finer points in the rules that govern dual compensation for a disability. That's because in the vast majority of cases, it makes more financial sense to accept full VA disability compensation and give up the right to any money from the military for a disability.

## DISABILITY COMPENSATION

Most veterans drawing pay for the lingering effects of illnesses or injuries related to military service are receiving—to use the precise term—"disability compensation" from the Department of Veterans Affairs.

Disability compensation is made in monthly payments to qualified veterans. Usually, Congress increases the amounts each year to keep pace with inflation. Payments are fully exempt from federal, state, and local income taxes.

### Eligibility

Disability compensation can be paid to anyone who has served in the military, including members of the reserves and National Guard. There is no minimum time that a person must spend in uniform to qualify.

Two major groups of veterans are ineligible:

• Veterans who receive discharges officially rated as "under dishonorable conditions."

• Veterans with disabilities caused by "willful misconduct," such as those incurred during commission of a crime or during unauthorized absences, or because of drug or alcohol abuse.

## Details of the Program

VA disability compensation is a monthly payment designed to offset the lost earning power caused by military-related health problems.

The severity of the disability is expressed as a percentage. The percentages start at 10 percent and go in increments of 10 percent up to 100 percent. There is a fixed amount of disability pay for each level of disability. In 1997, for example, the monthly payments ranged from less than $100 for a 10 percent disability to about $1,900 for a 100 percent disability. The amount usually increases each year by the same rate as the Consumer Price Index.

Not normally included in the rates for disability compensation are special payments for the loss of specific body parts—like eyes, hands, or legs—or the loss of the use of body parts, all for reasons connected with military service. These financial additions to regular VA disability compensation are called special monthly compensation, and can range up to nearly an additional $5,000 per month.

## Application

The earliest you can apply for VA disability compensation is during out-processing for your discharge. Application may be made at any time thereafter. Most applications are made years—even decades—after a veteran's discharge.

Application is made by filling out VA Form 21-526, "Veterans Application for Compensation or Pension." A copy can be obtained from any VA facility.

Claims are retroactive to the date of discharge only when made within a year of discharge.

## Other Benefits

Veterans who receive VA disability compensation are also eligible to apply for several other benefits:

- Free lifetime VA medical care for the disability.
- Vocational rehabilitation.
- Dependents' allowance (if the disability is rated at 30 percent or higher).
- Financial help to take care of a spouse who needs attendance (if the veteran's disability is rated at 30 percent or higher).

Veterans rated with 100 percent VA disabilities may be eligible to use exchanges and commissaries at military installations, plus on-base recreational facilities, as may their spouses and dependent children.

To obtain access to on-base facilities, veterans and their family members must have a military identification card.

## Fine Points

The foundation for a successful claim for VA disability compensation is laid in a military member's last weeks on active duty, specifically in the physical examination that everyone on active duty should receive before being discharged.

Sometimes military physicians will offer to waive it or to conduct an abbreviated exam. If you're still on active duty, insist on a thorough examination. You have a right to it. Besides, it may be the last time you receive a physical in a while. Many employer-paid health plans don't cover routine physicals.

You also have a right to apply for VA disability compensation as part of your out-processing from active duty. Many transition counselors advise servicemembers to apply for a minor problem—say, a hurt back that bothers you only some days or an injured joint that you feel only if a storm is coming. By filing a claim, even one that you know is going to be rejected, you're ensuring that the VA will preserve your medical records. Decades later, if that back problem or tricky joint worsens, it will be much easier to prove a connection between that problem and your military service.

Finally, whether you're approaching your discharge or you've been a civilian for decades, to ensure that you supply the proper details and documentation when applying for VA disability compensation, you should discuss the procedure beforehand with a VA counselor or a service officer from a veterans group.

## DISABILITY RETIREMENT

Long before the United States had the Department of Veterans Affairs or the Veterans Administration, it had people who were permanently disabled while serving their country in uniform. To protect the financial needs of those veterans, the military devised its own programs offering lifelong income and other benefits.

The military's disability retirement system has undergone many changes throughout the years. Usually, servicemembers are covered by the rules in effect on the day they came into the military.

The general provisions now in effect date to 1949. The specific details that follow cover the disability retirement rules for people who joined the military on or after September 7, 1980. Slightly different rules apply to veterans whose service began earlier.

> **B**oth VA and DoD disabilities are expressed as percentages. Beware comparing them. A 30 percent VA disability isn't the same as a 30 percent DoD disability.

As always, keep in mind that minor changes in the rules are made frequently, by the laws that Congress passes, by interpretations made by the courts, or by policies established by the military. Before taking major action affecting a disability retirement from the military, make sure you have an up-to-the-minute understanding of the rules.

### Eligibility

A military disability retirement is available to everyone in the military—active-duty and reservist—who becomes unable to perform military duties because of a permanent injury or illness.

To be eligible, servicemembers must meet two basic criteria:

1. The disability must be permanent.

2. The disability cannot result from "intentional misconduct," "willful neglect," or an unauthorized absence.

People with less than twenty years in the military—who are thus ineligible for a normal retirement—must be officially rated as being at least 30 percent disabled before they can qualify for a disability retirement from the military.

Veterans with at least twenty years in uniform, who are thus eligible for a regular retirement, can receive disability retired pay for disabilities rated smaller than 30 percent.

These retirement-eligible veterans can receive a portion of their regular retired pay as disability retired pay. Those with a 10 percent disability, for example, can have 10 percent of their retired pay come as disability retired pay.

Servicemembers who have less than eight years in the military have the additional burden of proving their disabilities were "incurred in the line of duty."

### Details of the Program

Two formulas are used to compute the size of a disability retirement check from the military. Veterans are entitled to use the formula that results in the most generous disability payment for them.

1. They can multiply the amount of basic pay in their last monthly paycheck by twelve, yielding a yearly average. That figure then is multiplied by 2.5 percent for each year of service. The yearly figure is divided by twelve again to compute the size of the monthly payment. This is called a "disability retirement based upon length of service."

2. Under a second option, veterans multiply the amount of basic pay in their last monthly paycheck by the percentage assigned to their disability. That's what they would receive as disability retired pay. This is called a "disability retirement based upon percentage of disability."

Payments for a disability retirement from the military cannot exceed 75 percent of the servicemember's monthly basic pay. Payments usually increase every year with cost-of-living adjustments, or COLAs, that typically offset purchasing power lost to inflation.

## Application

Generally, servicemembers don't have to take any action to apply for a disability retirement from the military. If medical problems cause a discharge before completion of an obligated period of service, a Physical Evaluation Board, or PEB, at the local military hospital determines whether a servicemember is disabled and recommends a percentage rating for the disability. The PEB's recommendation is forwarded to the Physical Review Council, or PRC, which reviews the medical record and makes a final recommendation. Each service has only one PRC.

This process governs people whose disabilities are evaluated as they leave active duty. Others, however, may wish to apply for a disability retirement from the military after they have already been discharged.

Technically, a veteran can apply for a military disability retirement at any time after leaving active duty. There is no time limit for applications.

For postdischarge applications, veterans first must petition their service's Board for the Correction of Military Records to change the discharge to a disability retirement. That petition is made by filling out DD Form 293, "Application for Review of Discharge or Separation from the Armed Forces," obtainable from any military personnel office, military retiree affairs office, or VA benefits office.

Second, if the corrections board rules in favor of a veteran, then a medical board must review the veteran's records and make the basic decision about eligibility for a disability retirement and set the level of the disability.

Anyone trying to correct a discharge—to obtain a military disability retirement or for any other reason—should take advantage of the free, expert advice obtainable from a military retiree affairs office, a veterans group, or a VA office.

## Other Benefits

Veterans with military disability retirements are like other military retirees: They retain their own military ID cards, and they continue to get access to on-base services and facilities. They keep these benefits even if they later apply for VA disability compensation and waive all their taxable military retired pay for the VA's tax-free payments.

Veterans eligible for disability retired pay from the military can have their spouses treated in military hospitals and clinics, under the same rules that apply to the spouses of other military retirees. The rights of a spouse to treatment in a military medical facility aren't taken away if a retiree waives all taxable military retired pay to receive tax-free VA disability compensation.

Again, like veterans with regular military retirements, an ex-servicemember eligible for disability retired pay from the military can provide an income for a spouse after the ex-servicemember's death by enrolling in the military's Survivor Benefit Plan (SBP). This DoD program can be used by veterans who waive military money for VA disability compensation.

## Fine Points

Once the military rates a disability by assigning it a percentage, that figure cannot be changed at another time. By contrast, veterans with VA disability compensation frequently have the government increase the percentage rating given to a disability.

It helps to understand why that happens. The military gives disability retirements to people because they cannot perform their most recent duties. If the disability worsens after discharge, the military expects veterans to turn to the VA system for redress. The military's disability rating system is, basically, a onetime deal.

As for the tax status of military disability retirements, this section has focused on the rules that apply to people leaving the military during the 1990s. Veterans of an earlier era are covered by different rules.

Military disability retirements are tax exempt for veterans who meet one of the following criteria regarding September 24, 1975:

- Were in the military on that date.
- Were already receiving disability retired pay on that date.
- Were in the military before that date.
- Became eligible for a disability retirement after that date because of a combat-related injury.

Veterans who entered the military after September 24, 1975, and who are leaving service with disabilities that are only partially based on combat-related injuries will be able to shield from taxes only that portion of their total military disability retirements that is based on the combat injuries.

## TEMPORARY DISABILITY RETIREMENT

Not all disabilities are permanent. Even with the latest medical technology, doctors aren't always able to tell which patients will recover and how much of their health they will regain.

When military people enter that fuzzy medical realm—with disabilities that make them incapable of serving but that might not be severe or permanent enough to justify a discharge—they are placed in a special status. The Temporary Disability Retired List, or TDRL, is an administrative category to which military people are assigned until their medical conditions stabilize. About 10,000 people on active duty end up on the TDRL each year.

### Eligibility

Personnel are placed on the TDRL after a lengthy, formal medical screening. Military people who are placed on the TDRL fall into two basic categories:

1. Disqualified from active duty because of a disability that may not be permanent.

2. Disqualified from active duty because of a disability that may be permanent, but whose severity (the percentage rating assigned to the disability) is unknown.

### Details of the Program

Servicemembers on the TDRL have no active-duty responsibilities, but they must report for periodic medical examinations at least every eighteen months. Those examinations or other formal reviews of medical records can result in a decision at any time to have the person return to active duty or be discharged.

Pay for people on the TDRL is at least 50 percent but cannot exceed 75 percent of their most recent basic pay.

Servicemembers can choose between two formulas to determine their pay while on the TDRL:

1. They can multiply the amount of basic pay in their last monthly paycheck by twelve, yielding a yearly average. That figure then is multiplied by 2.5 percent for each year of service. The yearly figure is divided by twelve again to compute the size of the monthly payment.

2. Under a second option, veterans multiply the amount of basic pay in their last monthly paycheck by the percentage

assigned to their disability. That's what they will receive as disability retired pay.

The longest anyone can spend on the TDRL is five years. There is no legal provision for waivers of the five-year limit.

## Application

Servicemembers cannot directly volunteer to go on the TDRL, but they can make their cases be placed in that category if their medical fitness to remain on active duty is being considered by a Physical Evaluation Board (PEB).

Military people who are being evaluated by a PEB can also argue to avoid the TDRL, seeking instead to be returned to active duty or to be discharged with a disability.

## Other Benefits

While on the TDRL, military members and their families have access to the same on-base facilities that are open to other active-duty retirees.

Especially important to many families is continuing eligibility of family members to military medical care, either on base or through CHAMPUS or Tricare.

TDRL recipients are also eligible for treatment in VA medical facilities and for VA disability compensation. VA medical treatment doesn't affect eligibility for military medical care, but accepting VA disability compensation makes people ineligible for TDRL pay.

## Fine Points

Since TDRL recipients have the same benefits as other military retirees, they also encounter the same restrictions.

A major benefit that's lost is eligibility for on-base housing. Military retirees don't continue to live in military housing and, as a general rule, neither do TDRL families. Base commanders have some authority to permit TDRL recipients to stay in on-base quarters for periods up to 180 days. That's the commander's call. Don't expect special treatment if an installation has a long line of active-duty families waiting for government quarters.

For servicemembers returned to active duty from the TDRL, their TDRL time counts toward pay purposes, but not toward retirement.

Take the case of an E-6 who goes into TDRL status after twelve years on active duty. If that enlisted person spends four years drawing TDRL pay, then returns to active duty, basic pay will be calculated as an E-6 with sixteen years. But that enlisted member will need to spend eight more years on active duty to qualify for retirement.

## DISABILITY SEVERANCE PAY

The disability retired pay administered by the military goes to veterans with severe medical problems or with enough time in uniform to qualify for a regular retirement.

If that and the VA's disability compensation were the only financial payments made to active-duty people with disabilities, however, thousands of people every year would fall through a huge crack in the rules.

A large number of servicemembers have injuries or illnesses that make them unfit for continued service on active duty, but they don't have enough time to meet the requirements for a military disability retirement. Or the medical problems may not be serious enough to retire from the military with the disability.

To meet the financial needs of the military folks who have disabling but "minor" medical problems, the armed forces maintain something called "disability severance pay." It is also often called "medical severance pay" or "medical separation pay."

## Eligibility

When military people are unable to perform the duties appropriate for their rank, they may be discharged with disability severance pay. Eligibility is based upon both length of service and the severity of the disability, as determined by the usual rating system for disabilities.

To qualify for disability severance pay, military people must have less than twenty years of military service. Their disability must be rated as less than 30 percent, and three conditions affecting the disability must be met:

1. It cannot result from "intentional misconduct" or "willful neglect."

2. It cannot have occurred during a period of unauthorized leave.

3. It cannot have existed before coming on active duty.

On this last point, there is a small loophole. If a medical condition exists before entering the military, and if that problem was aggravated by military service, then people may qualify for disability severance pay. Of course, they must meet all the other eligibility conditions for the payment.

It's important to note that two major groups of military people are ineligible for disability severance pay because they qualify for other payments. Not eligible are people with twenty years in uniform (who qualify for regular military retirements) and people with disabilities rated at 30 percent or more (who qualify for military disability retirements).

## Details of the Program

Disability severance pay is a payment made on a person's last day in the military. Unlike the other disability pays discussed above, which result in monthly checks, disability severance pay is a onetime payment.

The amount is determined by a specific formula. For each year on active duty a servicemember is entitled to receive two months' basic pay. In this formula, months are rounded to the nearest year. Someone with nine years and seven months active-duty time would be credited with ten years. Someone with nine years and five months would be credited with just nine years.

There's a cap on disability severance pay. No one can receive more than two years' basic pay. Generally, that means that the maximum payment comes after twelve years in the military, with no increase in disability severance pay for active-duty time beyond twelve years.

For most people, the figure for basic pay that's used in the formula is the amount appropriate for the servicemember's rank and years of service during the last month on active duty.

For people who have satisfactorily held a temporary higher grade on active duty, disability severance pay can be computed using basic pay currently given to military folks in that higher rank and years-of-service category.

## Application

As happens with the other DoD-administered disability pays, servicemembers cannot directly volunteer for disability severance pay. The closest they come to genuine input occurs if their medical fitness to remain on active duty is being considered by a Physical Evaluation Board.

For most people, disability severance pay is a benefit of last resort. It's better than being discharged with nothing, but it's usually inferior to a military disability retirement, or even assignment to the Temporary Disability Retirement List.

## Other Benefits

Recipients of disability severance pay have cut their relationship with the military. They aren't entitled to any ongoing, special benefits from the armed forces.

Usually, they are ineligible to join the reserves or National

Guard. The rationale is that if they're physically incapable of serving on active duty, they're physically incapable of serving in the reserves. People with special skills, however, may be able to wiggle into a reserve assignment at a lower rank. Since disability severance pay is specifically based on the inability to perform duties at one's active-duty rank, highly skilled veterans may be able to argue that they can perform reserve duties at a lower rank.

Recipients of disability severance pay, like other disabled veterans, are eligible for medical treatment in VA facilities. Because their disabilities are officially rated as service connected, it should be easier for them to receive treatment than veterans without disabilities or veterans with medical problems not related to military service.

## Fine Points

Before being discharged with military disability severance pay, active-duty people should go through the paperwork to apply for VA disability compensation.

By applying, you force the VA to open a file on your medical condition. Your military medical records will go into that VA file. That will make it easier to qualify for VA disability compensation in the future if your condition worsens.

Should you later receive VA disability compensation for the same medical problem for which you received the military's disability severance pay, you must repay the government for the severance pay. The repayment is made by withholdings from your VA disability compensation. If a later VA case is for a disability not related to the one that forced your discharge from the military, then no repayment is necessary.

Finally, beware the trap of "overcomparing" benefits, then assuming that you're entitled to all the perks of a similar benefit. Disability severance pay is a specific program, with clearly defined benefits set by federal law. It may be similar to a disability retirement, but you're not considered a military retiree if you receive disability severance pay. It also may seem quite similar to the exit bonuses that got heavy use during the drawdown. But don't count on getting continued access to exchanges and commissaries like recipients of the Voluntary Separation Incentive or Special Separation Benefit. Those are separate programs, operating quite differently from disability severance pay.

## VOCATIONAL REHABILITATION

Disability compensation is often not enough to live on, and not enough for a meaningful life. Despite their handicaps, many veterans want work that challenges their abilities and increases their income.

> Vocational rehabilitation is an individualized benefit. Before approving it, VA officials must be satisfied that each veteran's career goals are achievable.

For those disabled veterans, the Department of Veterans Affairs has a special program that helps disabled veterans prepare for suitable employment or achieve greater independence in daily living. Under this program, the government pays for all school-related expenses, while giving the veteran an allowance.

Some low-income veterans with disabilities that aren't connected to their military service are able to qualify for a similar program that provides vocational training and job placement.

### Eligibility

Although many veterans could benefit from a program of vocational training, this effort is targeted at a specific group of disabled people.

Participants must meet all of these three conditions:

1. They must have a discharge officially rated as "under other than dishonorable conditions" or be awaiting discharge from active duty for a disability.

2. They must be certified by VA officials as needing vocational rehabilitation to overcome a disability that prevents them from holding jobs consistent with their skills and interests.

3. Their disabilities must meet the official definition for being service connected, and those disabilities must meet one of the following criteria:

• Be rated by VA officials at 20 percent.

• Be rated by VA officials at less than 20 percent if the veteran first applied for vocational rehabilitation before November 1, 1990.

• Have been rated by VA officials at 10 percent after October 1, 1993, if a serious employment handicap exists.

Note that vocational rehabilitation is one of the few VA programs for which some people on active duty can qualify.

A form of vocational training is also available to some low-income veterans with disabilities not related to their military service. Specifically, these are veterans who receive a VA pension.

## Details of the Program

Vocational rehabilitation includes government-paid education or training, a subsistence allowance for people already discharged from the military, and counseling and other help.

For participants, the government will pay the costs of tuition, fees, books, supplies, and equipment, plus some transportation costs. Also included among fully paid services are tutorial assistance, prosthetic devices, and lip-reading training or signing for the deaf.

Usually, people can participate in vocational rehabilitation for up to forty-eight months. That period can be extended for veterans with severe handicaps to employment.

Vocational rehabilitation pays the bills for the following:

• College-level institutions, trade schools, and business or technical schools.

• On-the-job training and apprenticeship training.

• On-the-farm training.

• Combinations of classroom instruction and on-the-job experience.

• Special rehabilitative facilities.

• Some at-home study.

The subsistence allowance that's a part of vocational training isn't affected by what the government spends on tuition, fees, and other educational expenses. Nor is it affected by disability compensation, military retirement pay, or income from a work-study program.

The amount of subsistence is spelled out in VA charts that set different rates for the number of dependents, the kind of training, and whether the veteran is attending full time, half time, or at some other pace.

Amounts of subsistence allowance don't change automatically every year to keep up with inflation, like many other VA payments. Here are some examples of the monthly rates in effect in late 1997:

• Full-time instruction in an institution: veterans with no dependents, about $400; with one dependent, about $490; with two dependents, about $580; for each additional dependent, about $40.

• Full-time training on a farm, apprenticeship program, or on-the-job training: veterans with no dependents, about $350; with one dependent, about $420; with two dependents, about $480; for each additional dependent, about $30.

• Full-time evaluation or independent living program: veterans with no dependents, about $400; with one dependent, about $500; with two dependents, about $580; for each additional dependent, about $40.

The program will pay for up to four years of full-time vocational training, or for an equivalent period of part-time training—for example, eight years of half-time training. Payments will continue for two months after a veteran completes a training program or educational class.

Each program is individually designed and approved by VA officials, based on the needs and circumstances of the disabled veteran.

Normally, the training must be completed within twelve years after discharge from active duty. The start of the twelve-year eligibility period can be delayed in these two cases:

• A medical condition made the veteran unable to begin training.

• VA officials failed to notify a veteran of approval for a disability rating, which often sets the groundwork for eligibility for vocational training.

## VA Pensions

Most participants in the vocational rehabilitation program receive VA disability compensation because of injuries or illnesses linked to their military service, but a vocational training program is open to some recipients of VA pensions. That's a payment to low-income veterans with health problems not related to their military service.

For pension recipients, participation in vocational training is optional. They can receive up to twenty-four months of government-paid training.

If accepted for vocational training, recipients of VA pensions keep their full pensions during the training period. Afterward, their VA pensions will be reduced if their wages exceed the usual income limits for all VA pension recipients.

A special federal law makes some VA pension recipients eligible for vocational training. To be eligible, veterans must have been receiving VA pensions on December 31, 1995.

## Application

VA officials are supposed to notify disabled veterans who qualify for vocational rehabilitation that it is available, but there is no automatic notification for recipients of a VA pension.

Veterans can apply for vocational rehabilitation by completing VA Form 28-1900, "Disabled Veterans Application for Vocational Rehabilitation," which can be obtained from any VA office.

VA officials evaluate each applicant to determine eligibility and need. Then they put together a comprehensive, written plan detailing all the services that the veteran can expect to receive from the government.

## Other Benefits

All participants in vocational rehabilitation receive VA help after ending their formal programs. For eighteen months after the end of training, participants are eligible for counseling, job placement, and job assistance programs. License fees, supplies, travel expenses, medical services, and other help may be provided to them by VA officials during this period.

## Fine Points

Participating in vocational rehabilitation or vocational training and receiving a subsistence allowance won't affect the amount of either VA disability compensation or a VA pension.

If veterans taking part in vocational training lose their VA pensions, they can continue to participate in the program's training and employment services.

All veterans retain their rights to VA health care during vocational rehabilitation.

Again, since the VA vocational rehabilitation program is open to active-duty people, there's a provision in the rules that prevents them from receiving the subsistence allowance.

Once they leave active duty, they are treated like every other veteran and become eligible for the subsistence allowance. Spouses and dependent children can receive a veteran's subsistence allowance if the veteran isn't providing proper financial support.

Finally, veterans taking part in work-study programs under vocational rehabilitation must train, at a minimum, at three-quarters time.

# SEVEN

# Veterans Pensions

Military veterans were the beneficiaries of the original social safety nets that were erected by the federal government and by the states. At the time of the nation's first wars, veterans who were unable to take care of themselves were given a hand by their communities.

With the creation of the Veterans Administration and later the Department of Veterans Affairs, that legacy was systematized and continued. Today, the VA pension program is the major benefit that helps veterans who are unable to take care of themselves for reasons unrelated to their military service.

The VA pension program provides regular monthly checks for former servicemembers with limited incomes and health problems that prevent them from earning a living. Unlike recipients of VA disability compensation, recipients of a VA pension don't have to show a link between their medical problems and their military service.

It's often called "live pension" by specialists in veterans

affairs, to distinguish it from the so-called death pension paid to the widows, widowers, and other dependents of some veterans.

Recipients of VA pensions are eligible for a variety of other benefits, including a high priority for VA medical care, vocational training, death benefits, and continuing payments to widows, widowers, and dependent children.

Like many government programs, the VA's pension program has undergone fundamental changes over the years, and its rules have been completely rewritten several times. Currently, veterans are receiving VA pensions under three different versions of the pension program: the Improved pension, the Old-Law pension, and the Section 306 pension.

Since January 1, 1979, the Improved pension is the only one open for applications. People who received pensions under one of the earlier versions of the program have the option of switching to the current Improved pension.

## IMPROVED PENSION

The Improved pension plan is open to veterans with low incomes, meager financial resources, and poor health.

Recipients must have disabilities that aren't connected in any way with active duty. Those with health problems that stem from their military service are eligible for VA disability compensation.

Pension recipients get monthly checks from the government. The size of the checks varies, depending on the number of dependents and the severity of restrictions in day-to-day living that are imposed by the veteran's medical condition.

### Eligibility

Veterans must pass through a series of very specific legal hoops to qualify for a VA pension. Here are some of the major requirements:

- Service must include at least one day on active duty during wartime and ninety days total active-duty time. The ninety days don't have to be consecutive. Veterans discharged for a service-connected disability during wartime don't have to meet the ninety-day requirement.
- The veteran's discharge must be rated as "under other than dishonorable conditions."
- The veteran must have limited income and net worth. (Income must be less than the rates listed below, in "Details of the Program.") The size of allowable assets isn't specified by law, but veterans advocates say pensions are usually granted to people with less than $30,000 in assets.
- The veteran must have a disability that's officially rated as "permanent and total." VA rules outline very specific conditions that must be met before a disability can be given this rating.
- The disability cannot be due to "willful misconduct," which traditionally applies only to cases of alcoholism, drug addiction, and venereal disease.

The eligibility rules once were easier for veterans who were sixty-five years of age or older. Until 1990, VA guidelines waived the need for a "permanent and total" disability for those older veterans. In fact, they didn't have to have a disability to receive a VA pension.

All that changed on November 1, 1990. Since then, veterans aged sixty-five and older have had to meet the same eligibility rules as younger folks. Fortunately, those who qualified under the more liberal pre-1990 rules were allowed to continue their pensions without meeting the newer, stricter guidelines.

Recipients of the two earlier VA pension programs—the Old-Law pension and Section 306 pension—have the option of switching to the Improved pension at any time. Once they make that choice, they cannot return to an Old-Law pension or Section 306 pension at another time.

Two other eligibility rules for the Improved pension are worthy of note:

- Veterans will lose their pensions if their income or net worth exceeds certain levels. Usually, the pension will be restored if income or worth falls back to a qualifying level.

- No one can receive a VA pension while he or she is also being paid VA disability compensation. Anyone eligible for both programs will have to pick one.

## Details of the Program

The Improved pension provides a monthly income for qualified veterans. The exact amount varies with several factors, including the veteran's level of self-sufficiency and whether a spouse or other dependents live with the veteran.

The amount of the pension increases annually to keep up with inflation. Annual increases are the same amount and are given at the same time as increases in Social Security.

Below are listed the amounts of pension totals at the start of 1997 for veterans fitting the major categories of the pension program. Remember that rates are approximate yearly maximums. Many veterans who qualify for VA pensions never receive the full amount because if they have additional income, their pensions are reduced by one dollar for each dollar from another source.

- *Without a spouse or child:* $8,500.
- *With one dependent (spouse or child):* $11,000.
- *Without dependents and unable to care for self:* $13,600.
- *With one dependent (spouse or child) and unable to care for self:* $16,200.
- *Without dependents and housebound:* $10,300.
- *With one dependent and housebound:* $13,000.
- *Two veterans married to each other (total payment to couple):* $11,100.

- *Extra for veterans of Mexican Border War or World War I:* $1,900.
  - *Extra for each additional child:* $1,400.

Two other common conditions affect payments of Improved pensions: hospitalization and incarceration.

**Hospitalization:** Pensions for veterans receiving pensions at a with-spouse or with-dependents rate aren't affected by hospitalizations, even in a VA facility, or by admissions to domiciliaries or nursing homes; neither are the pensions of veterans without dependents or spouses who are hospitalized at VA expense.

Veterans without dependents or spouses who are admitted to a domiciliary or nursing home at VA expense have their checks reduced to a fixed amount monthly, which was $90 in 1997. The reduction begins four months after they enter the facility.

**Incarceration:** As a rule, veterans without spouses or other dependents cannot receive their Improved pensions if convicted and confined to a federal or state prison or to a local jail. Payments end on the sixty-first day of their confinement. After their release, veterans can resume receiving the pension if they still meet the eligibility rules.

For incarcerated veterans paid Improved pensions at the with-spouse or with-dependents rates, the monthly checks can continue to the spouse or children, but VA officials first must calculate what the spouse or children would receive under the VA's death benefit. The death benefit is compared with the Improved pension, and the spouse and children receive whichever monthly amount—Improved pension or death benefit—is smaller.

When a veteran's spouse or child is the one imprisoned, the Improved pension is recalculated. The veteran receives the pension at the rate applicable for people without a spouse or child.

To lose their pensions, veterans must be convicted. Payments are unaffected by pretrial confinement.

## Income Restrictions

VA's Improved pension is primarily for low-income veterans. Generally, for each dollar of outside income, veterans lose one dollar of their Improved pension.

Unfortunately, the dollar-for-dollar reduction is only a general rule. Some kinds of income will affect the size of an Improved pension. Other kinds of income have no effect on a pension check.

Until 1993, veterans had to submit annual statements to the VA about their income. Now, VA officials verify eligibility by checking the amount of income reported to the Internal Revenue Service on the veteran's annual income tax return.

Here are some sources of income that *reduce* the size of an Improved pension check:

- Wages, dividends, and interest.
- Income of spouse.
- Income of children under legal age.
- DoD exit bonuses.
- Military retired pay or civil service retirement, even if a veteran has waived rights or refused to accept military retired pay or civil service retirement.
- Social Security's Old Age, Survivors, and Disability Insurance.
- Social Security death benefits.
- Commercial annuities.
- Insurance dividends.
- Pay for jury duty.

The following sources of income *don't* reduce the size of an Improved pension:

- Social Security's Supplemental Security Income.

- Value of property owned and lived in by veteran.
- Financial gifts from relatives and friends.
- Profit from sale of property.

## Application

Veterans can apply for the Improved pension at any time after leaving active duty.

The formal method for requesting an Improved pension is submission of VA Form 21-526, "Veteran's Application for Compensation or Pension," which can be obtained from any VA facility.

Veterans may not know some of the precise information requested by the form, such as monthly Social Security benefits or exact periods of military service. When in doubt, applicants should provide their best understanding of the right information, followed by the notation "approx.," to indicate approximations.

Veterans filing their first request for VA benefits should include a copy of their discharge papers, typically DD Form 214. If the discharge papers have been lost, veterans can request new copies by filling out Standard Form 180, "Request Pertaining to Military Record," which is also obtainable from the nearest VA office.

The applications can be submitted without discharge papers and using approximate information in order to get the paperwork moving. However, before they actually begin receiving VA's Improved pension, veterans will have to provide VA officials with exact figures and the appropriate discharge papers.

Benefits can be paid retroactively to the date the application was received, but veterans usually have to request retroactive payments when they first file their VA Form 21-526. There is a block on the form for that request.

Certification that a veteran has a "permanent and total" disability can be done through a written statement by a private physician. The odds of VA officials accepting these statements improve when doctors back up their judgment with diagnostic results (e.g., X rays, lab tests) and submit their evaluations on a standardized form called FL 21-104, "Request for Medical Evidence from Non-VA Physician."

As you can see, the application procedures are very precise. This blizzard of paperwork can overpower many veterans. Before giving up, they should contact the nearest VA office or a veterans service officer working for a major veterans group. These professionals are paid to help. They understand the procedures, and they already have all the necessary forms.

## Other Benefits

The Improved pension alone will not solve the financial problem of many veterans and their families. For people with additional needs, there are additional programs.

- *VA health care:* High priority for free inpatient and outpatient VA medical care.
- *Aid and Attendance:* Increase in pension check for people in nursing homes or in need care. May also take the form of an increase in permitted additional income. The rates for Aid and Attendance include the housebound benefit described below.
- *Death pension:* Monthly payment to spouse of veterans eligible for—though not necessarily receiving—a VA pension at time of death.
- *Housebound benefit:* Increase in pension check for people permanently confined to their homes but otherwise capable of taking care of themselves.
- *Vocational training:* Up to twenty-four months of vocational training, followed by another eighteen months of job-placement help.

## Fine Points

VA pensions are closed to people with employment and health problems caused by alcoholism, drug abuse, and venereal disease. Those three conditions come under the category of "willful misconduct," which federal law says makes veterans ineligible for pensions. (Veterans with AIDS or the virus that causes AIDS have been able to receive VA pensions. The "willfull misconduct" restriction hasn't been applied to people with this illness.)

In the hands of an experienced advisor, however, many veterans with those problems have been able to qualify for VA pensions. For example, skilled advocates have been able to argue successfully that cirrhosis of the liver—not the alcoholism that caused the cirrhosis—has made a particular veteran disabled, unemployable, and therefore eligible for an Improved pension. Since cirrhosis isn't officially listed as "willful misconduct," the veterans have gotten their pensions.

Winning these borderline cases takes experience and skill. Veterans and family members should rely on attorneys and service officers from the major veterans groups who have successfully split these legal hairs before.

Pensions can be paid retroactively to the date of the application. Sometimes a letter can constitute that first official "application." Letter-applications must clearly specify who the veteran is—by name and Social Security number, service number, or VA identification number. They must state that the veteran is applying for a pension and include the dates of military service. Letter-applications must be followed up as soon as possible by the formal applications on the forms mentioned above.

A final fine point of great importance: Pension recipients must stay below the income limits discussed earlier. At one time, they had to file annual income reports. Now, VA computers automatically check tax returns veterans file with the Internal Revenue Service.

## OLD-LAW PENSION

VA pensions first became available to veterans after World War I. The initial pension program, now called the Old-Law pension, continued almost until the start of the Vietnam War.

The Old-Law pension was closed to new applications in 1960. Everyone who has been receiving it can continue to receive it but also has the option to switch at any time to the newer Improved pension.

Most of the rules listed above for the Improved pension also apply to the earlier Old-Law pension. The information in this section deals only with areas in which the Old-Law pension differs from the Improved pension.

### Eligibility

Eligibility rules are the same as for the Improved pension, with these two exceptions:

• Recipients must be veterans of World War I, World War II, or the Korean War.

• Recipients must have filed for the Old-Law pension before June 30, 1960.

### Details of the Program

The details for the Old-Law pension are the same as for the Improved pension, with these exceptions:

• Pensions are reduced, usually by 50 percent, when a veteran receiving the Old-Law pension at the without-dependents rate is admitted to a VA facility. Reductions begin after seven months.

• Most veterans receiving Aid and Attendance lose that monthly payment two months after entering a VA facility. Instead, they begin receiving the smaller "housebound benefit."

• Most veterans without families who receive Aid and Attendance have their housebound benefit cut in half seven months after being admitted to a VA facility.

## Income Restrictions

The following are exceptions to the income restrictions for the Improved pension:

> The Old-Law pension and Section 306 pension are sometimes called "protected pensions." That's because recipients were protected from change after the newer Improved pension began in 1979.

- In determining a veteran's income, the incomes of a spouse and children under age eighteen aren't included. Also not figured into those calculations are separation pay, exit bonuses, any federal retirement pay that the veteran can receive but has refused to accept, and dividends from commercial insurance.

- Net profit from the sale of personal property or most real property (i.e., land, buildings) is counted as income.

- Net profit from the sale of a veteran's home isn't counted as income if the money is used to purchase another home within the same calendar year or the next calendar year.

- Net profit is calculated as the sales price, minus the value of the property on the day the veteran began receiving a VA pension.

## Application

New applications for the Old-Law pension haven't been accepted since June 30, 1960. All new veterans must apply for the Improved pension. Everyone receiving the Old-Law pension is eligible, at any time, to switch to the Improved pension. Once made, that decision cannot be reversed.

## Other Benefits

Other benefits for the Improved pension also apply to recipients of the Old-Law pension. VA officials may require Old-Law pension recipients who apply for Aid and Attendance or the housebound benefit to switch to the Improved pension before approving the additional benefits.

## Fine Points

Recipients of the Old-Law pension who lost this VA benefit because their income exceeded official limits, and who later become eligible again for a VA pension because their income dropped below the limits, are given the Improved pension, not the Old-Law pension.

People who erroneously lost their Old-Law pensions because their income exceeded the official limits, but who are able to prove their income was within the limits all along, can have their Old-Law pensions restored.

## SECTION 306 PENSION

Between the original VA pension program, called here the Old-Law pension, and the current Improved pension, another pension program was on the books. It's commonly called the "Section 306 pension," a name derived from the section of the federal law that created it.

Section 306 pensions were closed to new applications in 1978. Everyone who had been receiving it can continue to receive it. They also have the option to switch at any time to the newer Improved pension.

Most of the rules listed above for the Improved pension also apply to the Section 306 pension. The information in this section deals only with areas in which the Section 306 pension differs from the Improved pension.

## Eligibility

The eligibility rules for this pension are the same as for the Improved pension.

## Details of the Program

All of the rules for the Improved pension apply, with this exception:

Some veterans will have their pensions reduced three months after admission to a VA domiciliary and four months after entering a VA medical facility or nursing home. This applies to veterans without dependents and to veterans who are paid Section 306 pensions at the without-dependents rate because they are not living with their spouse or supporting their children.

## Income Restrictions

Income restrictions are the same as for the Improved pension with these exceptions:

• In determining a veteran's income, wages of family members under age eighteen aren't counted; neither are dividends from commercial insurance.

• Some medical expenses can be subtracted from total income to reduce the amount of income listed on annual VA reports.

• In determining the net worth of Section 306 pension recipients, VA rules exclude home furnishings, personal effects, and a personal automobile.

## Other Benefits

Section 306 pension recipients are eligible for the other benefits of the Improved pension, except that federal rules prohibit payment of Aid and Attendance to Section 306 pension recipients who need help taking care of themselves at home. Veterans who are eligible for the extra monthly payments must switch to the Improved pension to receive Aid and Attendance.

## Application

Applications for the Section 306 pension were accepted only between July 1, 1960, and December 31, 1978. Everyone receiving a Section 306 pension is eligible, at any time, to switch to the Improved pension. Once made, that decision cannot be reversed.

Although Section 306 pensions were created after the Old-Law pension, recipients of an Old-Law pension are not entitled to switch to a Section 306 pension.

# EIGHT

# Spouses' Pensions

> **In This Chapter:**
>
> - *Dependency and Indemnity Compensation*
> - *Death Pension*
> - *Death Compensation*

The government's responsibility to individual veterans often lingers long after a former servicemember has been laid to rest in a national cemetery. A little-known fact about the Department of Veterans Affairs is that it sends checks every month to tens of thousands of people who never served in uniform.

Like all VA programs, the ones available to widows, widowers, and the children of veterans have very specific eligibility rules. If the rules often sound bureaucratic, it's because they are based on very specific language that has been written into federal law.

## DEPENDENCY AND INDEMNITY COMPENSATION

When people die while serving in the military, their spouses and children—and sometimes even their parents—become eligible for a variety of benefits from the government. Many of the same benefits are also offered to the survivors of disabled veterans who died years after their discharge.

The principal financial benefit for these family members is Dependency and Indemnity Compensation, commonly known by the acronym DIC.

DIC provides a monthly income for survivors. Like many government programs, it changes constantly. In 1993, a fundamental change legislated by Congress took effect. For people receiving their first DIC payments in 1993, the rates changed from amounts based on the rank of the veteran to a standard amount that everyone would receive. Survivors receiving DIC before 1993 will keep their old rank-based rates, unless they would receive more under the new system.

At least two other VA benefits are similar to DIC. The Death Pension is the principal VA program for the survivors of wartime veterans who died of medical problems that weren't related to their military service. Death Compensation goes to the parents of people who died before 1972, either on active duty or with service-connected disabilities.

### Eligibility

In order for a widow, widower, dependent child, or parent to receive DIC, the deceased veteran and the family member applying for DIC must both meet very specific eligibility rules.

The deceased veteran must have met one of the following criteria:

• Died on active duty, active duty for training, or inactive duty for training.

• Died after leaving the military as a result of medical problems caused or aggravated by situations officially rated as "in the line of duty" while on active duty, active duty for training, or inactive duty for training.

• Died for reasons unrelated to military service, so long as he or she left the military with a disability that was officially rated as total and service connected and that existed continuously for at least ten years immediately before death.

• Died for reasons unrelated to military service, so long as he or she left the military with a disability that was officially rated as total and service connected and that existed at least for the first five years after discharge.

When a claim for DIC is based on a death that occurred after a veteran was discharged from the military, the discharge must be rated as "under conditions other than dishonorable."

If the person applying for DIC is a widow or widower, that person also must meet one of these conditions:

• Have been married to the veteran for at least one year, if the marriage was childless.

• Have a child by the veteran if the death occurred less than a year after the marriage.

• Have lived with the veteran continuously from the time of the marriage, except if a separation was through no fault of the spouse.

• Have not remarried.

Several subtleties about remarriage are important. Normally, survivors permanently lose all rights to DIC if they remarry after a veteran's death. But if the new marriage ends by being voided or annulled by a court, the veteran's spouse can often qualify to receive DIC again. Usually, if the new marriage ends by divorce, the spouse cannot qualify for DIC.

Spouses can lose DIC if they live with another person in an undeclared, common-law marriage after the veteran's death.

If the person applying for DIC is a child of the deceased veteran, that child must be unmarried and meet one of these other criteria:

• Not have reached the eighteenth birthday.

• If older than eighteen, be incapable of supporting self because of a physical or mental disability incurred before the eighteenth birthday.

• Not have reached the twenty-third birthday and be attending a VA-approved school.

If the person applying for DIC is a parent of the deceased veteran, that parent must have little income. In 1997, the income limit for a parent living alone was about $9,000 a year to qualify for DIC. For both parents living together, the limit for their combined income had to be less than about $13,000 annually.

## Details of the Program

DIC provides a monthly income for qualified survivors of people who die on active duty or after being discharged with service-connected disabilities.

Since three basic groups of people are eligible for DIC— spouses, children, and parents—let's look at each group separately.

*Spouses:* If a veteran's death occurred on January 1, 1993, or afterward, qualified spouses receive a fixed monthly amount which in 1997 was $833. Normally, that amount will increase annually to keep pace with inflation.

That figure will be increased by another amount (in 1997, $182 monthly) if the veteran was totally disabled from an illness or injury that was officially rated as service connected. That disability must have existed for at least eight years before the veteran's death.

Generally, DIC isn't affected by the income of spouses, but DIC will cause an important decrease in another federal benefit: Spouses who receive monthly payments from the military's Survivor Benefit Plan, or SBP, will lose one dollar in SBP for each dollar in DIC.

*Children:* If the son or daughter of a veteran qualifies for DIC, these rates and rules apply:

1. If under eighteen, a monthly payment is made to the surviving parent or guardian. In 1997, it was $211.

2. If between eighteen and twenty-three and attending

school, payment is made directly to the child. In 1997, it was $179 monthly.

3. If under eighteen and disabled, a monthly payment is made to the surviving parent or guardian. It was $354 in 1997.

4. If there is no surviving parent, rates are based on the number of children. Rates in 1997 ranged from $354 monthly for one child to $662 monthly for three children.

5. If there is no surviving parent, and the child is older than eighteen but incapable of self-support, the regular no-parent rate is increased by $211 monthly.

> Do you think the government doesn't keep promises to veterans? In mid 1996, VA spouse pensions were still paid to three widows of veterans from the Indian Wars, which officially ended in 1898.

*Parents:* Rates for parents depend on the number of surviving parents, whether they live together, and whether they have divorced and remarried.

Again, the rates listed are for 1997. Often, they change annually to keep pace with inflation. Before making any financial decisions, make sure you have the latest rates and eligibility rules.

## Application

The application procedure differs slightly for each category of applicant.

Spouses and dependent children should submit VA Form 21-534, "Application for Dependency and Indemnity Compensation or Death Pension by a Surviving Spouse or Child." For a child with no surviving parent, submit VA Form 21-4183, "Application for Dependency and Indemnity Compensation by Child." A parent should submit VA Form 21-535, "Application for Dependency and Indemnity Compensation by Parent(s)."

These forms are all available at VA offices. Survivors should get help from a VA counselor or a trained professional from a veterans organization when submitting an application for DIC. Errors in paperwork can delay payments by months.

## Other Benefits

DIC alone will not meet the financial needs of many spouses and children of veterans. For people with additional needs, there are additional programs:

- *Aid and Attendance:* Increase in check for surviving spouses and parents who are in nursing homes or in need of care. In 1997, this benefit added about $211 to monthly DIC payments.

- *Housebound benefit:* Increase in monthly check for people permanently confined to their homes, but otherwise capable of taking care of themselves. This benefit applies to surviving spouses only, and in 1997 added about $102 to monthly DIC payments.

Eligibility for DIC and DIC rates aren't affected by receipt of Social Security, nor is there an impact on Social Security when people receive DIC.

## Fine Points

If a DIC recipient is imprisoned after being convicted of a felony, the DIC will be reduced to a token amount, usually about $50 monthly.

If that person has dependents who would be hurt financially by the loss of DIC, VA officials have the authority to make a reduced DIC payment directly to the dependents.

DIC is restored to its full amount after a beneficiary has been released from prison, begins participation in a work-release program, or enters a halfway house.

## DEATH PENSION

The death pension is the principal VA program for the survivors of low-income veterans whose deaths weren't related to their military service. Many of these veterans received a VA pension, as is discussed in the chapter entitled "Veterans Pensions."

### Eligibility

In order for a widow, widower, or dependent child to receive the death pension, the deceased veteran and the family member applying for the death pension must meet very specific eligibility rules.

The deceased veteran must have met the following criteria:

1. Spent at least ninety days on active duty, at least one day of which must have been during an official period of wartime.

2. Received a discharge that was officially rated as "under other than dishonorable conditions."

3. Died of a disability that was not related to military service.

If the person applying for the death pension is a widow or widower, that person also must do the following:

1. Meet the income limits discussed below.

2. Have documentary proof that the marriage began more than a year before the veteran's death. The proof may be a public record of marriage, an affidavit from a clergyman, certified statements from two eyewitnesses to the ceremony, or other documentation.

If the person applying for the death pension is a child of the deceased veteran, that person must meet the following conditions:

1. Meet income limits discussed below.

2. Be unmarried and under eighteen.

3. If a stepchild, be living in the veteran's household.

4. If older than eighteen, must have become permanently incapable of self-support before the eighteenth birthday.

5. If between eighteen and twenty-three, must be enrolled in training or education at an institution approved by the Department of Veterans Affairs.

## Details of the Program

The death pension provides a monthly income for qualified survivors of wartime veterans. The exact amount varies with several factors, including the survivor's income and whether dependents live with the survivor.

> DIC underwent a major change in 1993. Descriptions of this program before 1993 may be inaccurate, especially about rates.

The amount of the pension increases annually to keep up with inflation. Annual increases are the same amount and given at the same time as increases in Social Security.

Below are listed the amounts at the start of 1997 for survivors fitting the major categories of the death pension. These amounts are totals for the year:

- *Without a child:* $5,700.
- *With one dependent:* $7,400.
- *Without dependents and unable to care for self:* $9,000.
- *With one dependent and unable to care for self:* $10,800.
- *Without dependents and housebound:* $7,000.
- *With one dependent and housebound:* $8,700
- *Extra for each additional child:* $1,400.
- *Paid to each surviving child:* $1,400.

Again, these rates usually change every year to keep up with inflation and are yearly maximums. Many people who qualify for the death pension never receive the maximum annual amount. That's because if they have income from other sources, their monthly death pension check is reduced by one dollar for each dollar from another source.

## Income Restrictions

The VA's death pension is primarily for the low-income survivors of veterans. Generally, for each dollar of outside income, survivors lose one dollar from the maximum payable death pension.

Until recently, recipients had to fill out annual reports that set down their income. Now, VA computers automatically check income as reported to the Internal Revenue Service.

## Application

Survivors can apply for the death pension at any time, even years after a veteran's death. The formal method for requesting the death pension is submission of VA Form 21-534, "Application for Dependency and Indemnity Compensation or Death Pension by a Surviving Spouse or Child," which can be obtained from any VA facility.

If the application is made within forty-five days of the veteran's death, payments will be retroactive to the day of death. If the application is filed more than forty-five days after the veteran's death, payment will be retroactive only to the day of the application.

## Other Benefits

The death pension by itself will not solve the financial problem of many veterans and their families. For people with additional needs, there are additional programs that can help, including Aid and Attendance and the housebound benefit, as discussed on page 129.

## Fine Points

Spouses who had been receiving a death pension lose the monthly payments if they remarry. Those payments can be restored if the marriage is legally voided or annulled, but the death pension isn't restored if a marriage ends in divorce.

## DEATH COMPENSATION

One of the oddities of veterans benefits is that some programs have been on the books for years, even though few people receive them and no one ever applies for them anymore. Into that category falls death compensation.

Death compensation was originally established to provide a monthly income for the families of people who died on active duty and for the families of some veterans after their death.

A newer program, called Dependency and Indemnity Compensation (DIC), discussed earlier in this chapter, has replaced death compensation for most people, but some still receive death compensation because they don't quite fit the eligibility rules for DIC. Mostly, these are the low-income parents of folks who died on active duty or from service-connected causes after their discharge.

Death compensation shouldn't be confused with the death pension: They are two different programs, both administered by the Department of Veterans Affairs.

### Eligibility

Only a few thousand people still receive monthly death compensation payments, and VA officials say they rarely see any new application for the benefit.

Two basic factors determine eligibility—the date of the veteran's death (and some other particulars about the veteran), and who's seeking the monthly payment.

First, let's look at dates of death:

• A servicemember must have died on active duty before January 1, 1957.

• A discharged veteran must have died before January 1, 1957, from service-connected causes. That veteran's discharge must have been officially rated as "under conditions other than dishonorable."

• A discharged veteran receiving disability compensation must have died between May 1, 1957, and January 1, 1972.

Second, death compensation goes to only three groups of people: spouses, dependent children, and dependent parents.

For parents, who are the major group of people actually receiving death compensation today, a financial test is used to determine whether they were financially dependent on the deceased veteran. A parent living alone must have income less than $400 monthly to qualify for death compensation. If both parents live together—or if one has remarried and lives with a new spouse—total monthly income for the two parents must be below $660. These income totals increase by $185 monthly for every other person in the household.

### Details of the Program

Death compensation is paid monthly to eligible people by the Department of Veterans Affairs.

If both parents are alive and qualify as dependents, the payment is $40 monthly to each. If only one meets the eligibility requirements, the monthly payment is $75.

Rates exist for spouses and dependent children, although fewer than fifty people other than parents receive death compensation. For the record, the other monthly rates in effect in 1997 were these:

• $87 for a surviving spouse.

• $121 for a spouse and dependent child.

- $29 for each additional dependent child.
- $67 for a dependent child who has no surviving parent.

## Application

To apply for death compensation, parents should use VA Form 21-509, "Statement of Dependency of Parents."

## Fine Points

The death compensation for spouses ends upon their remarriage. For parents, the monthly payments continue if they remarry, but they still must meet the program's income limitations in their new households.

# NINE

# LIFE INSURANCE

---

***In This Chapter:***

- *Veterans Group Life Insurance*
- *Servicemen's Group Life Insurance*
- *Service-Disabled Veterans Insurance*
- *Veterans Mortgage Life Insurance*
- *Programs for Pre-1974 Discharges*

---

Financial obligations don't disappear while new veterans are reestablishing their civilian careers. Risks to life and limb aren't suspended while former servicemembers readjust to the private sector.

Bad things can happen to good people who've just taken off their uniforms and who haven't been able to build up their resources. And some of those bad things can jeopardize the financial welfare of families. To help protect against that, the government has backed a special life insurance program that veterans can purchase immediately after they leave the military.

It isn't "a freebie." To get the coverage, veterans must pay for it through regular contributions called "premiums." The rates, however, are at the low levels that are only available through large group policies.

Like many veterans programs, life insurance for veterans has changed many times over the years. About a dozen different programs are on the books, each with its own rules. Only four life insurance programs are open to people leaving the military since the post–Cold War drawdown of the mid-1990s.

## VETERANS GROUP LIFE INSURANCE

Most people leaving active duty can purchase coverage at low, group rates under a program called Veterans Group Life Insurance, or VGLI.

The current VGLI program is open to most people who have left active duty since August 1, 1974. Other programs, which are discussed later in this chapter, provided similar coverage for those discharged before that date.

VGLI was substantially improved on September 1, 1993. It went from being "term" insurance, which veterans could purchase only for the first five years after leaving the military, to a plan they can renew periodically for the rest of their lives.

### Eligibility

Many veterans programs have elaborate eligibility rules, but to qualify for VGLI, you must meet at least one of the following criteria:

- Have been released from active duty after August 1, 1974.
- Be a member of the Individual Ready Reserve (IRR) or Inactive National Guard (ING).
- Be a disabled reservist with a disability incurred while on inactive duty for training or while on active duty for less than thirty-one days.

What are the eligibility rules for military retirees? For

recipients of exit bonuses? For veterans with early releases or continued obligations for time in the reserves?

The answers to all those questions—and more—lie in the first, broad eligibility criterion. So long as veterans left active duty after August 1, 1974, they are eligible for VGLI.

> Life insurance is a low-cost, high-benefit investment for married veterans. Single people without children may find better uses for their money.

The improvement that officially took place September 1, 1993, created its own eligibility rules. Before that date, new veterans could sign up for VGLI for five years. After that date, veterans could have VGLI for the rest of their lives.

The 1993 change applies to people who have left active duty after September 1 of that year and to veterans who had VGLI coverage in force on that date.

## Dual Eligibility

VGLI is the insurance program for people who have left the military. A similar program, Servicemen's Group Life Insurance (SGLI), which is discussed in greater detail later in this chapter, has comparable coverage for folks who are still in uniform.

But many ex-servicemembers don't stay in the ex category forever. There's a constant movement of reservists, National Guardsmen, and discharged veterans back into active duty.

From time to time, many veterans will find themselves back in uniform and eligible again for SGLI, the active-duty insurance program. For them, it's possible to be covered by both VGLI and SGLI. The major restriction is that the combined coverage can't exceed $200,000. At least, that was the cap in effect in 1997.

## Rates and Rules

Coverage can be for as little as $10,000, as much as $200,000, or any amount in between. Those "in between" coverage amounts, however, must be in $10,000 increments.

Some veterans may face restrictions on the amount of coverage that they can obtain. In 1997, for example, every qualifying veteran could get at least $100,000 in coverage. But, between $100,000 and $200,000, the amount of VGLI couldn't be greater than the amount of SGLI coverage that people had on active duty.

As with any private insurance program, veterans must make regular contributions, called "premiums," to obtain the coverage. The government doesn't pay these premiums for veterans.

The amount of the premiums is determined by two factors: the age of the veteran and the amount of coverage. In 1997, for example, here were the monthly premiums for $10,000 in coverage for the major age groups:

- *Age 29 or younger:* $1.20.
- *Age 30 through 34:* $2.00.
- *Age 35 through 39:* $2.60.
- *Age 40 through 44:* $3.40.
- *Age 45 through 49:* $4.40.
- *Age 50 through 54:* $6.50.
- *Age 55 through 59:* $8.80.
- *Age 60 through 64:* $11.25.
- *Age 65 through 69:* $15.00.
- *Age 70 through 74:* $22.50.
- *Age 75 and older:* $45.00.

Each block of $10,000 has the same monthly premiums as those listed. VGLI participants who choose to pay in one lump sum each year get a discount.

Older veterans can obtain "decreasing term coverage" at

age sixty. For them, the amount of their premiums remains the same as they age, but the amount of coverage decreases.

## Beneficiaries

A VGLI beneficiary may be any person; it doesn't have to be a relative. It may also be a firm, corporation, the veteran's own estate, or any legal entity.

> VGLI veterans decide whether their beneficiaries will receive one lump-sum payment or thirty-six equal monthly payments.

To avoid legal complications, however, that decision should be submitted to the VGLI administrator on the official beneficiary designation forms provided by the administrator. The administrator is the office to whom the premium checks are mailed.

VGLI participants are permitted to change their beneficiaries at any time.

## Application

Veterans receive VGLI coverage only if they apply. There are two deadline applications for most veterans:

• Within 120 days after discharge: Qualify simply by paying your first VGLI premium.

• Between the 121st day after discharge and one year after discharge: Qualify by paying the first VGLI premium and demonstrating that you're in good health, which often requires a recent physical examination.

Veterans who qualify for VGLI by membership in the Individual Ready Reserve or Inactive National Guard have two similar deadlines. They can apply for VGLI within 120 days of joining the IRR or ING, along with paying the first premium.

At the end of that 120-day period, IRR and ING members have another year in which to apply, although for the extended application period they'll again have to submit proof that they're good insurance risks, a process often requiring a recent physical.

Veterans qualifying for VGLI because of a reserve-related disability have within a year of their discharge to apply for VGLI. Ironically, to qualify, they will have to prove that they are, in fact, poor risks for conventional insurance because they have disabilities.

## SERVICEMEN'S GROUP LIFE INSURANCE

The same government-backed insurance program—Servicemen's Group Life Insurance, or SGLI—that goes to active-duty people is also available to many members of the reserves and National Guard.

### Eligibility

SGLI is available to a wide spectrum of the military population, including the following:

- Everyone on active duty.
- Cadets and midshipmen at the four military academies.
- Members of the Ready Reserve.
- Reservists with part-time coverage.
- "Gray area" reserve retirees.

This last category—"gray area" reservists—refers to reservists and National Guardsmen who have been credited with twenty years' service toward their military retirement but who haven't begun receiving retired pay. For them, the retirement checks begin on their sixtieth birthday.

The term "Ready Reserve" also has a precise definition, usually reservists who are assigned to units and who take part in weekend drill periods every month.

Some reservists and National Guardsmen who don't meet the general membership provisions of SGLI are covered by this insurance plan during specific periods, usually lasting only a few days. This part-time SGLI coverage applies to people who have orders specifying that, for a period of less than thirty-one days, they will be on active duty or active duty for training. They have SGLI coverage during those days of service, plus during travel to and from the training site.

A more narrow kind of part-time coverage goes to folks who aren't members of the Ready Reserve but who are scheduled for brief periods of military service, such as attendance at a drill period. They have SGLI coverage from the moment they leave home until the moment they return home.

### Dual Eligibility

There is a perpetual flow of people from active duty to the Selected Reserve to the IRR to the civilian population and back again.

A VGLI reservist who becomes eligible for SGLI for a period may want to drop VGLI in favor of the less costly SGLI policy. Or the reservist can choose to keep both government-backed insurance policies. As noted before, the combined coverage can't exceed $200,000, as of 1997.

### Rates and Rules

The minimum amount of SGLI coverage available is $10,000; the maximum is $200,000. Between those two figures, people can obtain coverage in multiples of $10,000.

Although SGLI is government backed, it isn't government paid. People have to make monthly contributions for the coverage.

Those contributions are made through withholdings from the military paycheck. The only major group of SGLI recipients who would actually write a check monthly to the government are the reserve component's "gray area" retirees who no longer perform any reserve duties that lead to a paycheck.

Traditionally, a single SGLI rate applies to everyone. In

1997, the rate for most SGLI recipients was ninety cents monthly for each $10,000 in coverage.

### Beneficiaries

An SGLI beneficiary may be any person; it doesn't have to be a relative. It may also be a firm, corporation, the veteran's own estate, or any legal entity. To avoid legal complications, however, that decision should be submitted to the SGLI administrator on the official beneficiary designation forms, which can be obtained from military personnel offices or VA regional offices. SGLI participants can change their beneficiaries at any time.

### Application

When people become eligible for SGLI, a key provision of the insurance program goes "on automatic pilot." Everyone eligible for SGLI is automatically enrolled in the program at $100,000 of coverage. To obtain more or less coverage, or no coverage, folks have to request it.

To obtain the forms necessary to change the amount of SGLI coverage, contact the nearest military personnel office. Many family support centers also have information about the program.

### After Discharge

Active-duty members with SGLI and most reserve SGLI participants are covered by their insurance policies—at no cost—for 120 days after discharge.

## SERVICE-DISABLED VETERANS INSURANCE

To give veterans with permanent disabilities related to their military service an extra measure of financial protection, the government has put together a special insurance program called Service-Disabled Veterans Insurance, or SDVI. It's also known as the "RH" program, a name based on the letters at the beginning of individual policy numbers.

### Eligibility

SDVI is available to veterans who have left the military since April 24, 1951, and have disabilities that are officially rated as being service connected.

People discharged at earlier dates may be eligible for one of the insurance programs discussed in the section below, "Programs for Pre 1974 Discharges."

For SDVI, eligible veterans fall within two broad groups, each having slightly different policies:

1. Those who are officially rated as having a service-connected disability but are otherwise in good health.

2. Those who are totally disabled.

Possession of VA disability compensation isn't necessary to qualify for this insurance coverage. In fact, many SDVI participants are so-called zero-compensable disabled veterans, people with disabilities caused by military service that aren't severe enough to warrant disability compensation. But the official determination that a disability is service connected is necessary to be eligible for SDVI coverage.

### Details of the Program

Traditionally, SDVI coverage has been for much smaller amounts than the government-backed insurance plans for active-duty people and other veterans.

In 1997, the basic coverage was capped at $10,000. Participants could receive less coverage, in multiples of $500, to a minimum of $1,000.

Disabled veterans who are otherwise in good health must pay for the coverage from their own pockets. Government backing holds their insurance premiums to the same amounts normally paid by people without disabilities.

Totally disabled veterans can receive the basic coverage—$10,000 in 1997—at no cost. To get the free coverage, however, they must ask for it. They must apply in writing to the Department of Veterans Affairs for a waiver of premiums.

If they receive the waiver, they become eligible for an additional $20,000 in coverage. But, this time, they must pay for that additional coverage. Government support keeps premiums within the financial reach of many veterans.

### Application
Veterans must apply for SDVI coverage within two years after being notified that they have a service-connected disability.

A legal guardian can apply on behalf of an incompetent veteran. That application should be made within one year after the guardian has been appointed.

### Beneficiaries
Veterans with SDVI coverage have the same freedom in designating their beneficiaries as holders of other government-backed insurance policies.

To avoid legal complications, veterans should use the forms maintained by VA agencies to designate beneficiaries, and they should file that paperwork promptly at a VA regional office.

When the veteran isn't competent enough to name a beneficiary, the veteran's estate automatically becomes the beneficiary.

## VETERANS MORTGAGE LIFE INSURANCE
Veterans Mortgage Life Insurance, or VMLI, provides an extra measure of financial protection for the families of some disabled veterans who are in the process of buying homes. VMLI can permit such a family to keep its home if the veteran dies before the mortgage has been paid.

## Eligibility

This insurance policy is narrowly focused. It's for veterans with the most extreme disabilities. Relatively few recipients of VA disability compensation qualify.

To be eligible for VMLI, a veteran must first be eligible for the VA's Specially Adapted Housing program, which provides grants to veterans with severe disabilities requiring extensive modifications to their homes.

Among the veterans entitled to the special housing program are those who have suffered these injuries:

- Loss of both legs or the use of both legs.
- Loss of one leg or the use of one leg, plus blind in both eyes.
- Loss of one leg or the use of one leg, plus disease or injury that affects the sense of balance, confining the veteran to a wheelchair.
- Loss of one leg or the use of one leg, plus loss of an arm or the use of an arm, affecting balance and requiring special aids to movement.
- Loss of both hands or the use of both hands.

## Rules and Rates

The amount of VMLI coverage a veteran can obtain is linked to the value of the home the veteran is buying. The insurance policy cannot be worth more than the amount due on the home. As the veteran pays off the mortgage and the principal decreases, the amount of VMLI coverage will decrease, too.

Like most of the veterans insurance programs, VMLI coverage isn't free. Participants pay for it, usually by the government withholding a certain amount from their monthly VA disability compensation checks.

The exact amount of the premium is based on complex formulas that include the veteran's age, the unpaid principal due on the home, and the remaining length of the mortgage.

Despite the out-of-pocket premiums, VMLI coverage is a very good deal. The government pays for the administrative costs of the program, and the formulas to calculate the size of premiums use standard life-expectancy projections for the general population, not those for disabled people.

### Application

VMLI coverage is like the active-duty SGLI program in its automatic sign-up provision. If you're eligible and you want *not* to have VMLI, then you must take action. If you do nothing, you get the coverage.

### Fine Points

It's possible for veterans to have more than one piece of property that makes them eligible for VMLI coverage. When that happens, the overall coverage limits and rules apply to a combination of all the property. According to the 1997 rules, the total coverage would be held to $90,000, regardless of the value of all the property. And when the principal due on all mortgages, added together, fell below $90,000, the VMLI coverage would drop to that amount.

## PROGRAMS FOR PRE-1974 DISCHARGES

The U.S. government has offered insurance to its active-duty people, reservists, and veterans since the First World War.

At least one feature of those earlier programs still causes problems today. Many of the earlier insurance policies provide annual dividends to veterans. The news media frequently reports the amounts of those dividends, making newer veterans wonder what they're missing.

None of the government-backed life insurance plans now available to people who are leaving the military—or, generally, who have left the military since the mid-1960s—pay annual dividends.

> Some scam artists target veterans. If you're eligible for a dividend, you don't have to pay anyone to get your money.

This section lists provision highlights of some of the earlier government-backed life insurance programs. Rather than using their formal names, which can get quite confusing when all the programs are mentioned in a short space, we'll refer to them by the "policy letter."

Each individual insurance policy has an identification number. In front of those numbers is a letter or several letters. Each of the various life insurance plans used its own distinctive letter, called the policy letter. It's a useful, shorthand way of identifying which policy we're talking about.

## Dividends

On the anniversary of a veteran taking out a life insurance policy, most of the older programs will offer dividends. These can be paid directly to the veteran or kept in the VA insurance program and used to purchase more coverage.

The Internal Revenue Service has ruled that veterans have to pay taxes on the dividends only when they're paid to the veterans. If the dividends are left with the VA and used to buy more insurance, then they aren't taxable.

Dividends go regularly to veterans with policies in the following programs: K, V, RS, W, J, JR, and JS.

Not eligible for dividends are policies under VGLI, SGLI, or VMLI. Also not eligible are H and RH policies.

## Loans

Veterans can borrow up to 94 percent of the cash value of their insurance policies, while continuing to earn dividends for those policies. Like any other loan, a loan on the insurance policy must be repaid. Also like any other loan, the repayment includes an interest charge.

Veterans can learn about the repayment schedule and interest rates when applying for the loan. Generally, since November 2, 1987, there has been a variable interest rate for loans taken out against V and H policies. That interest rate changes annually. The government guarantees that the interest rate on these policies won't be more than 12 percent or less than 5 percent.

Interest on loans for all K policies is fixed for the life of the loan. That's also the rule for loans taken out before November 1987 that were based on V and H policies.

As with any loan, veterans should make sure they can handle the repayment schedule. Failure to keep up with the repayment scheme can result in the loss of the policy.

## Disabilities

Government-backed insurance programs have a variety of rules that come into play when policyholders become disabled.

For example, people with V and H policies can keep their life insurance without paying any more premiums if they become disabled before their sixty-fifth birthdays and if the disability is permanent.

Veterans with K policies may be eligible to receive the cash value of their insurance coverage if they become permanently and totally disabled.

Whatever the policy, veterans with government-backed life insurance should get some up-to-date, professional advice if confronting a disability that's likely to last several months. They should contact the nearest VA regional office, a benefits counselor at a VA medical facility, or a professional service officer for one of the major veterans groups.

## Disability Riders

Many commercial life insurance companies offer "riders," or special provisions to their policies that offer extra protection for a slightly larger premium.

A popular rider for many policyholders, both veterans and members of the general public, guarantees that the policyholder will receive an extra income if the policyholder becomes disabled.

Disability riders are available for many of the government-backed insurance policies, especially the K, V, and H policies. They are not available for RH, JR, or JS policies.

Another popular rider that's related to disabilities allows policyholders to keep their life insurance without having to pay any more premiums in the event of permanent disabilities.

## Other Policies

Not all the government-backed insurance programs for veterans were mentioned above. Here are the identifying letters and summaries of a few other programs:

- *A:* The bonus to World War I veterans that was the focus of the famous "Bonus March on Washington" in 1932. Some bonuses may still be unclaimed.

- *T:* Term insurance for World War I veterans, which ended in 1925.

- *AN:* Special free coverage for World War II veterans who didn't purchase any coverage and who later died before April 20, 1942.

- *N:* Term insurance for World War II veterans. It converted, over the years, into V policies. No N policies are still in force.

- *ARH:* A free version of the RH policy for people who were mentally incompetent because of a service-connected disability at the time of their discharge or within a year after discharge.

- *K:* Term insurance that World War I veterans could purchase until 1951. For active-duty members from 1919–1940.
- *V:* Permanent insurance for active-duty people from 1941–1951.
- *RS:* Issued to veterans discharged between April 25, 1951, and January 1, 1957.
- *W:* Term insurance that began in 1959 and ends at a veteran's 50th birthday.
- *J:* Permanent insurance for disabled veterans, which closed to new applicants in May 1966.
- *JR:* Same as J program, but for severe disabilities.
- *JS:* Same as J program, except disability must be rated as non-service-connected.
- *H:* Policies for people who served on active duty between October 8, 1940, and September 2, 1945, and who had service-connected disabilities.
- *RH:* Permanent insurance for veterans discharged after April 25, 1951, with service-connected disabilities.

# TEN

# HOME LOANS

### In This Chapter:

- *VA Home Loans*
- *Other Loan Programs*

Home ownership is still part of the American dream. Financial help from the government in purchasing a home is one of the most important benefits of military service.

That help comes in the form of a guaranty from the government to a financial institution that if the veteran stops making regular payments on a home loan, then the government will repay the lender for some of its losses.

No payments are made directly from the government to veterans under this program.

## VA HOME LOANS
### Eligibility

Home loan guaranties are one government benefit for which people outside the government have a prominent voice in making some basic decisions about eligibility. Remember that the actual loans that veterans receive come directly from a bank, savings and loan, or mortgage company. Those financial institutions have the right to decide whether someone applying for a home loan—veteran or nonveteran—is a good financial risk.

Veterans who believe they've been unfairly turned down for a home loan because of race, gender, or because they are veterans, should notify the nearest office of the Department of Veterans Affairs.

> There was no VA home loan program for World War I veterans or for veterans between the two world wars.

Unlike the GI Bill educational program, there's no deadline specifying that a veteran must use the home loan guaranty by a certain time after discharge. Eligible veterans may obtain a VA-backed home loan at any time after their discharge. They may even use it more than once to buy more than one home (but only one at a time).

Following are the eligibility rules for veterans of different eras.

*Now on Active Duty:* Current servicemembers must meet the following criteria:

- Served at least 90 days of continuous active duty. Increases to 180 days after formal end of Persian Gulf conflict.
- Not a six-month enlistee on active duty for training.

*Now in Selected Reserves:* Members of the Selected Reserves must have completed at least six years in the reserves or National Guard and meet one of following conditions:

- Still in Selected Reserves.
- Discharged under honorable conditions.
- Retired.
- Transferred to Ready Reserves.

Note: The legal authority for home loans for reservists is scheduled to expire October 28, 1999. Congress may reauthorize the benefits before they end.

**Spouses:** To qualify for a VA home loan, a person must be the spouse, widow, or widower of one of the following:

- Someone who died on active duty.
- Someone who died after discharge from service-connected causes.
- Someone officially listed as missing in action or prisoner of war for ninety days or longer.

Note: Spouses of deceased veterans lose eligibility when they remarry.

**Persian Gulf Vets:** Veterans of the Persian Gulf War must have served on active duty between August 2, 1990, and the formal end of conflict, which hadn't been set when this book went to press, and meet one of these other conditions:

- Served at least twenty-four months with discharge under conditions other than dishonorable.
- Served less than twenty-four months and been discharged under conditions other than dishonorable for hardship or early-out.
- Been a reservist or guardsman called to active duty during the official period of conflict who served at least ninety days and was discharged honorably.

**Most Peacetime Vets:** Veterans who served on active duty between July 26, 1947, and June 26, 1950, or between February 1, 1955, and August 4, 1964, or enlisted between May 8, 1975, and September 7, 1980, or been commissioned as officers between May 8, 1975, and October 16, 1981, must meet one of the following criteria to qualify for a VA home loan:

- Served at least 181 days continuous active duty and been discharged under conditions other than dishonorable.
- Served less than 181 days and been discharged under conditions other than dishonorable for service-connected disability.

**Other Peacetime Vets:** Those who enlisted between September 7, 1980, and August 1, 1990, or were commissioned as officers between October 16, 1981, and August 1, 1990, must meet one of the following requirements:

- Served the full period of active duty in stated time span.

- Completed twenty-four months of continuous active duty or full period (at least 181 days) for which called to active duty and discharged under conditions other than dishonorable.

- Completed at least 181 days on active duty and discharged for hardship or early-out.

- Discharged for service-connected disability, regardless of length on active duty.

***Other Wartime Vets:*** Also qualifying for VA home loans are people who served at least one day during the Vietnam War, from August 5, 1964, to May 7, 1975; the Korean War, from June 27, 1950, to January 31, 1955; or World War II, between September 16, 1940, and July 25, 1947, and meet both of the following conditions:

- Served at least ninety days on active duty or discharged with less than ninety days for a service-connected disability.

- Discharged under conditions other than dishonorable.

## Qualifying Homes

Homes that veterans wish to purchase with a government-backed loan must pass two tests—a specific test and a general test.

> VA loans cannot be used for investment property. Veterans must use the homes as their primary residences.

The specific test involves a VA-approved appraiser establishing the market value of the home. The goal is to ensure that, since the government is being asked to repay if the veteran defaults, the home itself is a reasonable financial risk for the government.

And here, things can get murky. The government assumes no responsibility for a veteran's choice of a home. It cannot act as an attorney or real estate agent for the veteran, nor can it guarantee that a home is free of defects.

But the government can refuse to back a loan if a home is in disrepair, and it can refuse to guarantee a loan if it is in excess of the fair market value.

There's also a general test to identify qualifying homes. Not every type of home or transaction can qualify for a government-backed VA home loan. Here are the major uses:

- To buy a home.
- To buy a townhouse or condominium.
- To buy a manufactured or mobile home.
- To buy a lot for a manufactured home.
- To build a home.
- To repair, alter, or improve a home.
- To make energy-efficient improvements.
- To simultaneously purchase and improve a home.
- To purchase a manufactured home and improve the lot.
- To refinance an existing home loan.
- To refinance an existing home loan in order to reduce the interest rate.
- To refinance a manufactured home loan and acquire a lot.

Additionally, VA home loan guaranties can be used to purchase or to build residential property containing more than one family unit. There cannot be more than four family units, however, and the veteran must occupy one of them.

If the veteran intends to use income from the other units to repay the mortgage, then VA rules require that the veteran must have a background that provides him with some qualifications to be a landlord. The veteran also must be able to repay the mortgage for at least six months without any rental income.

For a farm to qualify for VA home loans, it must have a home in which the veteran will live. If veterans intend to farm, they must show that the operation has a good chance of being successful. If nonfarming income permits the veteran to qualify for the loan, then farming operations aren't considered in the loan application process.

Businesses cannot be financed through the VA home loan guaranty program.

Cooperatively owned apartments rarely qualify for VA loans. To pass muster, all the cooperative members must be veterans who are using their own VA home loan benefits for the purchase.

VA home loans cannot be used to purchase homes overseas. To qualify, a home must be in one of the fifty states, the District of Columbia, Puerto Rico, Guam, the Virgin Islands, American Samoa, or the Northern Mariana Islands.

### Details of the Program

Although this VA program is commonly called a "home loan," a phrase that even appears here, remember that it's actually a guaranty. The government promises that it will pay the company issuing a mortgage if a veteran defaults on the loan.

The government places a cap on the amount of its liability. For most veterans, that cap was $50,750 in 1997. That dollar amount is often called "the entitlement." The cap doesn't mean that veterans must find a home that costs less than $50,750, but it is the most that the government will pay to a lender.

Manufactured or mobile homes have a guaranty limit of $20,000 if the home is not permanently affixed to a lot. Increases to $36,000 apply if the home is permanently attached to the lot and meets the state's legal definition of "real property."

### Application

Veterans seeking a VA home loan must take at least one of their formal discharge papers, the DD Form 214, to the nearest office of the Department of Veterans Affairs and obtain a second document called a "Certificate of Eligibility." This document can be issued on the spot, often in less than an hour.

## Occupancy

Everyone obtaining a VA home loan guaranty must certify in writing that he or she intends to use the home as the primary residence. This rules out the use of VA loans to purchase rental property and vacation homes.

There don't seem to be any written provisions that stipulate how long a veteran must live in a home before putting it up for rent. Again, VA rules give officials wide discretion. But, in general, it's permissible for veterans to retain their home loans if they move out and rent the property.

## Interest Rates

The government doesn't set the interest rate. That's between the veteran and the mortgage lender.

VA home loan guaranties must be obtained for a fixed-rate. Until 1995, adjustable-rate loans were permitted under the GI Bill program.

## Down Payments

VA rules require a down payment for a small number of specific kinds of purchases that don't apply to the vast majority of homeowners. This lack of a down payment is a major "plus" in the VA loan program for many veterans.

Who may have to make a down payment? The government requires them for the purchase of manufactured or mobile homes, for lots for manufactured or mobile homes, and for loans that exceed the government's appraisal of a property's fair market value.

With these exceptions, the government doesn't require veterans to make a down payment. Some veterans mistakenly believe that VA rules mean that lenders cannot require down payments. That's not the case.

Lenders make their own appraisals of the risks involved in

making a loan to a specific veteran. They can decide to ask a veteran for a down payment.

**Funding Fee**

Each veteran purchasing a home with a VA-backed home loan must pay a small amount, called a "funding fee," to offset the government's cost of running the program and to make up for some of the government's losses when veterans default on their loans.

The size of the funding fee is a certain percentage of, and can be included in, the overall home loan. Thus, if a veteran purchases a $100,000 home and the funding fee is $1,500, then the veteran might include the funding fee in the total loan and take out a loan for $101,500.

Here are the 1997 funding fee rates for specific categories:

• *Loans with no down payment or down payments less than 5 percent:* 2 percent for active-duty veterans; 2.75 percent for reserve veterans.

• *Loans for refinancing, home improvement, and home repair:* 2 percent for active-duty veterans; 2.75 percent for reserve veterans.

• *For second or subsequent use:* 3 percent with a down payment of less than 5 percent; 1.5 percent with a down payment of at least 5 percent; 1.25 percent with a down payment of at least 10 percent.

• *Loans for purchase or new construction with down payment of at least 5 percent but less than 10 percent:* 1.5 percent for active-duty veterans; 2.25 percent for reserve veterans.

• *Loans for purchase or construction with down payment of at least 10 percent:* 1.25 percent for active-duty veterans; 2 percent for reserve veterans.

• *Manufactured or mobile home:* 1 percent for both active-duty and reserve veterans.

- *Interest-rate reduction loans:* 0.5 percent for both active-duty and reserve veterans.

## Closing Costs

Incidental expenses are paid by everyone buying, building, or refinancing a home. Many of these incidental expenses are commonly lumped together and called "closing costs."

Closing costs may include title search, recording fees, a VA appraisal, credit report, survey fees, hazard insurance premiums, prepaid taxes, and a loan-origination fee.

Unlike the VA funding fee, which was discussed above, these closing costs cannot be included in loans for the purchase or construction of homes using VA-backed guaranties.

When a veteran refinances a home loan using the VA guaranty, however, these closing costs can be included in the overall loan.

## Discount "Points"

Frequently, home purchases include up-front payment of additional amounts to the lender. These amounts, called "discount points" or more simply "points," are computed as a percentage of the loan amount.

Except for what are formally known as "Interest Rate Reduction Refinancing Loans," points cannot be included in an overall VA-backed loan. Like closing costs and interest rates, details about the payment of points are worked out between the borrower and the lender.

## Prepayments

One of the commitments that the lender makes to the government is that there will be no penalty for veterans who pay off their mortgages early. That legal protection includes veterans who pay a little more each month than the required mortgage payment.

## Selling

The VA-backed home loan isn't a onetime deal. Veterans can buy several homes using VA guaranties, but they can own only one at a time.

Veterans who closed on a home loan after February 29, 1988, must formally notify the VA if someone else is assuming responsibility for the loan, and the VA must approve the transaction in writing. Application forms for that notification, called "a release from liability," can be obtained from the bank, mortgage company, or savings and loan association that made the loan.

A buyer who closed on a home before March 1, 1988, doesn't have to receive the VA's approval before letting someone else assume the home loan.

If a VA-backed loan is assumed by a nonveteran, the original veteran-owner may not be able to use VA benefits to buy a second home until the mortgage on the first one has been paid up. That's because the government is still liable if the new owner defaults.

One simple way to avoid this problem is for veterans not to let nonveterans assume a VA-backed loan. The veteran can avoid this trap by selling the home and repaying the original loan in full.

But if another veteran assumes a VA-backed loan, including the substitution of "entitlement," then the original owner may be free to seek a VA home loan guaranty to purchase another house.

Once property has been sold or a VA-backed loan has been assumed by another veteran, veterans don't automatically regain the right to seek another VA home loan. They must apply for the right in a process called "restoration of entitlement."

Any VA office has the forms necessary to apply for a restoration of entitlement. This review guarantees that the veteran isn't responsible for any debts to the government and that the veteran is still eligible for VA-backed loans.

### Financial Problems

If a temporary setback like a job loss or unusual expenses results in a veteran being unable to pay the regular monthly mortgage, there is some limited protection for people with VA-backed loans.

Lenders, in order to participate in this program, must formally agree with the Department of Veterans Affairs to offer "reasonable forbearance and indulgence" for veterans in temporary financial difficulty.

Usually, that means that lenders can't threaten to drive veterans out of their homes because a mortgage check was a day or two late.

### OTHER LOAN PROGRAMS

The Department of Veterans Affairs isn't the only federal agency with home loan guaranties for veterans. Another home loan program is run by the Department of Housing and Urban Development, and it's known as the HUD/FHA veterans program.

Here are some of the eligibility rules for HUD/FHA loans:

• At least ninety days of military service that began before September 8, 1980.

• For regular enlisted service that began after September 7, 1980, at least twenty-four months or the full period for which called to active duty or active duty for training.

• For all officers with service that began after October 13, 1982, at least twenty-four months or the full period for which called to active duty or active duty for training.

• Length-of-service times don't affect people discharged for hardship or disability.

• Veterans must have a discharge officially rated as "under other than dishonorable conditions."

Although this isn't a VA program, veterans applying for a HUD/FHA loan need to obtain a special certification of eligibility from a VA regional office.

Specifically, veterans must obtain VA Form 26-8261(a), "Request for Certificate of Veterans Status."

After completing the application and returning it to a VA office, a qualifying veteran will receive a document known as a "Certificate of Veterans Status." That certificate will get the legal wheels turning for a HUD/FHA loan.

# ELEVEN

# GI BILL EDUCATION

### In This Chapter:

- *Montgomery GI Bill*
- *Montgomery GI Bill (Selected Reserves)*
- *Veterans Educational Assistance Program*
- *Vietnam-Era GI Bill*

Since the end of World War II, government help in paying for education has been a major benefit of military service, designed to help people leaving the military make the adjustment back to civilian life. While the name "GI Bill" has remained on the books since the end of World War II, the program has been changed enough to justify slightly different names.

The three major wartime versions of the GI Bill—the World War II, Korean War, and Vietnam War programs—have expired. If you haven't already used your benefits under one of those programs, you can't get any government financial help now. Some veterans of the Vietnam War, however, can obtain government help in paying for civilian education by qualifying for the current program, called the Montgomery GI Bill.

## MONTGOMERY GI BILL

The major program during the 1990s to pick up the tab for veterans in civilian colleges and trade schools is the Montgomery

GI Bill. Like earlier versions of the GI Bill, it is open both to veterans who have been discharged and to people on active duty. And also like earlier versions, both groups have to meet very specific eligibility rules. Unlike the major wartime versions of the GI Bill, however, the Montgomery GI Bill requires participants to make a contribution before they can receive any benefits.

Trivia item: It's easy to understand how the Vietnam-Era GI Bill got its name. But where did the "Montgomery" in the Montgomery GI Bill come from?

G. V. "Sonny" Montgomery was a congressman from Mississippi who chaired the House Veterans Affairs Committee for many years during the final quarter of the twentieth century. He shepherded through Congress the GI Bill version that now bears his name. Until then, it had been simply called "the New GI Bill."

It's possible to earn Montgomery GI Bill benefits by serving either on active duty or in the reserves. Different rules apply in each case. This section covers the rules for people who are still on active duty and for discharged veterans who became eligible for the Montgomery GI Bill because they once served on active duty. For a summary of the rules for people who earned educational help because they served in the reserves, see the section entitled "Montgomery GI Bill (Selected Reserves)," later in this chapter.

## Eligibility

The Montgomery GI Bill is the government's basic educational benefit for people who come on active duty, serve their time, then leave with an honorable discharge.

Over the years, eligibility has been extended to different groups of veterans and active-duty people. That's created a confusing layer of rules. Let's try to examine one layer at a time.

**Who:** The Montgomery GI Bill is open to all enlisted members of all the armed services. It's also available to all officers who received their commissions through officer candidate school, direct commissioning, or as nonscholarship ROTC cadets.

In effect, this means the program is usually closed to graduates of a U.S. military academy and officers who received commissions as scholarship cadets in ROTC. Nevertheless, even these normally barred officers can sign up if they are being discharged with separation pay, Special Separation Benefit, or Voluntary Separation Incentive.

**When:** Participants must have entered the military for the first time after June 30, 1985. The phrase "for the first time" is important. It means what it says.

People who first came on active duty before that date may be eligible for more generous benefits under VEAP (see the section entitled "Veterans Educational Assistance Program," later in this chapter). Or they may be eligible to convert some benefits from the Vietnam-Era GI Bill into benefits under the Montgomery GI Bill.

People officially serving on full-time National Guard duty qualify if they assumed full-time status after November 29, 1989.

**How Long:** Montgomery GI Bill recipients must meet one of these minimum time-in-uniform rules:

• Continuous service for at least three years if the initial military obligation was for three years or for a longer period.

• Continuous service for at least three years, regardless of length of obligation.

• Continuous service of at least two years if the initial military obligation was for less than three years. This results in a reduced benefit.

- Continuous service of at least two years—regardless of length of obligation—followed by at least four years in Selected Reserves.

The normal required time periods for length of service can be shortened for certain involuntary discharges.

*High School Diploma:* If a person comes on active duty without a high school diploma, within the initial period of obligated service he or she must meet one of these three conditions:

- Earn a high school diploma.
- Earn an officially recognized equivalent.
- Complete twelve credit-hours toward a college degree.

*Discharge:* Regardless of the reason for the discharge or the time on active duty, a veteran must have an honorable discharge to take part in the Montgomery GI Bill.

## Approved Courses

To receive payments from the Montgomery GI Bill, veterans and active-duty people must enroll in classes or training that has been approved by the Department of Veterans Affairs.

In general, the following types of education and training are covered by the Montgomery GI Bill:

- College and university courses leading to associate, bachelor's, or graduate degree.
- Accredited independent study leading to a standard college degree.
- Cooperative training programs (for discharged veterans only, not for active-duty people).
- Approved correspondence courses.
- Apprenticeship and on-the-job training (for discharged veterans only, not for active-duty people).
- Courses leading to a diploma or certificate from an approved business, technical, or vocational school.
- Flight training for veterans who already have a private pilot's license; must pass a physical for a commercial license.

## Time Limit

Generally, the government stops writing checks for educational expenses after the tenth anniversary of a veteran's discharge. This "ten-year clock" can be reset if a veteran leaves active duty, then returns for at least ninety days. VA officials can also reset the ten-year clock for people prevented from using their Montgomery GI Bill benefits by a disability or by being detained by a foreign power.

Veterans with initial discharges from active duty that weren't good enough to qualify for educational benefits can have the ten-year limit extended if the discharge is upgraded to honorable.

## Payments and Contributions

Before a servicemember can receive any benefits from the Montgomery GI Bill, he or she must make a contribution. Normally, this takes the form of a nonrefundable monthly deduction from the paycheck. In 1997, the deduction was $100 per month for twelve months.

The basic benefit under the Montgomery GI Bill varies by the amount of active-duty and reserve time. Following are the major categories, plus maximum payment rates in effect for 1997:

- $428 monthly for thirty-six months to veterans with three years on active duty.
- $428 monthly for thirty-six months to veterans with two years on active duty, followed by four years in the Selected Reserves.
- $348 monthly for thirty-six months to veterans with less than three years on active duty.
- Up to $700 monthly in addition to one of these basic rates for people who enlisted or reenlisted in hard-to-fill jobs. This extra money is known as a "kicker". If you're eligible for a kicker, you already know it. You were officially notified when you enlisted or reenlisted.

## An Irrevocable Choice

Once a servicemember decides to participate in the Montgomery GI Bill, that decision cannot be changed. Likewise, people who don't sign up for the Montgomery GI Bill during their first few weeks in the military usually can't sign up at a later time.

Veterans cannot request refunds of their money contributed toward the Montgomery GI Bill. Even if they never enroll in a single class, the government will keep their $1,200.

Refunds are made only when participants die before receiving $1,200 in educational assistance and the death occurs on active duty or within one year of discharge. In such a case, the government will pay the veteran's survivors for the unused portion of the veteran's out-of-pocket contribution.

## MONTGOMERY GI BILL (SELECTED RESERVES)

Not everyone performing invaluable service for the U.S. military wears a uniform for forty hours each week. Reservists and National Guardsmen are an indispensable part of the military.

To recognize this contribution, Congress has extended the Montgomery GI Bill to the men and women who serve the nation's defense needs as members of the reserve component. The reserve version of the Montgomery GI Bill is sometimes referred to as the "Chapter 106" program. The name comes from the section of federal law that created it.

There are two major differences between the active-duty and reserve versions of the program. First, active-duty folks have $100 withheld monthly from their paychecks for a year in order to qualify, while reservists don't have a reduction in salary.

Second, many people taking part in the active-duty version of the Montgomery GI Bill don't begin using their benefits until they leave the military. For most reservists, eligibility for the Montgomery GI Bill ends when they leave the Selected Reserves.

Here are some technical nicknames for educational programs for veterans:

- Chapter 30 = Montgomery GI Bill.
- Chapter 31 = Vocational rehabilitation.
- Chapter 32 = Veterans Educational Assistance Program (VEAP).
- Chapter 34 = Vietnam-Era GI Bill.
- Chapter 106 = Montgomery GI Bill (Selected Reserves).

The nicknames come from the sections of federal law that created them.

## Eligibility

Most people in the reserves and the National Guard have served on active duty, where they may have earned Montgomery GI Bill benefits. If you qualified for this educational program through active-duty time, then you don't have to requalify as a reservist.

Not all reservists and guardsmen are eligible. Only participants in the Selected Reserves can qualify for the Montgomery GI Bill. The Selected Reserves consist of reservists and guardsmen who are assigned to units and members of the trained manpower pool called the Individual Mobilization Augmentation (IMA) program.

Here are some other eligibility rules:

- Enlisted members must have first enlisted after June 30, 1985, or they must have reenlisted or extended an enlistment after that date.
- Enlisted people must enlist or extend for not less than six years.
- Officers must have agreed to serve six years in addition to the original obligation.
- Participants must have completed initial active duty for training (IADT).

- Servicemembers must have earned high school diplomas or the equivalent before finishing IADT.
- Participants must remain in good standing with the Selected Reserves.

Unlike the active-duty version of the Montgomery GI Bill, most reservists and guardsmen lose eligibility for their educational benefits when they leave the Selected Reserves. Eligibility continues for ten years after discharge for people who leave the Selected Reserves because of a medical disability or because of a formal drawdown program. Reservists and guardsmen lose eligibility ten years after the date eligibility began. People who are receiving scholarships under the ROTC program may not use the reserve version of the Montgomery GI Bill.

## Payments and Contributions

Unlike the educational benefit for active-duty personnel, reservists and guardsmen don't have money withheld from their paychecks in order to qualify for their version of the Montgomery GI Bill. What they receive from the government to pay for their educational bills was placed, in 1997, at a maximum of $203 monthly. Generally, that figure should increase yearly at the same rate as inflation.

Reservists attending class full time can receive the maximum payments for thirty-six months. Besides full time, there are three other ways of measuring educational time for the Montgomery GI Bill: three-quarters time, half time, and one-quarter time.

## Fine Points

Some reservists are eligible to participate in both the active-duty and the reserve versions of the Montgomery GI Bill. There are limits on what they can do. For example, federal law prohibits them from being paid twice for the same class.

Nevertheless, it may be possible for some people to use all their benefits under the active-duty program, then to use their benefits under the reserve version, or vice versa. For them, there's a forty-eight-month limit.

Other reservists are eligible, simultaneously, for the reserve version of the Montgomery GI Bill and the Veterans Educational Assistance Program, or VEAP.

They may be able to qualify for payments from both programs at different times, but they cannot use the same period of active duty to qualify for both VEAP and the reserve version of the Montgomery GI Bill.

## VETERANS EDUCATIONAL ASSISTANCE PROGRAM

Between the end of the Vietnam-Era GI Bill and the creation of the Montgomery GI Bill, a program was put on the books with the name of the Veterans Educational Assistance Program.

Although commonly called VEAP, it is sometimes referred to in legal shorthand as the "Chapter 32" program. By any name, it was a milestone for veterans. VEAP was the first educational program for veterans that required an out-of-pocket contribution from participants.

Although no one has been able to sign up for VEAP since 1987, there are still plenty of veterans and active-duty people receiving benefits under this program.

### Eligibility

As with all versions of the GI Bill, VEAP's participants are defined by the period during which they came into the military. To be eligible, people must have first joined the military between January 1, 1977, and July 1, 1985. The word "first" means what it says. If you came on active duty during the eligibility period, then left the military, then returned after the eligibility window had closed, you still could receive financial help for education under the VEAP program.

There's another important eligibility criterion for late users of VEAP benefits, however. In order to get benefits *now,* they must have made some sort of financial contribution before April 1, 1987: Remember that VEAP required military people to make an out-of-pocket contribution before they would receive any matching benefits from the government.

### Contributions

Essentially, VEAP is a matching program: For every dollar contributed by a servicemember, the government adds two dollars to be used to pay educational bills.

The maximum contribution by a servicemember toward VEAP is $2,700. After the government adds its share, the most the majority of veterans will receive from VEAP is $8,100.

Some Army veterans, however, receive more. That service's Army College Fund offered improved VEAP benefits to soldiers who enlisted in some high-skill or hard-to-fill jobs. Those benefits were known as kickers, and could be worth as much as $18,300. If you're eligible for a kicker, you already know it. Everyone who received a kicker signed a written contract with the Army at the time of enlistment that spelled out those rights and benefits.

### Payments

The easiest way to figure out how much a veteran will receive from VEAP is to multiply that person's total contribution by the number three.

Payments to veterans are made monthly. Usually, veterans receive VEAP payments for the same number of months that they contributed money into the program.

### Time Limits

Payments for education under VEAP end ten years after a veteran's discharge.

For veterans who have broken service—that is, they've been discharged at least once and returned to active duty—VEAP payments end ten years after the most recent discharge.

The ten-year limit can be extended if a veteran is unable to attend class or take a training course because of a disability.

## Refunds

While VEAP more closely resembles the current Montgomery GI Bill than earlier versions of the GI Bill, it has some provisions that are unique.

Unlike the Montgomery GI Bill, a veteran can drop out of the VEAP program and receive a refund. The refund includes only the veteran's contribution, not the government's matching funds. Nor will the government pay interest on a servicemember's contribution.

Refunds also are made to survivors when VEAP-eligible veterans die without using all of their educational benefits.

Veterans who haven't used their entire benefits under VEAP by the tenth anniversary of discharge are entitled to receive refunds for their unused contributions to the program. Refunds for unused VEAP benefits should be automatic after the tenth anniversary of discharge.

The nearest VA office can help veterans or their survivors apply for refunds.

## Reenrollments

A unique provision of VEAP allows people to drop out of the program and receive refunds, then to sign up for it again.

This affects veterans who qualified for VEAP during an early stint in the military, who leave the armed forces and get refunds of their unused VEAP contributions, and who later return to active duty.

They would be unable to qualify for the Montgomery GI Bill because VEAP was the educational benefit that was on the books when they first joined the military. Consequently, if they rejoin the military, they can rejoin VEAP.

### Drawdown Conversions

For most veterans, VEAP isn't as useful or as generous as the Montgomery GI Bill. Lawmakers have recognized that, and they have been allowing different categories of VEAP participants who are facing discharge to switch to the Montgomery GI Bill.

If your discharge date is approaching, check with a military education office or transition office to find out whether you qualify for one of the conversion programs.

### VIETNAM-ERA GI BILL

Although the Vietnam-Era GI Bill has elapsed and no payments are being made to anyone under this program, there are still people who are affected by it.

These are the veterans and the military people who served on active duty during the switch from the Vietnam-Era GI Bill to the Montgomery GI Bill, roughly the period 1984 to 1987. More precise dates are listed below.

For them, it's possible to convert their eligibility for the Vietnam-Era GI Bill into eligibility for the Montgomery GI Bill, known as "a Chapter 34 to 30 Conversion."

If they qualify, they will receive the same Montgomery GI Bill rates as everyone else, plus a little more. That additional payment is about $200 monthly for full-time educational study.

### Eligibility

To make the conversion, Vietnam-era veterans must have been eligible for the Vietnam-Era GI Bill. They also must have benefits remaining, technically, under the educational program. Who has benefits remaining? Everyone who never used the Vietnam-Era GI Bill, plus everyone who used it but for less than the maximum time or for less than the maximum amounts for full-time study.

Typically, veterans of that era were entitled to forty-five months of education under the Vietnam-Era GI Bill. If they received checks for less than forty-five months, or checks that were for less than full-time study for forty-five months, then they have benefits remaining under the Vietnam-Era GI Bill.

## Deadlines

Like participants in the Montgomery GI Bill, Vietnam-era veterans who are switching educational programs generally have ten years from the date of their last discharge to use the benefit.

As a rule, VA officials keep the ten-year clock running for any period that a veteran spent off active duty between January 1, 1977, and June 30, 1985.

For veterans who spent two years on active duty and four years in the Selected Reserves, the ten-year clock begins on the date of discharge from active duty or at the end of the four years in the Selected Reserves, whichever is later.

# TWELVE

# Tying Up Loose Ends with the Military

The military can cast a long shadow over a veteran's life. Job skills and personal relationships developed while on active duty can have a decisive impact on lives even decades after taking off the uniform.

Unpleasant aspects of military service can also persist for decades. The injury that was a nuisance when it occurred during military maneuvers can deteriorate into a true disability. Or a scrape that resulted in a hasty departure from the armed forces—along with something less than an honorable discharge—can block passage to important benefits.

Fortunately, the Pentagon and the Department of Veterans Affairs recognize the lasting imprint made by the military on the lives of veterans. Officials have created administrative channels that enable veterans to bring their concerns to the right offices or agencies.

As anyone who has explored those channels can tell you, however, they're not quick. And it's not always clear what's important, why certain decisions were made, or what a veteran should do next.

Before you go it alone or hire a lawyer, it's always best to check into the free sources of help available. VA officials may be restricted in the advice they can give, but they are able to offer copies of forms and written information about procedures.

The major veterans organizations also have full-time professionals, called "service officers," who handle these sorts of problems every week. Their help is free and offered equally to members and nonmembers. They have desks at VA regional offices.

## COPIES OF DISCHARGES

Your discharge papers—known to veterans during the last several decades as DD Form 214—are the basic ticket of admission to a full range of veterans benefits, from disability pay to burial in a national cemetery. Duplicate DD Form 214s can be obtained, free of charge, from the federal government.

### Eligibility

Everyone who has received a discharge from the military can obtain a copy of his or her personal DD Form 214.

If a veteran is incapacitated or otherwise unable to sign a request, a spouse may request a copy on the veteran's behalf. To prevent unnecessary delays, a spouse should clearly explain why the veteran isn't making the request and include documentation—such as a note from a doctor or an admission form to a nursing home—that supports the explanation. If a widow or widower is requesting a copy, he or she should include a copy of the veteran's death certificate.

## Application

If possible, everyone—veterans and family members—requesting a copy of a discharge should use Standard Form 180, "Request Pertaining to Military Records." That form is available from VA regional offices and veterans organizations.

A safety deposit box at a local bank is a good place to keep discharge papers, but make sure family members have access to it.

The government will fulfill requests made in a letter, which should be typed or clearly printed and specify exactly what is being sought, such as a DD Form 214 or any other portion of the military member's official record.

The request should include as much of the following information as possible:

- The veteran's legal name.
- The veteran's Social Security number or service number.
- The veteran's service (e.g., the Army).
- The date the veteran entered the military (or an approximate date).
- The date the veteran left the military (or an approximate date).

The veteran, spouse, widow, or widower should sign the request and make sure it includes a return address. The request, whether made in Standard Form 180 or in a letter, should be mailed to: National Personnel Records Center, Military Personnel Records, 9700 Page Boulevard, Saint Louis, MO 63132-5100.

## Emergencies

It's possible to obtain duplicates of a DD Form 214 by making a request over the telephone, but this option is limited to people with genuine emergencies.

What's a legitimate emergency depends on a case-by-case decision. People who feel they have an immediate need for a DD Form 214 should contact the nearest VA regional office. Officials there can explain the procedure for making a telephone request.

## UPGRADING DISCHARGES

Because most VA benefits depend on receiving at least a general discharge, the government has created several avenues for veterans who believe they were erroneously given an unfavorable discharge.

Using any one of these options, a veteran can have his or her original discharge canceled and receive a new discharge. This process is commonly called "upgrading" a discharge.

The most direct approach for an upgrade is to file an appeal with a discharge review board. Each military department has one of these boards. The U.S. Transportation Department oversees a board for the Coast Guard, and former members of the Marine Corps use the board operated by the Department of the Navy.

### Eligibility

Every veteran who has received a discharge that wasn't rated as honorable can apply for an upgrade.

### Details of the Program

Discharge review boards are empowered to have most discharges changed or replaced.

Veterans applying to a board can present documentation on their own behalf or call witnesses. They can appear in person. They have a right to hire an attorney, be represented by an accredited member of a major veterans organization, or be aided by an employee of a state department of veterans affairs.

Veterans are responsible for paying their own way if they choose to appear personally before a board.

To be successful, a veteran must prove that a discharge was illegally or unfairly given. Boards can review discharges in light of current standards. The boards will commonly upgrade an unfavorable discharge from years ago if someone currently discharged would receive an honorable or general discharge for the same problem or infraction.

Normally, the five-member discharge review boards hold hearings in Washington, D.C. Occasionally, however, they conduct hearings in selected sites around the country. The boards also sometimes send a single person called a hearing examiner to take testimony from veterans across the country.

The decisions made by the discharge review boards must be approved by the secretary of the appropriate military department.

Discharge review boards cannot change any document in a veteran's military personnel file except discharge papers. Other limitations on the boards' authority are significant:

• They cannot review a discharge ordered by a general court-martial.

• They cannot directly determine eligibility for any VA benefit. (But access to more VA benefits usually comes from an upgraded discharge.)

• They cannot change a discharge to a disability discharge. Nor can they change a disability discharge to something else.

• They cannot revoke any discharge or recall any veteran to active duty.

On this last point, it's important to note that discharge review boards commonly recommend to service secretaries that a veteran be given a chance to return to active duty. That's just a recommendation. The final decision rests with the service secretary.

## Application

Requests for a discharge review board hearing to examine a veteran's case must be made within fifteen years after leaving the military.

Applications must be made on DD Form 293, "Application for Review of Discharge or Dismissal." It's available at most VA facilities and from service officers for the major veterans groups. Applications should be accompanied by copies of the original discharge and any supporting materials.

When veterans have died or if they are unable to manage their own affairs, then their applications can be made by a spouse, next of kin, or legal representative. Written evidence of the veteran's death, incapacity, relationship to the applicant, or power of attorney should accompany applications made by other people.

## Fine Points

Congress created the discharge review boards to right discharges that were wrongly given. They weren't created to help people get VA benefits. Historically, the boards have turned a deaf ear to veterans who argued that their discharges should be upgraded just to ensure access to VA programs.

Discharge review boards were set up *solely* to review discharges. Another panel, the military's Board for the Correction of Military Records, discussed next, can also authorize upgrades.

## CORRECTING MILITARY RECORDS

Problems that began in the military as minor, sometimes even clerical mistakes on official documents, can linger for years and cause serious consequences.

Congress has created special three-person boards in each military department that have wide-ranging authority to correct any military document, including discharge papers. This review board is called "Board for the Correction of Military Records" in the Army and Air Force. The Navy and Marine Corps call it "Board for the Correction of Naval Records."

## Eligibility

Everyone who has served in the military can petition one of these boards to correct a military record. Also eligible are people who are still on active duty or still in the reserves.

## Details of the Program

Boards for the correction of records have broad powers that are rare for such administrative operations. By law, they can "correct any military record . . . to correct an error or remove an injustice."

Veterans and military members applying to a board can present documentation on their own behalf. If a board takes up a case, the panel will obtain the person's military records.

Most of the work of the boards is done by studying official records and documentation submitted by people requesting a correction. Hearings are rare, occurring in only a small percentage of cases.

When a board agrees to a hearing, people can be represented by an attorney or an accredited member of a major veterans organization. Veterans can call their own witnesses, but the board has no authority to require anyone to testify.

All hearings are held in Washington, D.C. People petitioning the board are responsible for paying their own expenses related to a hearing.

Typically, it takes more than a year between the time an application is filed with a board and the board issues a final decision. All decisions are reviewed by the secretary of the appropriate military department.

To be successful, a veteran must show that a military record is erroneous or unjust. Often, in disciplinary cases, that means showing that a punishment was too severe for the offense committed. Decisions of the boards for the correction of records must be approved by the secretary of the appropriate military department.

These boards have considerable authority to change official documents in ways affecting the benefits available from the military and the Department of Veterans Affairs. In particular, these boards can do the following:

- Place veterans on the retired rolls.
- Change a previous discharge to a disability retirement.
- Reinstate a veteran on active duty.
- Order a promotion.
- Change performance evaluations.
- Credit a veteran with additional active-duty time, with the result of making the veteran eligible for VA benefits.
- Change the date of a discharge to show completion of an enlistment or active-duty obligation.
- Upgrade discharges ordered by a general court-martial.

On this last item, it's important to note that the boards can upgrade discharges—on the basis that a sentence was unfairly severe—but they cannot overturn convictions.

## Application

Requests for reviews by a board for the correction of records should be made within three years after a veteran discovers an error or injustice.

The boards have the authority to waive the three-year rule if a veteran has a good reason for failing to file within that time. The trend in recent years has been for the boards to follow the three-year rule closely.

Applications must be made on DD Form 149, "Application for Correction of Military or Naval Record." It's available at most VA facilities, from on-base military legal offices, and from service officers for the major veterans groups.

> Correct problems with your military records now. You might not have the time later, when that problem keeps you from getting a vital VA benefit.

If possible, applications should be accompanied by copies of the document that a person wants to change, plus any supporting materials.

A veteran who wants to present his or her case in person before a board must specifically request a hearing when submitting the DD Form 149. The forms have a block for entering those requests.

When veterans have died or if they are unable to manage their own affairs, then their applications can be made by a spouse, parent, next of kin, or legal representative. Written evidence of the veteran's death, incapacity, relationship to the applicant, or power of attorney should accompany applications made by other people.

## Fine Points

The boards for the correction of records do most of their work with paper. Hearings are rare. This has major consequences for anyone who asks a board to correct something on the official record.

The application and the supporting documentation submitted by a veteran must be enough to persuade the board that an error or injustice has occurred. If a board takes up a case, it will study the pertinent portions of the veteran's personnel file. Again, the paperwork initially submitted with the application must make the veteran's case, clearly and persuasively.

Assistance from a professional who has dealt with boards for the correction of records is invaluable. Service officers from the major veterans organizations can provide assistance free of charge. Civilian attorneys who specialize in military law can also help, although they charge for their services.

A typical problem encountered by "go-it-alone" applicants is that they fail to exhaust other available administrative remedies. This is common for active-duty members and reservists, and for veterans with cases more properly handled by a discharge review board.

## COPIES OF MEDALS

Awards and decorations given for military service often become more important—not less—as veterans age and their time in uniform slips farther into the past. Unfortunately, the decorations that veterans originally received on active duty often get misplaced or even lost over the years.

Provisions are on the books to provide veterans with copies of the awards and decorations they received on active duty or while members of the reserves.

### Eligibility

Anyone who was officially awarded a military decoration can request a copy of that medal at any time. Family members and survivors can make those requests when the veteran is unable to do it.

### Details of the Program

If possible, requests should be submitted using VA Standard Form 180, "Request Pertaining to Military Records," which is obtainable from VA offices as well as most major veterans organizations.

Written requests are also accepted. Requests should be typed or printed very clearly and contain the following:

- The veteran's name.
- The veteran's Social Security or military service number.
- The veteran's branch of service.
- The veteran's dates of service (or approximate dates).
- The specific medal being sought.

If possible, include a copy of the veteran's discharge papers, known in recent years as DD Form 214.

All requests, whether by the veteran, a family member acting on the veteran's behalf, or a survivor, should be signed.

## Applications

Whether the request is made on the appropriate VA form or in a letter, it should be sent to the office maintained by each service for these issues.

- *Army:* U.S. Army Reserve Personnel Center, Attn.: DARP-PAS-EAW, 9700 Page Boulevard, Saint Louis, MO 63132-5100.
- *Navy, Marine Corps, Coast Guard:* Navy Liaison Office, Room 3475, 9700 Page Boulevard, Saint Louis, MO 63132-5100.
- *Air Force:* National Personnel Records Center, Military Personnel Records, 9700 Page Boulevard, Saint Louis, MO 63132-5100.

## Fine Points

These procedures were set up for veterans who were awarded medals, misplaced them, and now want the government to replace them. They won't help people who think they should have been given a certain decoration while they were in uniform.

Commercial firms that sell medals often advertise in publications catering to veterans and active-duty military personnel. Sometimes it's quicker to deal with these companies than with the government.

A copy of a medal purchased from a commercial outfit is no less authentic than one given, free, by the government. In fact, the government buys its medals from commercial sources.

When dealing by mail or telephone with a commercial supplier, make sure the medal meets all the formal government specifications and that it's suitable for wear on an active-duty uniform.

# THIRTEEN

# Taps

Old soldiers may "just fade away," but the nation's obligation to them and their families doesn't end.

Survivors of veterans may be entitled to ongoing benefits, especially if the veterans were military retirees, if they were drawing VA disability compensation or VA pensions at the time of their death, or if there were children in the household who were underage or disabled. (You may want to recheck the earlier chapter entitled "Spouses' Pensions.")

The government also provides financial assistance for the burial of certain kinds of veterans, space in national cemeteries, headstones and markers for burials outside national cemeteries, and occasionally honor guards.

Burial-related benefits are the one category of veterans programs for which the local VA office might not be the best, quickest authority. Instead, the directors of local funeral homes usually have the most up-to-date and comprehensive summaries of benefits, along with the forms necessary to file for various programs.

Of course, survivors can go to the nearest VA office or major veterans group for help in understanding and securing their benefits. It may be easier, though, for them to start with the funeral director handling arrangements for their veteran.

## BURIAL ALLOWANCES

The government provides some financial help in paying for the burial expenses of some veterans, but this is a limited benefit that goes only to specific categories of veterans.

The families of Just-Plain-Veteran veterans aren't entitled to this financial support unless the veteran can meet some other eligibility rule, as discussed below.

### Eligibility

As happens with many veterans benefits, the rules pertaining to burial allowances were written at different times and apply to different categories of veterans.

In general, some sort of burial allowance is available for the following:

- People who die on active duty.
- Military retirees.
- Veterans who die directly from service-connected injuries.
- Recipients of VA disability compensation.
- Recipients of VA pensions.
- Disabled vets without next of kin or financial resources.
- Veterans who die in VA facilities.

### Amount of Benefits

As expected, the most generous benefits go to people who die on active duty. They are eligible for separate allowances for body preparation, transportation, and interment in a cemetery. In 1997, the maximum was close to $5,000, although many survivors received less.

The families of veterans whose deaths were directly related to some disability caused by their military service could receive, in 1997, a burial allowance of $1,500. According to federal law, those deaths must be "as a result of a service-connected disability." It doesn't count if a veteran with a service-connected disability dies of some other cause.

Recipients of VA disability compensation and VA pensions and disabled veterans without next of kin or financial resources qualify for a modest burial allowance. In 1997, it was $300. That amount could be increased to $450, in some cases, for burial in a private cemetery.

When veterans die in VA facilities, their survivors are entitled to a $300 burial allowance, plus government-paid transportation of the remains to the community in which the veteran will be buried.

## Application

Application forms are available from funeral directors, VA regional offices, and military survivors assistance and casualty assistance offices.

## HEADSTONES AND MARKERS

Until the early 1990s, the federal government provided either a free headstone or a marker for a veteran's grave, or the government provided a token payment—usually about $50—that could be used by the family toward the purchase of one. Legal authority for the government to pay that allowance is no longer on the books, but headstones and markers are still being provided by the government.

## Eligibility

The rules for free government headstones and markers are broadly written. Those eligible for this benefit include the following:

- Almost all veterans.
- Everyone who dies on active duty.
- Reservists with twenty years' service.
- When buried in national cemeteries, spouses and dependent children of veterans and active-duty people.

Spouses and dependent children of veterans and active-duty people are ineligible for government-paid headstones and markers if they are buried anywhere but in a national, federal, or state veterans cemetery.

Two major categories of former servicemembers ineligible for headstones or markers are those discharged "under dishonorable conditions" and those convicted of "subversive activities."

## Description

The headstones and markers can be flat bronze, flat granite, flat marble, or upright marble. Also covered are niche markers for cremated remains.

Inscriptions at government expense include the following information:

- Name.
- Years of birth and death.
- Branch of service.
- Military rank.
- War service.
- Religious symbol.
- Awards for valor.
- Purple Heart.

Survivors can include other inscriptions or symbols at their own expense.

## Transportation

The government assumes all costs for transporting and emplacing headstones and markers. For veterans not buried in national or state cemeteries, however, the family may have to pay the costs of placing the headstone or marker on the grave.

## Application

Applications for headstones and markers are available from funeral directors, VA regional offices, and military survivors assistance and casualty assistance offices.

## NATIONAL CEMETERIES

National cemeteries are special final resting places for the men and women who have served their country in uniform. There are no costs to a veteran's family for burial in a national cemetery, nor for the maintenance of the plot. The Department of Veterans Affairs has a full-time professional staff that guarantees the finest care for those gravesites. The government has put its full faith and credit behind preserving the national cemeteries, in perpetuity, as dignified resting places for the nation's veterans.

Some national cemeteries are "closed." That means they've used up available land and they're not burying any more veterans.

## Eligibility

Virtually everyone who has ever worn a uniform of a U.S. armed service qualifies for burial in a national cemetery, including the following:

- All veterans of active-duty service.
- Everyone who dies on active duty.
- Reservists who die on active duty.
- Reservists who die while being treated for service-connected causes.

• Members of the Reserve Officers Training Corps (under specific circumstances).

Two major categories of former servicemembers usually ineligible for burial in national cemeteries are those discharged "under dishonorable conditions" and those convicted of "subversive activities."

The following are also eligible for burial in a national cemetery:

• Spouses and dependent children of veterans eligible for burial in a national cemetery.

• Former spouses of veterans who married nonveterans and whose new marriages ended in death or divorce, so long as the new marriage began before October 31, 1990.

Except for this last category, the survivors of other veterans who married nonveterans after the death of the veteran lose the right to burial in a national cemetery.

Spouses and dependent children are buried in the same plot as the veteran. If some other family member dies before the veteran, he or she can be buried in a national cemetery if the veteran also plans to be buried in the same plot.

## Columbaria

Increasingly, national cemeteries have columbaria for the burial of cremated remains. Everyone eligible for burial in a national cemetery is also eligible for admission to a columbarium.

## Arlington

Veterans eligible for burial at Arlington National Cemetery outside Washington, D.C., are limited to the following:

• Military retirees.

• People who die on active duty.

• Veterans who were honorably discharged before October 1, 1949, with disabilities rated at 30 percent or more.

- Recipients of the Medal of Honor, Distinguished Service Cross, Air Force Cross, Navy Cross, Distinguished Service Medal, Silver Star, or Purple Heart.

Rules also authorize burial of other federal officials, at the discretion of the secretary of the Army.

Access to the columbarium at Arlington is less limited. Basically, everyone eligible for burial in a national cemetery is eligible for inurnment at Arlington.

## Application

Unlike private cemeteries, national cemeteries do not accept reservations for plots. Applications are accepted only after the death of a veteran. Funeral directors know the necessary application procedures.

## FINAL HONORS

Normally, other honors, such as flags, honor guards, and special certificates, are also available for the burial of veterans.

## Flag

The government will provide a flag to drape the coffin of most veterans during their funerals and at graveside. This includes the following:

- Veterans of any wartime period.
- Retired military personnel.
- "Gray area" reserve retirees.
- Veterans who served at least one enlistment or obligated period of service since January 31, 1955.
- Veterans who were discharged since January 31, 1955, with a disability.

The flag is presented at the gravesite to a next of kin. Provisions exist authorizing it to be given to "a close friend or associate" of the deceased.

## Honor Guard
Veterans buried in national cemeteries and private cemeteries don't have any legal right to an honor guard to render services at the grave site.

> Can veterans in your area receive military honors during local burials? If not, maybe it's time to work with a veterans group to establish a local honor guard.

Active-duty installations frequently dispatch riflemen and a trumpeter for the nearby burial of veterans. Honor guards are assigned only when it doesn't conflict with military duties. Veterans groups and schools often provide honor guards.

## Presidential Certificates
The survivors of veterans with honorable discharges are entitled to receive a "Presidential Memorial Certificate," a parchment certificate with the veteran's name, an inscription noting the veteran's service to the nation, and the signature of the president.

## Application
Funeral directors know the procedures for obtaining flags and presidential certificates. They also know contact points at military installations and veterans groups who may be able to provide honor guards.

# VA FACILITIES

## ALABAMA

### Medical Centers

Birmingham: More than 500 beds, including nearly 50 in blind rehabilitation center. Open-heart surgery, organ transplant, hemodialysis, Vietnam veterans outreach. *(700 S. 19th Street, Zip: 35233. Phone: 205/933-8101)*

Montgomery: About 200 beds. General medicine, surgery, outpatient psychiatry. Intensive care unit, telemetry unit for medical, surgical, and cardiology. *(215 Perry Hill Road, Zip: 36109. Phone: 205/223-4670)*

Tuscaloosa: More than 700 beds, plus nearly 200 for nursing care. Acute and long-term psychiatry, addictions treatment, rehabilitation medicine, post-traumatic stress. *(3701 Loop Road, East, Zip: 35404. Phone: 205/554-2000)*

Tuskegee: More than 700 beds, plus more than 150 for nursing care. Post-traumatic stress, homeless and chronically mentally ill, geriatric evaluation, female veterans, podiatry, substance abuse program. *(Zip: 36083. Phone: 205/727-0550)*

### Clinics

Anniston: *(226 E. 9th Street, Zip: 36201. Phone: 205/236-1661)*

Decatur: *(401 Lee Street, N.E., Suite 606, Zip: 35602. Phone: 205/350-1531)*

Florence: *(401 E. Spring Street, Zip: 35630. Phone: 205/776-5683)*

Huntsville: *(201 Governor's Drive, S.W., Zip: 35801. Phone: 205/533-1645)*

Huntsville: *(2006 Franklin Street, S. E., Suite 104, Zip: 35801. Phone: 205/534-1691)*

Mobile: *(1359 Springhill Avenue, Zip: 36604. Phone: 205/415-3900)*

Tuscaloosa: *(2017 Rainbow Drive, Zip: 35404. Phone: 205/546-9239)*

### Regional Office

Montgomery: *(345 Perry Hill Road, Zip: 36109. Local: 205/279-4866. Statewide: 800/827-1000)*

### Vet Centers

Birmingham: *(1425 S. 21st Street, Suite 108, Zip: 35205. Phone: 205/933-0500)*

Mobile: *(3725 Airport Boulevard, Suite 143, Zip: 36608. Phone: 205/304-0188)*

## National Cemeteries

Fort Mitchell: *(553 Highway 165, Seale, Zip: 36875. Phone: 205/855-4731)*

Mobile: *(1202 Virginia Street, Zip: 36604. Phone: 904/452-3357)*

## ALASKA

### Clinics

Anchorage: Outpatient services include general medicine, alcohol and drug treatment, mental health, and pharmacy. Arranges for comprehensive medical care with civilian and military facilities, plus VA hospitals in lower forty-eight states. Senior companion program, contract nursing, alcohol halfway houses. *(2925 De Barr Road, Zip: 99508. Phone: 907/257-4700)*

Fort Wainwright: Bassett Army Hospital *(Zip: 99703. Phone: 907/353-5112)*

### Regional Office

Anchorage: *(2925 De Barr Road, Zip: 99508. Local: 907/257-4700. Statewide: 800/827-1000)*

### Benefits Office

Juneau: *(709 W. 9th Street, Zip: 99802. Phone: 907/586-7472)*

### Vet Centers

Anchorage: *(4201 Tudor Centre Drive, Suite 115, Zip: 99508. Phone: 907/563-6966)*

Fairbanks: *(5219 E. 5th Avenue, Suite 102, Zip: 99701. Phone: 907/456-4238)*

Kenai: *(445 Coral Street, Zip: 99611. Phone: 907/283-5205)*

Wasilla: *(851 E. Westpoint Avenue, Suite 109, Zip: 99654. Phone: 907/376-4318)*

## National Cemeteries

Fort Richardson: *(P.O. Box 5-498, Bldg. 997, Davis Highway, Zip: 99505. Phone: 907/384-7075)*

Sitka: *(P.O. Box 1065, Saw Mill Creek Road, Zip: 99835. Phone: 907/384-7075)*

## ARIZONA

### Medical Centers

Phoenix: Nearly 500 beds, plus more than 100 in nursing care unit. Post-traumatic stress, day hospital. *(650 East Indian School Road, Zip: 85012. Phone: 602/277-5551)*

Prescott: More than 200 beds, plus about 50 in nursing care unit and 200 in domiciliary. Intensive care unit, pulmonary disease, physical therapy, pharmacy. *(Highway 89 North, Zip: 86313. Phone: 602/445-4860)*

Tucson: More than 300 beds, plus more than 100 for nursing care. Cancer, cardiology, neurology, kidney transplants, blindness rehabilitation, spinal cord injury. *(3601 S. 6th Avenue, Zip: 85723. Phone: 602/792-1450)*

### Regional Office

Phoenix: *(3225 N. Central Avenue, Zip: 85012. Local: 602/263-5411. Statewide: 800/827-1000)*

### Vet Centers

Phoenix: *(141 E. Palm Lane, Suite 100, Zip: 85004. Phone: 602/379-4769)*

Prescott: *(637 Hillside Avenue, Suite A, Zip: 86301. Phone: 602/778-3469)*

Tucson: *(3055 N. 1st Avenue, Zip: 85719. Phone: 602/332-0333)*

**National Cemeteries**

Phoenix: National Memorial Cemetery of Arizona *(23029 N. Cave Creek Road, Zip: 85024. Phone: 602/379-4615)*

Prescott: *(VA Medical Center, 500 Highway 89N, Zip: 86301. Phone: 602/445-4860)*

## ARKANSAS

**Medical Centers**

Fayetteville: More than 150 beds. Post-traumatic stress, ambulatory surgery, mental hygiene clinic. *(1100 N. College Avenue, Zip: 72703. Phone: 501/443-4301)*

Little Rock: Nearly 1,100 beds, plus another 200 in nursing home and 50 in domiciliary. Open-heart surgery, post-traumatic stress, geriatrics, rehabilitation medicine, cancer center, neurosurgery, ophthalmology, dentistry. *(4300 W. 7th Street, Zip: 72205. Phone: 501/370-6601)*

**Regional Office**

North Little Rock: *(Bldg. 65, Fort Roots, P.O. Box 1280, Zip: 72115. Local: 501/370-3800. Statewide: 800/827-1000)*

**Vet Center**

North Little Rock: *(201 W. Broadway, Suite A, Zip: 72114. Phone: 501/324-6395)*

**National Cemeteries**

Fayetteville: *(700 Government Avenue, Zip: 72701. Phone: 501/444-5051)*

Fort Smith: *(522 Garland Avenue, Zip: 72901. Phone: 501/783-5345)*

Little Rock: *(2523 Confederate Boulevard, Zip: 72206. Phone: 501/324-6401)*

## CALIFORNIA

**Medical Centers**

Fresno: More than 250 beds. Respite care, sleep lab, hospice, nursing home care unit. *(2615 E. Clinton Avenue, Zip: 93703. Phone: 209/225-6100)*

Livermore: Nearly 200 hospital beds, plus more than 100 beds in nursing care unit. Long-term care, respite care, geriatric evaluation, neurology, ophthalmology, hospice, preventative medicine. *(4951 Arroyo Road, Zip: 94550. Phone: 415/447-2560)*

Loma Linda: More than 500 beds. Intensive care, alcohol dependency, cardiac catheterization lab, nuclear medicine, electron microscopy, hemodialysis center, sleep disorders, post-traumatic stress. *(11201 Benton Street, Zip: 92357. Phone: 714/825-7084)*

Long Beach: More than 1,200 beds, plus nearly 200 beds in nursing care unit. Lithotripsy unit, laser center. *(5901 E. 7th Street, Zip: 90822. Phone: 310/494-2611)*

Palo Alto: Nearly 1,500 beds. Spinal cord injury, blindness rehab center, schizophrenia research center, women's trauma recovery, post-traumatic stress. *(3801 Miranda Avenue, Zip: 94304. Phone: 415/493-5000)*

San Diego: More than 400 beds. Cardiac surgery, spinal cord injury, AIDS, diabetes. Extended care, hospice, geropsychiatry. Substance abuse, Alzheimer's, neurology. *(3350 La Jolla Village Drive, Zip: 92161. Phone: 619/552-8585)*

San Francisco: More than 300 beds, plus more than 100 in nursing care. AIDS, pacemaker center, post-traumatic stress, open-heart surgery, prosthetics, hemodialysis, orthopedics, angioplasty. *(4150 Clement Street, Zip: 94121. Phone: 415/221-4810)*

West Los Angeles: More than 1,300 beds, plus 300 in domiciliary and more than 200 for nursing care. Neuropsychiatry, AIDS, cardiac clinic, major dental lab, hemodialysis, hospice, post-traumatic stress, prosthetics. *(Wilshire & Sawtelle Boulevards, Zip: 90073. Phone: 310/478-3711)*

**Clinics**
Berkeley: *(841 Folger Avenue, Zip: 94710. Phone: 510/486-3902)*
East Lost Angeles: *(5400 E. Olympic Boulevard, Zip: 90040. Phone: 213/894-5339)*
Los Angeles: Substance abuse, post-traumatic stress, neuromuscular disease program, geriatric evaluation, gastroenterology. *(351 E. Temple, Zip: 90012. Phone: 213/253-2677)*
Martinez: *(1111 Haven Street, Zip: 94553. Phone: 510/372-2665)*
Martinez: *(150 Muir Road, Zip: 94553. Phone: 510/372-2179)*
Oakland: *(2221 Martin Luther King Jr. Way, Zip: 94612. Phone: 510/273-7096)*
Pleasant Hill: *(Northern California System of Clinics, 2300 Contra Costa Boulevard, Zip: 94523. Phone: 510/372-2000)*
Redding: *(2787 Eureka Way, Zip: 96001. Phone: 916/246-5444)*
Sacramento: *(4600 Broadway, Zip: 95820. Phone: 916/731-7300)*
San Diego: *(2022 Camino Del Rio North, Zip: 92108. Phone: 619/220-4065)*
Santa Barbara: *(4440 Calle Real, Zip: 93110. Phone: 805/683-1491)*
Sepulveda: *(1611 Plummer Street, Zip: 91343. Phone: 818/891-7711)*

**Regional Offices**
Los Angeles: Serving counties of Inyo, Kern, Los Angeles, Orange, San Bernardino, San Luis Obispo, Santa Barbara, and Ventura. *(Federal Building, 11000 Wilshire Boulevard, Zip: 90024. Local: 310/479-4011. Statewide: 800/827-1000)*
Oakland: Serving remaining counties in California, except for Alpine, Lassen, Modoc, and Mono. *(1301 Clay Street, Room 1300, North, Zip: 94612. Local: 510/637-1325. Statewide: 800/827-1000)*
San Diego: Serving counties of Imperial, Riverside, and San Diego. *(2022 Camino Del Rio North, Zip: 92108. Local: 619/297-8220. Statewide: 800/827-1000)*
Counties of Alpine, Lassen, Modoc, and Mono are served by the regional office in Reno, Nevada.

**Benefits Office**
East Los Angeles: *(5400 E. Olympic Boulevard, Zip: 90022. Phone: 213/722-4927)*

**Vet Centers**
Anaheim: *(859 S. Harbor Boulevard, Zip: 92805. Phone: 714/776-0161)*
Burlingame: *(1234 Howard Avenue, Zip: 94010. Phone: 415/344-3126)*
Chico: *(25 Main Street, Zip: 95926. Phone: 916/899-8549)*
Commerce: *(VA East L.A. Clinic, 5400 E. Olympic Boulevard, Room 140, Zip: 90022. Phone: 213/728-9966)*
Concord: *(1899 Clayton Road, Suite 140, Zip: 94520. Phone: 510/680-4526)*
Eureka: *(305 V Street, Zip: 95501. Phone: 707/444-8271)*
Fresno: *(3636 N. 1st Street, Suite 112, Zip: 93726. Phone: 209/437-5660)*
Los Angeles/South Central: *(251 West 85th Place, Zip: 90003. Phone: 310/215-2380)*

Los Angeles/West: *(2000 Westwood Boulevard, Zip: 90025. Phone: 310/475-9509)*
Marina: *(455 Reservation Road, Suite E, Zip: 93933. Phone: 408/384-1660)*
Oakland: *(287 Seventeenth Street, Zip: 94612. Phone: 510/273-7341)*
Riverside: *(4954 Arlington Avenue, Suite A, Zip: 92571. Phone: 909/276-6342)*
Rohnert Park: *(6225 State Farm Drive, Suite 101, Zip: 94928. Phone: 707/586-3295)*
Sacramento: *(1111 Howe Avenue, Suite 390, Zip: 95825. Phone: 916/978-5477)*
San Diego: *(2900 Sixth Avenue, Zip: 92103. Phone: 619/294-2040)*
San Francisco: *(25 Van Ness Avenue, Zip: 94102. Phone: 415/431-6021)*
San Jose: *(278 N. 2nd Street, Zip: 95112. Phone: 408/993-0729)*
Santa Barbara: *(1300 Santa Barbara Street, Zip: 93101. Phone: 805/564-2345)*
Sepulveda: *(16126 Lassen Street, Zip: 91343. Phone: 818/892-9227)*
Upland: *(313 N. Mountain Avenue, Zip: 91786. Phone: 909/982-0416)*
Vista: *(1830 West Drive, Tri City Plaza, Suite 103, Zip: 92083. Phone: 619/945-8941)*

**National Cemeteries**
Fort Rosencrans/Point Loma: *(P.O. Box 6237, San Diego, Zip: 92166. Phone: 619/553-2084)*
Golden Gate: *(1300 Sneath Lane, San Bruno, Zip: 94066. Phone: 415/589-7737)*
Los Angeles: *(950 S. Sepulveda Boulevard, Zip: 90049. Phone: 310/824-4311)*
Riverside: *(22495 Van Buren Boulevard, Zip: 92508. Phone: 909/653-8417)*

San Francisco/Presidio of San Francisco: *(P.O. Box 29012, Zip: 94129. Phone: 415/561-2008)*
San Joaquin Valley: *(32053 W. McCabe Road, Gustine, Zip: 95322. Phone: 209/854-1041)*

## COLORADO
**Medical Centers**
Denver: Nearly 400 beds, plus more than 50 beds in nursing unit. Sleep laboratory, AIDS, hospice, and hemodialysis. *(1055 Clermont Street, Zip: 80220. Phone: 303/399-8020)*
Fort Lyon: Nearly 350 beds, plus 150 beds in nursing home units. Specializes in long-term care for chronic psychiatric problems and medical impairments. *(Zip: 81038. Phone: 719/384-3100)*
Grand Junction: Nearly 100 beds, plus another 50 in nursing care units. Respiratory care, mental hygiene, computerized tomography imaging, diagnostic nuclear medicine, substance abuse. *(2121 North Avenue, Zip: 81501. Phone: 303/242-0731)*

**Clinic**
Colorado Springs: *(1785 N. Academy Boulevard, Zip: 80909. Phone: 719/380-0004)*

**Regional Office**
Denver: *(44 Union Boulevard, P.O. Box 25126, Zip: 80225. Local: 303/980-1300. Statewide: 800/827-1000)*

**Vet Centers**
Boulder: *(2128 Pearl Street, Zip: 80302. Phone: 303/440-7306)*
Colorado Springs: *(416 E. Colorado Avenue, Zip: 80903. Phone: 719/471-9992)*
Denver: *(1815 Federal Building, Zip: 80204. Phone: 303/433-7123)*

## National Cemeteries

Fort Logan: *(3698 S. Sheridan Boulevard, Denver, Zip: 80235. Phone: 303/761-0117)*

Fort Lyon: *(VA Medical Center, Zip: 81038. Phone: 719/384-3152)*

## CONNECTICUT
### Medical Centers

Newington: About 150 beds. Intensive care units. Acute medicine, ambulatory care, chronic psychiatry, dental, acute and chronic geriatric, rehabilitation medicine, neurology, respite care, same-day minor surgery. *(555 Willard Avenue, Zip: 06111. Phone: 203/666-6951)*

West Haven: Nearly 600 beds, plus almost 100 for nursing care. Blindness rehabilitation, cardiac arrhythmia center, comprehensive cancer, respite, stroke, post-traumatic stress, epilepsy, open-heart surgery. *(W. Spring Street, Zip: 06516. Phone: 203/932-5711)*

### Regional Office

Hartford: *(450 Main Street, Zip: 06103. Local: 203/278-3230. Statewide: 800/827-1000)*

### Vet Centers

Hartford: *(370 Market Street, Zip: 06120. Phone: 203/240-3543)*

New Haven: *(141 Captain Thomas Boulevard, Zip: 06516. Phone: 203/932-9899)*

Norwich: *(100 Main Street, Zip: 06360. Phone: 203/887-1755)*

## DELAWARE
### Medical Center

Wilmington: More than 200 beds, plus about 50 for nursing care. Hemodialysis, respiratory care, cardiopulmonary, rehabilitation medicine, geriatric evaluation, substance abuse (including detoxification). *(1601 Kirkwood Highway, Zip: 19805. Phone: 302/994-2511)*

### Regional Office

Wilmington: *(1601 Kirkwood Highway, Zip: 19805. Local: 302/998-0191. Statewide: 800/827-1000)*

### Vet Center

Wilmington: *(VAMROC Bldg. 2, 1601 Kirkwood Highway, Zip: 19805. Phone: 302/994-1660)*

## DISTRICT OF COLUMBIA
### Medical Center

Washington: More than 700 beds, plus more than 100 for nursing care. Alcoholism, AIDS, hypertension, cardiovascular disease, spinal cord regeneration, pain clinic, sleep lab, Persian Gulf illnesses. *(50 Irving Street, N.W., Zip: 20422. Phone: 202/745-8000)*

### Regional Office

Washington: *(1120 Vermont Avenue, N.W., Zip: 20421. Phone: 202/418-4343)*

### Vet Center

Washington: *(801 Pennsylvania Avenue, S.E., Zip: 20003. Phone: 202/543-8821)*

## FLORIDA
### Medical Centers

Bay Pines: Nearly 700 beds, with almost 250 beds in nursing unit and 200 in domiciliary. Large community nursing home care program. Substance abuse, mental hygiene, speech pathology, stress, gynecology. *(10000 Bay Pines Boulevard, N., Zip: 33504. Phone: 813/398-6661)*

Gainesville: Nearly 500 beds, plus more than 100 in nursing home care units. Geriatric research lab, post-traumatic stress. *(1601 Southwest Archer Road, Zip: 32608. Phone: 904/376-1611)*

Lake City: More than 300 beds, including nearly 250 in nursing care unit. Vietnam veterans outreach program. Acute psychiatry, recreational therapy, female veterans program, noninvasive cardiology, speech therapy. *(801 S. Marion Street, Zip: 32055. Phone: 904/755-3016)*

Miami: Nearly 700 beds, plus more than 200 in nursing care unit. Centers for AIDS, day treatment, hemodialysis, prosthetics, spinal cord injury, substance abuse. Oral surgery and implantology, open-heart surgery. *(1201 N.W. 16th Street, Zip: 33125. Phone: 305/324-4455)*

Tampa: Nearly 700 beds, plus more than 200 for nursing care. Intensive care, spinal cord injury, traumatic brain injury, eye clinic, magnetic resonance imaging, hemodialysis, open-heart surgery, homeless vets program, orthopedic surgery. *(13000 Bruce B. Downs Boulevard, Zip: 33612. Phone: 813/822-6011)*

West Palm Beach: More than 500 beds, with 120 in nursing unit. Adult day health care, dialysis, noninvasive cardiology, eye clinic.

*(7305 N. Military Trail, Zip: 33240. Phone: 407/882-6700)*

### Clinics

Daytona Beach: *(1900 Mason Avenue, Zip: 32117. Phone: 904/274-4600)*

Fort Myers: *(2070 Carrell Road, Zip: 33901. Phone: 813/939-3939)*

Jacksonville: *(1833 Boulevard, Zip: 32206. Phone: 904/232-2712)*

Key West: *(1111 Twelfth Street, Suite 207, Zip: 33040. Phone: 305/536-6696)*

Oakland Park: *(5599 N. Dixie Highway, Zip: 33334. Phone: 305/771-2101)*

Orlando: *(5201 Raymond Street, Zip: 32803. Phone: 407/629-1599)*

Pensacola: *(312 Kenmore Road, Zip: 32503. Phone: 904/476-1100)*

Port Richey: *(8911 Ponderosa, Zip: 34668. Phone: 813/869-3203)*

Riviera Beach: *(301 Broadway, Executive Plaza, Zip: 33404. Phone: 407/845-2800)*

Tallahassee: *(1607 St. James Court, Zip: 32308. Phone: 904/878-0191)*

### Regional Office

Saint Petersburg: *(144 First Avenue, South, Zip: 33701. Local: 813/898-2121. Statewide: 800/827-1000)*

### Benefits Offices

Fort Myers: *(2070 Carrell Road, Zip: 33901)*

Jacksonville: *(1633 Boulevard, Room 3109, Zip: 32206)*

Miami: *(Federal Building, 51 S.W. 1st Avenue, Room 120, Zip: 33130)*

Oakland Park: *(5599 N. Dixie Highway, Zip: 33334)*

Orlando: *(83 West Columbia Street, Zip: 32806)*

Pensacola: *(312 Kenmore Road, Room 1-G-250, Zip: 32503)*

Riviera Beach: *(310 Broadway, Executive Plaza, Zip: 33404)*

## Vet Centers

Fort Lauderdale: *(315 N.E. 3rd Avenue, Zip: 33301. Phone: 305/356-7926)*

Jacksonville: *(1833 Bowlevard Street, Zip: 32206. Phone: 904/232-3621)*

Lake Worth: *(2311 Tenth Avenue, North, Room 13, Palm Beach, Zip: 33461. Phone: 407/585-0441)*

Miami: *(2700 S.W. 3rd Avenue, Suite 1-A, Zip: 33129. Phone: 305/859-8387)*

Orlando: *(5001 S. Orange Avenue, Suite A, Zip: 32809. Phone: 407/857-2800)*

Pensacola: *(202 W. Jackson Street, Zip: 32501. Phone: 904/435-8761)*

Saint Petersburg: *(2837 First Avenue, N., Zip: 33713. Phone: 813/893-3791)*

Sarasota: *(1800 Siesta Drive, Zip: 34239. Phone: 813/952-9406)*

Tallahassee: *(249 E. 6th Avenue, Zip: 32303. Phone: 904/942-8810)*

Tampa: *(1507 W. Sligh Avenue, Zip: 33604. Phone: 813/228-2621)*

## National Cemeteries

Barrancas: *(Pensacola Naval Air Station, Zip: 32508. Phone: 904/452-3357)*

Bay Pines: *(P.O. Box 477, Zip: 33504. Phone: 813/398-9426)*

Florida/Bushnell: *(P.O. Box 337, Bushnell, Zip: 33513. Phone: 904/793-7740)*

Saint Augustine: *(104 Marine Street, Zip: 32084. Phone: 904/793-7740)*

## GEORGIA

### Medical Centers

Augusta: More than 1,000 beds, with about 40 beds in nursing unit. Regional facility for spinal cord injury, post-traumatic stress, long-term psychiatry, hemodialysis, open-heart surgery. Sleep, speech, and stroke rehabilitation. *(1 Freedom Way, Zip: 30910. Phone: 706/733-0188)*

Decatur: About 550 beds, plus about 120 beds in nursing unit. Open-heart surgery, geriatrics, AIDS, Alzheimer's, prosthetics, psychiatric, alcohol and drug treatment. *(1670 Clairmont Road, Zip: 30033. Phone: 404/321-6111)*

Dublin: Nearly 800 beds, including about 350 for domiciliary care and nearly 100 in nursing unit. Intensive care, respiratory care, rehabilitation medicine, long-term psychiatric. *(1826 Veterans Boulevard, Zip: 31021. Phone: 912/258-2000)*

### Clinics

Columbus: *(1008 Broadway, Zip: 31902. Phone: 706/649-7879)*

Savannah: *(325 W. Montgomery Crossroad, Zip: 31406. Phone: 912/920-0214)*

### Regional Office

Atlanta: *(730 Peachtree Street, N.E., Zip: 30365. Local: 404/881-1776. Statewide: 800/827-1000)*

### Vet Centers

Atlanta: *(77 Peachtree Place, N.W., Zip: 30309. Phone: 404/347-7264)*

Savannah: *(8110 White Bluff Road, Zip: 31406. Phone: 912/927-7360)*

### National Cemetery

Marietta: *(500 Washington Avenue, Zip: 30060. Phone: 404/428-5631)*

# HAWAII
## Medical Center
Honolulu: Clinic-based home care, substance abuse rehabilitation, post-traumatic stress. *(P.O. Box 50188, 300 Ala Moana Boulevard, Zip: 96850. Phone: 808/566-1000)*

## Regional Office
Honolulu: *(P.O. Box 50188, 300 Ala Moana Boulevard, Zip: 96850. Local: 808/566-1000. Statewide: 800/827-1000)*

## Vet Centers
Hilo: *(120 Keawe Street, Suite 201, Zip: 96720. Phone: 808/969-3833)*
Honolulu: *(1680 Kapiolani Boulevard, Suite F, Zip: 96814. Phone: 808/566-1764)*
Kailua-Kona: *(Pottery Terrace, Fern Building, #415, Zip: 96740. Phone: 808/329-0574)*

## National Cemetery
Honolulu: National Memorial Cemetery of the Pacific *(2177 Puowaina Drive, Zip: 96813. Phone: 808/566-1430)*

# IDAHO
## Medical Center
Boise: More than 120 beds. Intensive care unit. Speech pathology, hemodialysis, mental health clinic, respiratory care. *(500 West Fort Street, Zip: 83702. Phone: 208/336-5100)*

## Clinic
Pocatello: *(1651 Alvin Rickin Drive, Zip: 83201. Phone: 208/232-6214)*

## Regional Office
Boise: *(805 W. Franklin Street, Zip: 83702. Local: 208/334-1010. Statewide: 800/827-1000)*

## Vet Centers
Boise: *(1115 W. Boise Avenue, Zip: 83706. Phone: 208/342-3612)*
Pocatello: *(1975 S. 5th Street, Zip: 83201. Phone: 208/232-0316)*

# ILLINOIS
## Medical Centers
Chicago/Lakeside: Nearly 500 beds. Emphasis on neurosurgery, neurology, allergies. Intensive-care unit. Speech pathology, sickle-cell screening, hemodialysis. VA national allergy program, ambulatory surgery. *(333 E. Huron Street, Zip: 60611. Phone: 312/943-6600)*
Chicago/Westside: More than 400 beds. Post-traumatic stress, drug and alcohol dependency, Alzheimer's, geriatrics. *(820 S. Damen Avenue, P.O. Box 8195, Zip: 60680. Phone: 312/666-6500)*
Danville: More than 850 beds, including nearly 200 nursing care beds. Long-term psychiatric care, alcohol treatment, mental health, visual impairment services, rehabilitation services. Regional signage program. *(1900 E. Main Street, Zip: 61832. Phone: 217/442-8000)*
Hines: Nearly 1,000 acute-care hospital beds, plus nearly 300 in extended-care facility. Heart and kidney transplants, spinal cord injury, magnetic resonance imaging, comprehensive rehabilitation center, adult day care center. *(Roosevelt Road & 5th Avenue, Zip: 60141. Phone: 703/343-7200)*
Marion: Nearly 200 beds, plus more than 50 in nursing care unit. Respite care, geriatric evaluation, general dentistry, women's health, cardiology, nuclear medicine, kinesiotherapy, urology, psychiatry. *(2401 W. Main Street, Zip: 62959. Phone: 618/997-5311)*

North Chicago: More than 700 beds, plus more than 300 in nursing care unit and more than 60 in domiciliary. Stress disorder unit, geriatric evaluation, psychiatric day treatment. Independent-living program, respite care. *(3001 Green Bay Road, Zip: 60064. Phone: 708/688-1900)*

### Clinic

Peoria: *(411 W. Martin Luther King Drive, Zip: 61605. Phone: 309/671-7350)*

### Regional Office

Chicago: *(536 S. Clark Street, P.O. Box 8136, Zip: 60680. Local: 312/663-5510. Statewide: 800/827-1000)*

### Vet Centers

Chicago: *(1514 E. 63rd Street, Zip: 60637. Phone: 312/684-5500)*
Chicago Heights: *(1600 Halsted Street, Zip: 60411. Phone: 708/754-0340)*
East Saint Louis: *(1269 N. 89th Street, Suite 1, Zip: 62203. Phone: 618/397-6602)*
Evanston: *(565 Howard Street, Zip: 60202. Phone: 708/332-1019)*
Moline: *(1529 16th Avenue, Room 6, Zip: 61265. Phone: 309/762-6954)*
Oak Park: *(155 S. Oak Park Avenue, Zip: 60302. Phone: 708/383-3225)*
Peoria: *(3310 N. Prospect Street, Zip: 61603. Phone: 309/671-7300)*
Springfield: *(624 S. 4th Street, Zip: 62702. Phone: 217/492-4955)*

### National Cemeteries

Alton: *(600 Pearl Street, Zip: 62003. Phone: 314/263-8691)*
Camp Butler: *(Rural Route 1, Springfield, Zip: 62707. Phone: 217/522-5764)*
Danville: *(1900 E. Main Street, Zip: 61832. Phone: 217/431-6550)*

Mound City: *(P.O. Box 38, Zip: 62963. Phone: 314/263-8691)*
Quincy: *(36th & Maine Streets, Zip: 62301. Phone: 319/524-1304)*
Rock Island: *(P.O. Box 737, Moline, Zip: 61265. Phone: 309/782-2094)*

## INDIANA
### Medical Centers

Fort Wayne: More than 100 beds, with about 50 in nursing care unit. Specializes in hospital-based home care, cancer treatment, gerontology, and optometry. *(2121 Lake Avenue, Zip: 46805. Phone: 219/426-5431)*
Indianapolis: More than 550 beds. Acute medical, surgical, psychiatric, neurological, and nursing home care. Kidney transplants, intensive care, orthopedic services. *(1481 W. 10th Street, Zip: 46202. Phone: 317/635-7401)*
Marion: More than 800 beds, plus nearly 100 in nursing care unit. AIDS, combat veterans treatment program, geriatric evaluation, halfway house, oral surgery, podiatry, pulmonary function, rehabilitation medicine, respite care. *(E. 38th Street, Zip: 46952. Phone: 317/674-3321)*

### Clinics

Crown Point: *(9330 Broadway, Zip: 46307. Phone: 219/662-0001)*
Evansville: *(500 E. Walnut, Zip: 47713. Phone: 812/865-6202)*

### Regional Office

Indianapolis: *(575 N. Pennsylvania Street, Zip: 46202. Local: 317/226-5566. Statewide: 800/827-1000)*

### Vet Centers

Evansville: *(311 N. Weinbach Avenue, Zip: 47711. Phone: 812/473-5993)*

Fort Wayne: *(528 West Berry Street, Zip: 46802. Phone: 219/460-1456)*
Gary: *(2236 West Ridge Road, Zip: 46403. Phone: 219/887-0048)*
Indianapolis: *(3833 Meridian, Zip: 46208. Phone: 317/927-6440)*

## National Cemeteries
Crown Hill: *(700 W. 38th Street, Indianapolis, Zip: 46208. Phone: 317/674-0264)*
Marion: *(1700 E. 38th Street, Zip: 46952. Phone: 317/674-0284)*
New Albany: *(1943 Ekin Avenue, Zip: 47150. Phone: 502/893-3852)*

## IOWA
### Medical Centers
Des Moines: About 150 beds. Laser eye surgery, wheelchair sports, joint replacements, cardiac catheterization. *(30th & Euclid Avenue, Zip: 50310. Phone: 515/255-2173)*
Iowa City: Nearly 300 beds, plus nearly 50 psychiatric beds. Regional center for cancer services. Kidney transplants, sleep studies, women's health clinic, burn clinic, cardiac bypass. *(Highway 6 West, Zip: 52246. Phone: 319/338-0581)*
Knoxville: About 650 beds, plus more than 100 in domiciliary facility. Acute and long-term care referrals. Special programs for substance abuse, Alzheimer's, and homelessness. Ventilator-dependent unit. Residential program for post-traumatic stress. *(1515 W. Pleasant Street, Zip: 50138. Phone: 515/842-3101)*

### Clinic
Bettendorf: *(2979 Victoria Drive, Zip: 52722. Phone: 319/338-0581)*

### Regional Office
Des Moines: *(210 Walnut Street, Zip: 50309. Local: 515/284-0219. Statewide: 800/827-1000)*

### Vet Centers
Des Moines: *(2600 Martin Luther King Parkway, Zip: 50310. Phone: 515/284-4929)*
Sioux City: *(706 Jackson, Zip: 51101. Phone: 712/255-3808)*

### National Cemetery
Keokuk: *(1701 J Street, Zip: 52632. Phone: 319/524-1304)*

## KANSAS
### Medical Centers
Leavenworth: Nearly 300 beds, plus more than 100 in nursing care unit and 450 in domiciliary. Geriatrics, acute medical, surgical, and psychiatric programs. Intensive-care unit. Centralized mail-out pharmacy. *(4101 S. 4th Street, Zip: 66048. Phone: 913/682-2000)*
Topeka: More than 500 beds, with nearly 100 for nursing care. Intensive care, post-traumatic stress, alcohol and drug treatment, biofeedback, respiratory care, inpatient rehabilitation. *(2200 Gage Boulevard, Zip: 66622. Phone: 913/272-3111)*
Wichita: More than 200 beds, plus about 50 for nursing care. Women's clinic, mental hygiene, inpatient alcohol, visual impairment services, prosthetics lab. *(5500 E. Kellogg, Zip: 67218. Phone: 316/685-2221)*

### Regional Office
Wichita: *(5500 E. Kellogg, Zip: 67211. Local: 316/682-2301. Statewide: 800/827-1000)*

### Vet Center
Wichita: *(413 S. Pattie, Zip: 67211. Phone: 316/265-3260)*

## National Cemeteries
Fort Leavenworth: *(Zip: 66027. Phone: 913/758-4105)*
Fort Scott: *(P.O. Box 917, Zip: 66701. Phone: 316/223-2840)*
Leavenworth: *(P.O. Box 1694, Zip: 66048. Phone: 913/758-4105)*

## KENTUCKY
### Medical Centers
Lexington: More than 700 beds, plus 100 in nursing care unit. Intensive-care units, cardiac labs, ventilator-dependent unit, electronmicroscopy, geriatric evaluation, pulmonary function lab, hemodialysis. *(Leestown Road, Zip: 40511. Phone: 606/233-4511)*
Louisville: Nearly 350 beds. Diabetics, cancer, hypertension, shock, laser therapy, orthopedics, geriatric evaluation, rehabilitation medicine, nuclear medicine, day treatment center. *(800 Zorn Avenue, Zip: 40206. Phone: 502/895-3401)*

### Regional Office
Louisville: *(545 S. Third Street, Zip: 40202. Local: 502/584-2231, Statewide: 800/827-1000)*

### Vet Centers
Lexington: *(301 E. Vine Street, Zip: 40503. Phone: 606/233-4511)*
Louisville: *(1355 S. 3rd Street, Zip: 40208. Phone: 502/636-4002)*

### National Cemeteries
Camp Nelson: *(6980 Danville Road, Nicholasville, Zip: 40356. Phone: 606/885-5727)*
Cave Hill: *(701 Baxter Road, Louisville, Zip: 40204. Phone: 502/893-3852)*
Danville: *(377 N. First Street, Zip: 40442. Phone: 606/885-5727)*
Lebanon: *(RR 1, Box 616, Zip: 40033.*
*Phone: 502/893-3652)*
Lexington: *(833 W. Main Street, Zip: 40508. Phone: 606/885-5727)*
Mill Springs: *(Rural Route 2, Nancy, Zip: 42544. Phone: 606/885-5727)*
Zachary Taylor: *(4701 Brownsboro Road, Louisville, Zip: 40207. Phone: 502/893-3852)*

## LOUISIANA
### Medical Centers
Alexandria: Nearly 400 beds, including 200-plus beds in nursing home. Adult day care, alcohol and drug treatment, long-term psychiatric services. Top-of-line microsurgery and microimaging. *(Shreveport Highway, Zip: 71301. Phone: 318/487-0084)*
New Orleans: Nearly 400 beds, plus more than 100 in nursing unit. Open-heart surgery, outpatient spinal cord injury, intensive-care unit, cardiac catheterization, electron microscopy, hemodialysis, nuclear medicine, geriatric evaluation. *(1601 Perdido Street, Zip: 70146. Phone: 504/568-0811)*
Shreveport: More than 300 beds. Visual impairment team, readjustment counseling, respite care, ambulatory surgery, drug dependence, cardiac catheterization, nuclear medicine, neurology, mental hygiene. *(510 E. Stoner Avenue, Zip: 71130. Phone: 318/221-8411)*

### Clinics
Baton Rouge: *(216 S. Foster Drive, Zip: 70806. Phone: 318/389-0628)*
Jenningss: *(1624 Elton Road, Zip: 70546. Phone: 318/473-0010)*

### Regional Office
New Orleans: *(701 Loyola Avenue, Zip: 70113. Local: 504/589-7191. Statewide: 800/827-1000)*

## Vet Centers

New Orleans: *(1529 N. Claiborne Avenue, Zip: 70116. Phone: 504/943-8386)*

Shreveport: *(Building 3, Suite 260, 2620 Centenary Boulevard, Zip: 71104. Phone: 318/425-8387)*

## National Cemeteries

Alexandria: *(209 Shamrock Avenue, Pineville, Zip: 71360. Phone: 318/449-1793)*

Baton Rouge: *(220 N. 19th Street, Zip: 70806. Phone: 504/654-3767)*

Port Hudson: *(20978 Port Hickey Road, Zachary, Zip: 70791. Phone: 504/654-3767)*

## MAINE

### Medical Center

Togus: About 400 beds. Post-traumatic stress, substance abuse, day treatment, psychiatry. *(Route 17 East, Zip: 04330. Phone: 207/623-8411)*

### Regional Office

Togus: *(Route 17 East, Zip: 04330. Local: 207/623-8000. Statewide: 800/827-1000)*

### Benefits Office

Portland: *(475 Stevens Avenue, Zip: 04101. Phone: 207/780-3569)*

### Vet Centers

Bangor: *(352 Harlowe Street, Zip: 04401. Phone: 207/947-3391)*

Caribou: *(228 Sweden Street, Zip: 04736. Phone: 207/496-3900)*

Lewiston: *(475 Pleasant Street, Zip: 04240. Phone: 207/783-0068)*

Portland: *(63 Prebie Street, Zip: 04101. Phone: 207/780-3584)*

Sandford: *(441 Maine Street, Zip: 04073. Phone: 207/490-1513)*

### National Cemetery

Togus: *(VA Medical Center, Zip: 04330. Phone: 207/623-8411)*

## MARYLAND

### Medical Centers

Baltimore: More than 300 beds. Comprehensive geriatrics, cancer treatment, AIDS, infectious diseases, post-traumatic stress, substance abuse, psychiatry, neurosurgery, acute rehabilitation. *(10 N. Greene Street, Zip: 21201. Phone: 410/605-7000)*

Fort Howard: About 200 beds, and nearly 50 in nursing home unit. Rehabilitation medicine, long-term care, geriatrics, alcohol rehabilitation, hospice. *(N. Point Road, Zip: 21052. Phone: 410/477-1800)*

Perry Point: Nearly 700 beds, plus almost 100 in nursing care unit. Geriatric evaluation, geropsychiatry, Alzheimer's, noninvasive cardiology, post-traumatic stress, cocaine rehabilitation, readjustment counseling. *(Zip: 21902. Phone: 301/642-2411)*

### Prosthetic Assessment Information Center

Baltimore: *(103 S. Gay Street, Zip: 21201. Phone: 410/962-3934)*

### Clinic

Cumberland: *(710 Memorial Avenue, Zip: 21502. Phone: 301/724-0061)*

### Regional Office

Baltimore: Serving all counties except Montgomery and Prince Georges, which are served by the regional office in Washington, D.C. *(31 Hopkins Plaza, Zip: 21201. Local: 410/685-5454. Statewide: 800/827-1000)*

### Vet Centers

Baltimore: *(777 Washington Boulevard, Zip: 21230. Phone: 410/539-5511)*

Elkton: *(7 Elkton Commercial Plaza, South Bridge Street, Zip: 21921. Phone: 410/398-0171)*
Silver Spring: *(1015 Spring Street, Suite 101, Zip: 20910. Phone: 301/589-1073)*

## National Cemeteries
Annapolis: *(800 West Street, Zip: 21401. Phone: 410/644-9696)*
Baltimore: *(5501 Frederick Avenue, Zip: 21228. Phone: 410/644-9696)*
Loudoun Park: *(3445 Frederick Avenue, Baltimore, Zip: 21229. Phone: 410/644-9696)*

## MASSACHUSETTS
### Medical Centers
Bedford: More than 750 beds, with another 250 beds in nursing unit and 50 in domiciliary. Intensive-care unit. Emphasis on psychiatry, geriatrics, alcohol and drug treatment, Alzheimer's, geriatric dentistry. *(200 Spring Road, Zip: 01730. Phone: 617/275-7500)*
Boston: More than 550 beds. State-of-the-art diagnostic resources, transplants, renal dialysis. Mental health center, post-traumatic stress, POW support group and women's veterans program, mammography. *(150 S. Huntington Avenue, Zip: 02130. Phone: 617/278-4591)*
Brockton/West Roxbury: More than 1,200 beds. Regional center for spinal cord injury, cardiac catherization, cardiac surgery, thoracic surgery, and neuropsychiatry. Drug and alcohol detoxification, mammography. *(940 Belmont Street, Zip: 02401. Phone: 508/583-4500)*
Northampton: Nearly 500 beds. Post-traumatic stress, geriatric evaluation, nutrition counseling, respite care, speech therapy, hospice, dentistry, optometry, occupational therapy. *(421 N. Main Street, Zip: 01060. Phone: 413/584-4040)*

### Clinics
Boston: *(251 Causeway Street, Zip: 02114. Phone: 617/248-1364)*
Lowell: *(130 Marshall Road, Zip: 01851. Phone: 508/459-3866)*
Springfield: *(1550 Maine Street, Zip: 01103. Phone: 413/785-0301)*
Worcester: *(605 Lincoln Street, Zip: 01605. Phone: 508/856-0104)*

### Regional Office
Boston: Serving all communities except the towns of Fall River and New Bedford, and counties of Barnstable, Dukes, Nantucket, Bristol, and part of Plymouth, which are served by the regional office in Providence, Rhode Island. *(JFK Federal Building, Zip: 02203. Local: 617/227-4600. Statewide: 800/827-1000)*

### Vet Centers
Brockton: *(1041 Pearl Street, Zip: 02401. Phone: 508/580-2730)*
Boston: *(665 Beacon Street, Zip: 02215. Phone: 617/424-0665)*
Lowell: *(73 East Merrimack Street, Zip: 01853. Phone: 508/453-1151)*
Lowell: *(81 Bridge Street, Zip: 01852. Phone: 508/934-9124)*
New Bedford: *(468 North Street, Zip: 02740. Phone: 508/999-6920)*
Northhampton: *(228 Pleasant Street, Zip: 01060. Phone: 413/582-3079)*
Pittsfield: *(199 South Street, Zip: 01201. Phone: 413/499-2672)*
Springfield: *(1985 Main Street, Zip: 01103. Phone: 508/737-5167)*
Springfield: *(583 State Street, Zip: 01133. Phone: 413/732-9966)*
Winchendon: *(Town Hall, Zip: 01475. Phone: 508/297-3028)*

Worcester: *(108 Grove Street, Zip: 01605. Phone: 508/856-7046)*

**National Cemetery**
Bourne: *(Zip: 02532. Phone: 508/563-7113)*

## MICHIGAN

**Medical Centers**
Allen Park: More than 500 beds, with about 80 more beds in nursing home. Comprehensive psychiatry and comprehensive cancer care. Post-traumatic stress, female veterans, hemodialysis, sleep center. *(Southfield & Outer Drive, Zip: 48101. Phone: 313/562-6000)*
Ann Arbor: About 220 beds, with more than 100 additional beds in nursing units. Acute medical, surgical, and psychiatric care. Spinal cord injury, open-heart surgery, alcohol treatment, state-of-the-art diagnostic resources. *(2215 Fuller Road, Zip: 48105. Phone: 313/769-7100)*
Battle Creek: Nearly 600 beds, with another 200 beds in nursing unit. Intensive-care unit, substance abuse, alcohol halfway houses, geriatric evaluation, post-traumatic stress, psychiatry. *(5500 Armstrong Road, Zip: 49016. Phone: 616/966-5600)*
Iron Mountain: Nearly 200 beds. Intensive care, substance abuse, psychology, pulmonary function, respite care, audiology and speech pathology. *("H" Street, Zip: 49801. Phone: 906/774-3300)*
Saginaw: More than 100 beds, plus nearly 50 in nursing care unit. Intensive care, respiratory care, gastroenterology, computerized tomography, nuclear medicine, optometry, cancer. *(1500 Weiss Street, Zip: 48602. Phone: 517/793-2340)*

**Clinics**
Gaylord: *(850 N. Otsego, Zip: 49735. Phone: 517/732-7525)*
Grand Rapids: *(3019 Coit, N.E., Zip: 48505. Phone: 616/365-9575)*

**Regional Office**
Detroit: *(McNamara Federal Building, 477 Michigan Avenue, Zip: 48226. Local: 313/964-5110. Statewide: 800/827-1000)*

**Vet Centers**
Grand Rapids: *(1940 Eastern Avenue, S.E., Zip: 49507. Phone: 616/243-0385)*
Lincoln Park: *(1766 Fort Street, Zip: 48146. Phone: 313/381-1370)*
Oak Park: *(20820 Greenfield Road, Zip: 48237. Phone: 313/967-0040)*

**National Cemetery**
Fort Custer: *(15501 Dickman Road, Augusta, Zip: 49012. Phone: 616/731-4164)*

## MINNESOTA

**Medical Centers**
Minneapolis: More than 700 acute-care beds, plus 100 in extended care. AIDS, brain sciences, cardiac surgery, geriatrics, prosthetic treatment center, post-traumatic stress, radiation therapy, orthopedics, alcohol-related diseases. *(One Veterans Drive, Zip: 55417. Phone: 612/725-2000)*
Saint Cloud: More than 300 beds, plus more than 50 in domiciliary and 200 in nursing care unit. Geriatrics, ventilator-dependent unit, mental health, day treatment, chemical dependency, independent-living unit. *(4801 Eighth Street, N., Zip: 56303. Phone: 612/252-1670)*

### Regional Office

Saint Paul: Serving all communities except counties of Becker, Beltrami, Clay, Clearwater, Kittson, Lake of the Woods, Mahnomen, Marshall, Norman, Otter Tail, Pennington, Polk, Red Lake, Roseau, and Wilkin, which are served by the regional office in Fargo, North Dakota. *(Federal Building, Fort Snelling, Zip: 55111. Local: 612/726-1454. Statewide: 800/827-1000)*

### Vet Centers

Duluth: *(405 E. Superior Street, Zip: 55802. Phone: 218/722-8654)*
Saint Paul: *(2480 University Avenue, Zip: 55114. Phone: 612/644-4022)*

### National Cemetery

Fort Snelling: *(7601 Thirty-fourth Avenue, S., Minneapolis, Zip: 55450. Phone: 612/726-1127)*

## MISSISSIPPI

### Medical Centers

Biloxi: More than 1,100 beds, including beds in nursing unit and domiciliary. Substance abuse program, Vietnam veterans outreach, and new programs for Gulf War veterans. *(400 Veterans Avenue, Zip: 39531. Phone: 601/388-5541)*
Jackson: More than 400 beds, plus another 100 in nursing care unit. Special programs for cancer treatment, acute and chronic dialysis, spinal cord injury, post-traumatic stress, and chemical dependency. *(1500 E. Woodrow Wilson Drive, Zip: 39216. Phone: 601/364-1201)*

### Regional Office

Jackson: *(100 W. Capital Street, Zip: 39269. Local: 601/965-4873. Statewide: 800/827-1000)*

### Vet Centers

Biloxi: *(2196 Pass Road, Zip: 39531. Phone: 601/388-9938)*
Jackson: *(4436 N. State Street, Suite A-3, Zip: 39206. Phone: 601/965-5727)*

### National Cemeteries

Biloxi: *(P.O. Box 4968, Zip: 39535. Phone: 601/388-6668)*
Corinth: *(1551 Horton Street, Zip: 38834. Phone: 901/386-8311)*
Natchez: *(41 Cemetery Road, Zip: 39120. Phone: 601/445-4981)*

## MISSOURI

### Medical Centers

Columbia: More than 200 beds, plus nearly 100 beds in nursing unit. Intensive-care, coronary care units. Neurosurgery, open-heart surgery, substance abuse, hospital-based home care. *(800 Hospital Drive, Zip: 65201. Phone: 314/443-2511)*
Kansas City: More than 300 beds. Referral center for audiology services, cardiac catheterization, neurosurgery, orthopedic surgery, plastic and reconstructive surgery, renal transplants, and low-vision care. *(4801 Linwood Boulevard, Zip: 64128. Phone: 816/861-4700)*
Poplar Bluff: More than 150 beds, plus about 50 in nursing care unit. Diabetes, hypertension, optometry, dermatology, rheumatology, podiatry, female veterans, post-traumatic stress, Persian Gulf illnesses. *(1500 N. Westwood Boulevard, Zip: 63901. Phone: 314/686-4151)*

Saint Louis: More than 1,000 beds in two units, Jefferson Barracks and Grand Boulevard or John Cochran division. Organ transplants, spinal cord injury, prosthetics, psychiatry, drug and alcohol dependence. *(John Cochran Division: 915 N. Grand Boulevard, Zip: 63106. Phone: 314/652-4100. Jefferson Barracks Division: Zip: 63125. Phone: 314/487-0400)*

### Clinic

Mount Vernon: *(600 N. Main Street, Zip: 65712. Phone: 417/466-4000)*

### Regional Office

Saint Louis: *(400 S. 18th Street, Zip: 63103. Local: 314/342-1171, Phone: 800/827-1000)*

### Benefits Office

Kansas City: *(Federal Office Building, 601 E. 12th Street, Zip: 64106)*

### Vet Centers

Kansas City: *(3931 Main Street, Zip: 64111. Phone: 816/753-1866)*
Saint Louis: *(2345 Pine Street, Zip: 63103. Phone: 314/231-1260)*

### National Cemeteries

Jefferson Barracks: *(2900 Sheridan Road, Zip: 63125. Phone: 314/263-8691)*
Jefferson City: *(1024 McCarty Street, Zip: 65101. Phone: 314/263-8691)*
Springfield: *(1702 E. Seminole Street, Zip: 65804. Phone: 417/881-9499)*

## MONTANA

### Medical Centers

Fort Harrison: About 150 beds. Respite care, dentistry, orthopedics, ophthalmology, imaging services, audiology. Psychiatry and substance abuse. *(William Street, Zip: 59636. Phone: 406/442-6410)*
Miles City: Nearly 100 beds, plus nursing care unit. Specialty clinics for ophthalmology, cardiology, neurology, cancer, rehabilitation medicine, vascular, urology, podiatry. *(210 S. Winchester, Zip: 59301. Phone: 406/232-3060)*

### Clinic

Billings: *(1127 Alderson Avenue, Zip: 59102. Phone: 406/657-6786)*

### Regional Office

Fort Harrison: *(Zip: 59636. Local: 406/447-7975. Statewide: 800/827-1000)*

### Vet Centers

Billings: *(1948 Grand Avenue, Zip: 59102. Phone: 406/657-6071)*
Missoula: *(500 N. Higgins Avenue, Zip: 59802. Phone: 406/721-4918)*

## NEBRASKA

### Medical Centers

Grand Island: About 100 beds, plus another 100 beds in nursing care unit. Comprehensive rehabilitative medicine, hemodialysis, speech pathology, dental and outpatient surgery, intensive-care unit, geriatric evaluation, female veterans. *(2201 N. Broadwell, Zip: 68803. Phone: 308/382-3660)*
Lincoln: More than 100 beds. General surgery, urology, orthopedics, dentistry, alcohol detoxification, respiratory therapy, computerized tomography, carotid Doppler. *(600 S. 70th Street, Zip: 68510. Phone: 402/489-3802)*

Omaha: More than 250 beds. Audiology and speech, gastroenterology, immunology, allergy, cardiology, nephrology, hypertension, endocrinology, oncology, diabetes, orthopedics and prosthetics. *(4101 Woolworth Avenue, Zip: 68105. Phone: 402/346-8800)*

**Regional Office**
Lincoln: *(5631 S. 48th Street, Zip: 68516. Local: 402/437-5001. Statewide: 800/827-1000)*

**Vet Centers**
Lincoln: *(920 "L" Street, Zip: 68508. Phone: 402/476-9736)*
Omaha: *(5123 Leavenworth Street, Zip: 68106. Phone: 402/553-2068)*

**National Cemetery**
Fort McPherson: *(HCO 1, Box 67, Maxwell, Zip: 69151. Phone: 308/582-4433)*

## NEVADA
**Medical Centers**
Las Vegas: More than 100 beds for general patients, plus programs for AIDS and infectious diseases. Clinics for cholesterol, diabetes, dentistry, and hypertension. Women's program, geriatric evaluation, osteoporosis, pharmacy, prosthetics, psychiatry. *(1703 W. Charleston, Zip: 89102. Phone: 702/385-3700)*
Reno: More than 150 beds, including 60 in nursing care unit. Geriatric rehabilitation, addictive disorders, hematology, Alzheimer's, colon cancer, hypertension, heart disease, respite care, Parkinson's. *(1000 Locust Street, Zip: 89520. Phone: 702/786-7200)*

**Regional Office**
Reno: Serves all communities in Nevada plus California counties of Alpine, Lassen, Modoc, and Mono. *(1201 Terminal Way, Zip: 89520. Local: 702/329-9244. Statewide: 800/827-1000)*

**Vet Centers**
Las Vegas: *(704 S. 6th Street, Zip: 89101. Phone: 702/388-6368)*
Reno: *(1155 W. 4th Street, Suite 101, Zip: 89503. Phone: 702/323-1294)*

## NEW HAMPSHIRE
**Medical Center**
Manchester: About 150 beds, plus more than 100 in nursing care unit. Pulmonology, gastroenterology, neurology, urology, cardiology, adult day care. *(718 Smyth Road, Zip: 03104. Phone: 603/624-4366)*

**Regional Office**
Manchester: *(Cotton Federal Building, 275 Chestnut Street, Zip: 03101. Local: 603/666-7785. Statewide: 800/827-1000)*

**Vet Center**
Manchester: *(103 Liberty Street, Zip: 03104. Phone: 603/668-7060)*

## NEW JERSEY
**Medical Centers**
East Orange: More than 900 beds. AIDS, cancer screening, diabetes education, electron microscopy, intensive-care unit, methadone maintenance, spinal cord injury, women's health programs, Persian Gulf family support center. *(Tremont Avenue & S. Center, Zip: 07019. Phone: 201/676-1000)*
Lyons: Nearly 1,000 beds, nearly 350 in nursing care unit. Head trauma unit, post-traumatic stress, female veterans, compul-

sive gambling program, geriatric evaluation, alcohol rehabilitation. *(Valley & Knollcrott Road, Zip: 07939. Phone: 908/647-0180)*

**Clinics**

Brick: *(970 Route 70, Zip: 08724. Phone: 908/206-8900)*
Linwood: *(222 New Road, Building 2, Zip: 08221. Phone: 609/926-1180)*
Vineland: *(New Jersey Vets Home, Northwest Boulevard. Zip: 08360. Phone: 609/692-2881)*

**Regional Office**

Newark: *(20 Washington Place, Zip: 07102. Local: 201/645-2150. Statewide: 800/827-1000)*

**Vet Centers**

Jersey City: *(115 Christopher Columbus Drive, Zip: 07302. Phone: 201/645-2038)*
Linwood: *(222 New Road, Building 2, Suite 4, Zip: 06221. Phone: 609/927-8387)*
Newark: *(77 Halsey Street, Zip: 07102. Phone: 201/645-5954)*
Trenton: *(171 Jersey Street, Zip: 08611. Phone: 609/989-2260)*

**National Cemeteries**

Beverly: *(R.D. #1, Bridgeboro Road, Zip: 08010. Phone: 609/989-2137)*
Finn's Point: *(RFD #3, Fort Mott Road, Salem, Zip: 08079. Phone: 609/989-2137)*

## NEW MEXICO
**Medical Center**

Albuquerque: Nearly 500 beds, with another 50 in nursing home. Provides services to entire state through rural health program. Spinal cord injury unit, heart surgery, magnetic imaging. *(2100 Ridgecrest Drive, S.E., Zip: 87108. Phone: 505/265-1711)*

**Clinics**

Artesia: *(1700 W. Main Street, Zip: 88210. Phone: 505/746-3531)*
Farmington: *(1001 W. Broadway, Zip: 87401. Phone: 505/326-4383)*
Gallup: *(1806 E. 66th Avenue, Zip: 87301. Phone: 505/722-7234)*
Raton: *(1275 S. 2nd Street, Zip: 87740. Phone: 505/445-2391)*
Silver City: *(1302 Thirty-Second Street, Zip: 88061. Phone: 505/538-2921)*

**Regional Office**

Albuquerque: *(Dennis Chavez Federal Building, 500 Gold Avenue, S.W., Zip: 87102. Local: 505/766-3361. Statewide: 800/827-1000)*

**Vet Centers**

Albuquerque: *(1600 Mountain Road, N.W., Zip: 87104. Phone: 505/766-5900)*
Farmington: *(4251 E. Main Street, Suite B, Zip: 87402. Phone: 505/327-9684)*
Santa Fe: *(1996 Warner Street, Warner Plaza, Suite 5, Zip: 87505. Phone: 505/988-6562)*

**National Cemeteries**

Fort Bayard: *(P.O. Box 189, Zip: 88036. Phone: 915/540-6182)*
Santa Fe: *(501 N. Guadalupe St., P.O. Box 88, Zip: 87504. Phone: 505/988-6400)*

## NEW YORK
**Medical Centers**

Albany: About 640 beds, including intensive-care unit, with another 100 beds in nursing home. Adult day care, twenty-four-hour outpatient care, alcohol rehabilitation, post-traumatic stress, psychiatry, hemodialysis, state-of-the-art cancer treatment, eye institute. *(113 Holland Avenue, Zip: 12208. Phone: 518/462-3311)*

Batavia: More than 200 beds, with nursing unit. Intensive-care unit, rehabilitative services, geriatric evaluation. *(222 Richmond Avenue, Zip: 14020. Phone: 716/343-7500)*

Bath: More than 200 beds, plus another 150 in nursing unit and 500 in domiciliary. Alzheimer's, speech and hearing, blindness rehabilitation, brain injury, chemical dependency, female veterans, geriatric evaluation, vocational rehabilitation. *(Veterans Avenue, Zip: 14810. Phone: 607/776-2111)*

Bronx: More than 700 beds, with another 120 beds in nursing unit. Spinal cord, alcohol and drug dependency, schizophrenia and Alzheimer's, kidney dialysis, prosthetics, pain management. *(130 W. Kingsbridge Road, Zip: 10406. Phone: 718/584-9000)*

Brooklyn: About 1,000 beds at three different sites, plus 300 beds in nursing home unit, 50 in homeless domiciliary. Hemodialysis, peritoneal dialysis, laser endoscopy and bronchoscopy, AIDS, electroconvulsive therapy, post-traumatic stress, aphasia treatment, adult day care program, geriatric psychiatry. *(800 Poly Place, Zip: 11209. Phone: 718/836-6600)*

Buffalo: Nearly 800 beds, plus almost 70 beds in nursing unit. Regional cancer center. Open-heart surgery, heart transplant, pacemaker, drug and alcohol treatment, post-traumatic stress, hemodialysis, geriatrics, neurodiagnostics. *(3495 Bailey Avenue, Zip: 14215. Phone: 716/834-9200)*

Canandaigua: More than 900 beds, with another 100 beds in nursing unit and 40 in domiciliary. Emphasis on long-term care.

Drug and alcohol abuse, mental health, post-traumatic stress. *(Fort Hill Avenue, Zip: 14424. Phone: 716/394-2000)*

Castle Point: Nearly 180 beds, with almost 150 beds in nursing unit. Long-term care for spinal cord injury, plastic surgery, rehabilitation medicine. *(Zip: 12511. Phone: 914/831-2000)*

Montrose: Nearly 900 beds, including more than 300 pyschiatric, 200 in nursing care, and nearly 50 in domiciliary. Intensive-care unit. Geriatrics, substance abuse, post-traumatic stress, dentistry, respite care. *(Route 9-A, Zip: 10548. Phone: 914/737-4400)*

New York City: More than 1,000 beds. Inpatient and outpatient AIDS. Specializes in open-heart surgery, cardiac catheterization, extracorporeal photophoresis, neurosurgery, prosthetics, and orthotics. *(423 E. 23rd Street, Zip: 10010. Phone: 212/686-7500)*

Northport: More than 800 beds, plus nearly 200 in nursing care unit. Neurosurgery, dialysis, prosthetic sensory aids, radiation therapy, respite care, Vietnam veterans, female veterans. *(79 Middleville Road, Long Island, Zip: 11749. Phone: 516/261-4400)*

Syracuse: About 300 beds, plus 50 for nursing care. Laser treatments, cardiac catheterization, respiratory care, lithotripsy, female veterans, audiology, speech pathology, nuclear medicine, computerized axial tomography. *(800 Irvine Avenue, Zip: 13210. Phone: 315/476-7461)*

## Clinics

Albany: *(91 Central Avenue, Zip: 12206. Phone: 518/432-1068)*

Brooklyn: *(35 Ryerson Street, Zip: 11205. Phone: 718/330-7851)*

Buffalo: *(2963 Main Street, Zip: 14209. Phone: 716/834-4270)*
Elizabethtown: *(Park Street, Zip: 12932. Phone: 518/873-2179)*
Fort Drum: *(Building T-2407, Dunn Avenue, Zip: 13602. Phone: 315/773-7231)*
Massena: *(1 Hospital Drive, Zip: 13662. Phone: 315/764-1711)*
New York City: *(423 E. 23rd Street, Zip: 10036. Phone: 212/951-5983)*
Plattsburgh: *(380th Medical Group, Zip: 12903. Phone: 518/565-7482)*
Rochester: *(100 State Street, Zip: 14614. Phone: 716/263-5734)*
Sidney: *(39 Pearl Street West, Zip: 13838, Phone: 607/563-3970)*
St. Albans: *(179th Street & Linden Boulevard, Zip: 11425. Phone: 718/526-1000)*
Syracuse: *(1031 E. Fayette Street, Zip: 13210. Phone: 315/423-5690)*

## Regional Offices
Buffalo: *(Federal Building, 111 W. Huron Street, Zip: 14202. Local: 716/846-5191. Statewide: 800/827-1000)*
New York City: Serving counties of Albany, Bronx, Clinton, Columbia, Delaware, Dutchess, Essex, Franklin, Fulton, Greene, Hamilton, Kings, Montgomery, Nassau, New York, Orange, Otsego, Putnam, Queens, Rensselaer, Richmond, Rockland, Saratoga, Schenectady, Schoharie, Suffolk, Sullivan, Ulster, Warren, Washington, and Westchester. *(245 West Houston Street, Zip: 10001. Local: 212/807-7229. Statewide: 800/827-1000)*

## Benefits Offices
Albany: *(O'Brien Federal Building, Clinton Avenue & N. Pearl Street, Zip: 12207)*

Rochester: *(Federal Office Building & Courthouse, 100 State Street, Zip: 14614)*
Syracuse: *(344 W. Genesee Street, Zip: 13202)*

## Vet Centers
Albany: *(875 Central Avenue, Zip: 12206. Phone: 518/438-2505)*
Babylon: *(116 West Main Street, Zip: 11702. Phone: 516/661-3930)*
Bronx: *(226 East Fordham Road, Rooms 216–217, Zip: 10458. Phone: 718/367-3500)*
Brooklyn: *(165 Cadman Plaza, East, Zip: 11201. Phone: 718/330-2825)*
Buffalo: *(351 Linwood Avenue, Zip: 14209. Phone: 716/882-0505)*
Harlem: *(55 West 125th Street, Zip: 10027. Phone: 212/870-8126)*
New York: *(120 West 44th Street, Zip: 10036. Phone: 212/944-2931)*
Rochester: *(134 S. Fitzhugh Street, Zip: 14614. Phone: 716/263-5710)*
Staten Island: *(150 Richmond Terrace, Zip: 10301. Phone: 718/816-4499)*
Syracuse: *(716 E. Washington Street, Zip: 13203. Phone: 315/423-5690)*
White Plains: *(200 Hamilton Avenue, Zip: 10601. Phone: 914/682-6251)*
Woodhaven: *(75-10B 91st Avenue, Zip: 11421. Phone: 718/296-2871)*

## National Cemeteries
Bath: *(VA Medical Center, Zip: 14810. Phone: 607/776-5480)*
Calverton: *(210 Princeton Boulevard, Zip: 11933. Phone: 516/727-5410)*
Cypress Hills: *(625 Jamaica Avenue, Brooklyn, Zip: 11208. Phone: 516/454-4949)*
Long Island: *(Farmingdale, Zip: 11735. Phone: 516/454-4949)*
Woodlawn: *(1825 Davis Street, Elmira, Zip: 14901. Phone: 607/776-2111)*

## NORTH CAROLINA
### Medical Centers
Asheville: More than 350 beds, plus another 50 beds in nursing care unit. Open-heart surgery, speech pathology, psychiatry, alcohol treatment. *(1100 Tunnel Road, Zip: 28805. Phone: 704/298-7911)*
Durham: More than 500 beds. Regional referral center for high-risk heart surgery, other patients. AIDS, transplant programs, ophthalmology, epilepsy center, dialysis, pain clinic, post-traumatic stress. *(508 Fulton Street, Zip: 27705. Phone: 919/286-0411)*
Fayetteville: About 350 beds and nearly 50 in nursing home unit. Acute psychiatry, sickle-cell screening, speech pathology, respite care. *(2300 Ramsey Street, Zip: 28301. Phone: 910/822-7059)*
Salisbury: More than 800 beds. Neuropsychiatric services, rehabilitation medicine, psychiatric intensive-care unit, nuclear medicine, pulmonary function, geropsychiatry, substance abuse. *(1601 Brenner Avenue, Zip: 28144. Phone: 704/638-9000)*

### Clinic
Winston-Salem: *(Federal Building, 251 N. Main Street, Zip: 27155. Phone: 910/631-5517)*

### Regional Office
Winston-Salem: *(251 N. Main Street, Zip: 27155. Local: 910/748-1800. Statewide: 800/827-1000)*

### Vet Centers
Charlotte: *(223 S. Brevard Street, Suite 103, Zip: 28202. Phone: 704/333-6107)*
Fayetteville: *(4 Market Square, Zip: 28301. Phone: 910/323-4908)*
Greensboro: *(2009 Elm-Eugene Street, Zip: 27406. Phone: 910/333-5366)*
Greenville: *(150 Arlington Boulevard, Suite B, Zip: 27858. Phone: 919/355-7920)*

### National Cemeteries
New Bern: *(1711 National Avenue, Zip: 28560. Phone: 919/637-2912)*
Raleigh: *(501 Rock Quarry Road, Zip: 27610. Phone: 919/832-0144)*
Salisbury: *(202 Government Road, Zip: 28144. Phone: 704/636-2661)*
Wilmington: *(2011 Market Street, Zip: 28403. Phone: 910/637-2912)*

## NORTH DAKOTA
### Medical Center
Fargo: About 200 beds, plus 50 in restorative care unit. Acute psychiatry, inpatient substance abuse, intensive-care unit. *(2101 Elm Street, Zip: 58102. Phone: 701/232-3241)*

### Regional Office
Fargo: *(2101 Elm Street, Zip: 58102. Local: 701/293-3656. Statewide: 800/827-1000)*

### Vet Centers
Fargo: *(1322 Gateway Drive, Zip: 58103. Phone: 701/237-0942)*
Minot: *(2041 3rd Street, N.W., Zip: 58701. Phone: 701/852-0177)*

## OHIO
### Medical Centers
Chillicothe: About 600 beds, including nursing unit and 50 beds for extended psychiatric care. Specialty in neuropsychiatry. Post-traumatic stress, substance abuse. *(17273 State Route 104, Zip: 45601. Phone: 614/773-1141)*
Cincinnati: Nearly 250 beds, plus about 150 beds in nursing unit

and 60 beds in domiciliary. Cardiology, infectious diseases, vascular surgery, neuro-oncology, Vietnam-era readjustment. *(3200 Vine Street, Zip: 45220. Phone: 513/861-3100)*

Cleveland: More than 900 beds, including nursing unit and domiciliary. Acute and chronic psychiatry, geriatrics, post-traumatic stress, electrical stimulation center. *(10701 East Boulevard, Zip: 44106. Phone: 216/791-3800)*

Dayton: About 350 beds, not including nearly 300 in nursing home and 600 in domiciliary facilities. Homeless veterans, hyperbaric oxygen programs. *(4100 W. 3rd Street, Zip: 45428. Phone: 513/268-6511)*

### Clinics

Canton: *(221 Third Street, S.E., Zip: 44702. Phone: 216/489-4660)*

Columbus: *(2090 Kenny Road, Zip: 43221. Phone: 614/469-5164)*

Toledo: *(3333 Glendale Avenue, Zip: 43614. Phone: 419/259-2000)*

Youngstown: *(2031 Belmont, Zip: 44505. Phone: 216/740-9200)*

### Regional Office

Cleveland: *(1240 E. 9th Street, Zip: 44199. Local: 216/621-5050. Statewide: 800/827-1000)*

### Benefits Offices

Cincinnati: *(The Society Bank Center, 36 E. 7th Street, Suite 210, Zip: 45202)*

Columbus: *(Federal Building, 200 N. High Street, Room 309, Zip: 43215)*

### Vet Centers

Cincinnati: *(30 E. Hollister Street, Zip: 45219. Phone: 513/569-7140)*

Cleveland: *(11511 Loraine Avenue, Zip: 44111. Phone: 216/671-8530)*

Cleveland Heights: *(2134 Lee Road, Zip: 44118. Phone: 216/932-8471)*

Columbus: *(30 Spruce Street, Zip: 43215. Phone: 614/253-3500)*

Dayton: *(6 S. Patterson Boulevard, Zip: 45402. Phone: 513/461-9150)*

### National Cemetery

Dayton: *(4100 W. Third Street, Zip: 45428. Phone: 513/262-2115)*

## OKLAHOMA

### Medical Centers

Muskogee: More than 100 beds. Internal medicine, general surgery, family practice, geriatrics, psychiatry, hospice, substance abuse, ex-POWs. *(Honor Heights Drive, Zip: 74401. Phone: 918/683-3261)*

Oklahoma City: Nearly 400 beds. Open-heart surgery, cardiac catheterization, hemodialysis, gastroenterology, audiology and speech, laser eye surgery, quantitative fluorescence imaging. *(921 N.E. 13th Street, Zip: 73104. Phone: 405/270-0501)*

### Clinics

Ardmore: *(1015 S. Commerce, Zip: 73401. Phone: 405/223-2266)*

Clinton: *(Highway 183, P.O. Box 1209, Zip: 73601. Phone: 405/323-5540)*

Lawton: *(Comanche County Hospital, Zip: 73502. Phone: 405/357-6611)*

Tulsa: *(1855 E. 15th Street, Zip: 74101. Phone: 918/581-7105)*

### Regional Office

Muskogee: *(125 S. Main Street, Zip: 74401. Local: 918/687-2500. Statewide: 800/827-1000)*

### Benefits Office

Oklahoma City: *(200 N.W. 5th Street, Zip: 73102)*

## Vet Centers

Oklahoma City: *(3033 N. Walnut, Suite 101-W, Zip: 73105. Phone: 405/270-5184)*

Tulsa: *(1408 S. Harvard, Zip: 74112. Phone: 918/581-7105)*

## National Cemetery

Fort Gibson: *(1423 Cemetery Road, Zip: 74434. Phone: 918/478-2334)*

## OREGON
## Medical Centers

Portland: More than 500 beds, plus 100 in nursing care unit and 50 in domiciliary. Liver transplant, cardiology, cardiac surgery, ophthalmology, Moh's surgery, sleep apnea, seizure monitoring, Alzheimer's, geriatric evaluation. *(3710 S.W. U.S. Veterans Hospital Road, Zip: 97207. Phone: 503/273-5246)*

Roseburg: More than 200 beds, with nearly 90 in nursing care unit. Fifteen-bed Alzheimer's unit, geriatric evaluation, vocational rehabilitation, psychiatric and long-term care. *(913 New Garden Valley Boulevard, Zip: 97470. Phone: 503/440-1000)*

## Clinics

Bandon: *(1010 First Street S. E., Suite 100, Zip: 97411. Phone: 503/347-2620)*

Eugene: *(138 W. 8th Street, Zip: 97401. Phone: 503/465-6966)*

Portland: *(8909 S.W. Barbur Boulevard, Zip: 97207. Phone: 503/293-2946)*

## Domiciliary

White City: Over 900 beds; only independent domiciliary in VA system. *(8495 Crater Lake Highway, Zip: 97503. Phone: 503/826-2111)*

## Regional Office

Portland: *(1220 S.W. 3rd Avenue, Zip: 97204 Local: 503/221-2431. Statewide: 800/827-1000)*

## Vet Centers

Eugene: *(1966 Garden Avenue, Zip: 97403. Phone: 503/465-6918)*

Grants Pass: *(211 S.E. 10th Street, Zip: 97526. Phone: 503/479-6912)*

Portland: *(8383 N.E. Sandy Boulevard, Suite 110, Zip: 97220. Phone: 503/273-5370)*

Salem: *(318 Church Street, N.E., Zip: 97301. Phone: 503/362-9911)*

## National Cemeteries

Eagle Point: *(2763 Riley Road, Zip: 97524. Phone: 503/826-2511)*

Roseburg: *(VA Medical Center, Zip: 97470. Phone: 503/440-1000)*

Williamette: *(11800 S.E. Mount Scott Boulevard, Portland, Zip: 97266. Phone: 503/273-5250)*

## PENNSYLVANIA
## Medical Centers

Altoona: Nearly 200 beds, including nursing home. Intensive-care unit, psychiatry, detoxification center. Scheduled for inpatient psychiatric facility. *(2907 Pleasant Valley Boulevard, Zip: 16602. Phone: 814/943-8164)*

Butler: About 250 beds, plus 100 beds in nursing unit and nearly 70 in domiciliary. Geriatrics, respite care, substance abuse, hospital-based home care, adult day care, mental hygiene. *(325 New Castle Road, Zip: 16001. Phone: 412/287-4781)*

Coatesville: Nearly 840 beds, plus more than 200 in nursing unit and about 50 in domiciliary. Neuropsychiatric facility, post-traumatic stress, extended care, substance abuse, inpatient

Alzheimer's. *(1400 Black Horse Road, Zip: 19230. Phone: 215/384-7711)*

Erie: More than 150 beds, including about 40 in nursing care unit. Female veterans programs, intensive-care unit, stress lab, pulmonary blood gas, optometry, audiology and speech pathology. *(135 E. 38th Street, Zip: 16504. Phone: 814/868-8661)*

Lebanon: More than 500 beds, plus nearly 200 in nursing care unit. Geriatrics, rehabilitation, substance abuse, long-term care, mobile health-screening van, respite care, podiatry, mental health. *(1700 South Lincoln Avenue, Zip: 17042. Phone: 717/272-6621)*

Philadelphia: More than 400 beds, plus nearly 250 in nursing care unit. Rheumatology and immunology center, geriatric evaluation, laser surgery, hemodialysis, inpatient and outpatient post-traumatic stress, female veterans. *(University & Woodland Avenues, Zip: 19104. Phone: 215/383-2400)*

Pittsburgh (Highland Drive): More than 600 beds. Specializes in neuropsychiatry. Ex-POW center, sleep laboratory, domestic relations clinic, substance abuse, post-traumatic stress, schizophrenia, neurobehavioral unit. *(7180 Highland Drive, Zip: 15206. Phone: 412/363-4900)*

Pittsburgh (University Drive): More than 500 beds, plus more than 200 in nursing care units. Open-heart surgery, liver transplant, intensive-care units, home dialysis, geriatric care, hypertension, alcoholism, neurology. *(University Drive C, Zip: 15240. Phone: 412/683-3000)*

Wilkes-Barre: More than 300 beds, plus nearly 200 for nursing care. Angiography, audiology and speech pathology, hematology, neurology, cardiopulmonary, hospice, post-traumatic stress, inpatient alcohol. *(1111 E. End Boulevard, Zip: 18711. Phone: 717/824-4304)*

## Clinics

Allentown: *(2937 Hamilton Boulevard, Zip: 18103. Phone: 610/776-4304)*

Camp Hill: *(25 N. 32nd Street, Zip: 17011. Phone: 717/730-9782)*

Sayre: *(Guthrie Square, Zip: 18840. Phone: 717/888-8062)*

Springfield: *(1489 Baltimore Pike, Zip: 19064. Phone: 215/543-1588)*

## Regional Offices

Philadelphia: Serves counties of Adams, Berks, Bradford, Bucks, Cameron, Carbon, Centre, Chester, Clinton, Columbia, Cumberland, Dauphin, Delaware, Franklin, Juniata, Lackawanna, Lancaster, Lebanon, Lehigh, Luzerne, Lycoming, Mifflin, Monroe, Montgomery, Montour, Northampton, Northumberland, Perry, Philadelphia, Pike, Potter, Schuylkill, Snyder, Sullivan, Susquehanna, Tioga, Union, Wayne, Wyoming, and York. *(RO & Insurance Center, 5000 Wissahickon Avenue, Zip: 19101. Local: 215/438-5225. Statewide: 800/827-1000)*

Pittsburgh: Serves rest of Pennsylvania and West Virginia counties of Brooke, Hancock, Marshall, and Ohio. *(1000 Liberty Avenue, Zip: 15222. Phone: 412/281-4233)*

## Benefits Office

Wilkes-Barre: *(100 N. Wilkes-Barre Boulevard, Zip: 18702)*

## Vet Centers

Erie: *(1000 State Street, Suites 1 & 2, Zip: 16501. Phone: 814/453-7955)*

Harrisburg: *(1007 N. Front Street, Zip: 17102. Phone: 717/782-3954)*

McKeesport: *(500 Walnut Street, Zip: 15132. Phone: 412/678-7704)*

Philadelphia: *(1026 Arch Street, Zip: 19107. Phone: 215/627-0238)*

Philadelphia: *(101 E. Olney Avenue, Zip: 19120. Phone: 215/924-4670)*

Pittsburgh: *(954 Penn Avenue, Zip: 15222. Phone: 412/765-1193)*

Scranton: *(959 Wyoming Avenue, Zip: 18509. Phone: 717/344-2676)*

## National Cemeteries

Fort Indiantown Gap: *(Annville, Zip: 17003. Phone: 717/865-5254)*

Philadelphia: *(Haines Street & Limekiln Pike, Zip: 19138. Phone: 609/989-2137)*

## THE PHILIPPINES

### Clinic, Regional Office

Manila: Outpatient clinic and VA regional center, for U.S. veterans and Filipinos who qualify under U.S. law. General medicine, minor surgery, psychiatry, radiology, pharmacy, diabetic clinic, prosthetics, orthopedic rehabilitation. *(1131 Roxas Boulevard, Zip: 96440. Local: 810/521-7521. From U.S.: 011-632-521-7116, Ext. 2501)*

## PUERTO RICO

### Medical Center

San Juan: More than 600 beds, plus more than 100 in nursing care. Inpatient blind rehab center, post-traumatic stress, psychiatric intervention, sickle-cell anemia, prosthetics, speech pathology, geriatric evaluation, hypertension. *(1 Veterans Plaza, Zip: 00927. Phone: 809/758-7575)*

## Clinics

Mayaguez: *(Carr. Estatal #2, Frente A Res. Sultana, Zip: 00708. Phone: 809/831-3400)*

Ponce: *(Reparada Industrial—Lot #1, Calle Principal, Zip: 00731. Phone: 809/841-3115)*

St. Croix: *(Box 12, Rural Route 02, Zip: 00853. Phone: 809/778-5553)*

## Regional Office

San Juan: *(U.S. Courthouse & Federal Building, Carlos E. Chardon Street, Hato Rey, Zip: 00936. Local: 809/766-5141. Long distance: 800/827-1000)*

## Vet Centers

Arecibo: *(52 Gonzalo Marin Street, Zip: 00612. Phone: 809/879-4510)*

Ponce: *(35 Mayor Street, Zip: 00731. Phone: 809/841-3260)*

Rio Piedras: *(Condomino Medical Center Plaza, Suite LCBA and LC9, Zip: 00921. Phone: 809/783-8794)*

## National Cemetery

Bayamon: *(Zip: 00960. Phone: 809/785-7281)*

## RHODE ISLAND

### Medical Center

Providence: More than 300 beds. Intensive-care unit, dialysis, alcohol treatment, respiratory diseases, coronary care, speech and language pathology, nuclear medicine, post-traumatic stress, alcohol and chemical addictions. *(830 Chalkston Avenue, Zip: 02908. Phone: 401/273-7100)*

## Regional Office

Providence: *(380 Westminster Mall, Zip: 02903. Local: 401/273-4910. Statewide: 800/827-1000)*

## Vet Centers

Cranston: *(789 Park Avenue, Zip: 02910. Phone: 401/467-2046)*
Providence: *(909 N. Main Street, Zip: 02904. Phone: 401/528-5271)*

## SOUTH CAROLINA

### Medical Centers

Charleston: More than 400 beds. Open-heart surgery, fetal alcohol syndrome, diabetes, lipid disorders. *(109 Bee Street, Zip: 29401. Phone: 803/577-5011)*
Columbia: More than 450 beds, plus more than 100 beds in nursing unit. Advanced resources for eyes, cancer. Acute psychiatric care, substance abuse. *(Garners Ferry Road, Zip: 29209. Phone: 803/776-4000)*

### Clinics

Greenville: *(3510 Augusta Road, Zip: 29601. Phone: 803/299-1600)*
Savannah: *(325 W. Montgomery Crossroads, Zip: 31406. Phone: 912/920-0214)*

### Vet Centers

Columbia: *(1513 Pickens Street, Zip: 29201. Phone: 803/765-9944)*
Greenville: *(14 Lavinia Street, Zip: 29601. Phone: 803/271-2711)*
North Charleston: *(5603-A Rivers Avenue, Zip: 29418. Phone: 803/747-8387)*

### National Cemeteries

Beaufort: *(1601 Boundary Street, Zip: 29902. Phone: 803/524-3925)*
Florence: *(803 E. National Cemetery Road, Zip: 29501. Phone: 803/669-8783)*

## SOUTH DAKOTA

### Medical Centers

Fort Meade: About 350 beds, including more than 50 in nursing care units. Intensive care, rehabilitation therapy, mobile CAT scan, pulmonary function lab. *(Interstate 90 & Highway 34, Zip: 57741. Phone: 605/347-2511)*
Hot Springs: About 150 beds, plus 400 beds in domiciliary units. Audiology and speech pathology, dentistry, cardiac stress testing, mobile imaging scanners, mental health clinic. *(5th Street, Zip: 57747. Phone: 605/745-4101)*
Sioux Falls: Nearly 200 beds, plus almost 100 in extended-care unit. Substance abuse, women's health, geriatric evaluation, hearing aid center, podiatry, optometry, cardiac electrophysiology. *(2501 W. 22nd Street, Zip: 57117. Phone: 605/336-3230)*

### Regional Office

Sioux Falls: *(2501 W. 22nd Street, Zip: 57117. Local: 605/336-3496. Statewide: 800/827-1000)*

### Vet Centers

Rapid City: *(610 Kansas City Street, Zip: 57701. Phone: 605/348-0077)*
Sioux Falls: *(601 S. Cliff Avenue, Zip: 57102. Phone: 605/332-0856)*

### National Cemeteries

Black Hills: *(Sturgis, Zip: 57785. Phone: 605/347-3830)*
Fort Meade: *(Zip: 57785. Phone: 605/347-3830)*
Hot Springs: *(VA Medical Center, Zip: 57747. Phone: 605/745-4101)*

## TENNESSEE

### Medical Centers

Memphis: More than 800 beds. Spinal cord injury, prosthetic treament, ambulatory surgery, blood and bone marrow matching, neurology, psychiatry, rehabilitation, cardiology. *(1030 Jefferson Avenue, Zip: 38104. Phone: 901/523-8990)*

Mountain Home: Nearly 500 beds, plus 600 in domiciliary and more than 100 in nursing care. Post-traumatic stress, pacemaker implant, joint replacement, respiratory care, alcohol treatment, psychiatry. *(Sidney & Lamont Streets, Zip: 37684. Phone: 615/926-1171)*

Murfreesboro: More than 700 beds, plus about 100 in nursing care. Geriatric evaluation, halfway house. Outpatient care in cardiology, internal medicine, gastroenterology, neurology, gynecology. *(3400 Lebanon Road, Zip: 37129. Phone: 615/893-1360)*

Nashville: More than 400 beds. Angioplasty, arthroscopic surgery, brain stem testing, gerontology, laser surgery, open-heart surgery, organ transplants, head and neck tumors, major prosthetic surgery, dialysis. *(1310 Twenty-fourth Avenue, South, Zip: 37212. Phone: 615/327-4751)*

### Clinics

Chattanooga: *(Building 6200, East Gate Center, Zip: 37411. Phone: 615/855-6550)*

Cookville: *(121 S. Dixie Avenue, Zip: 38501. Phone: 615/893-1360)*

Knoxville: *(9031 Cross Park Drive, Suite 100, Zip: 37923. Phone: 615/545-4592)*

### Regional Office

Nashville: *(110 Ninth Avenue, South, Zip: 37203. Local: 615/736-5251. Statewide: 800/827-1000)*

### Vet Centers

Chattanooga: *(425 Cumberland Street, Suite 140, Zip: 37404. Phone: 615/752-5234)*

Johnson City: *(1615-17 Market Street, Zip: 37604. Phone: 615/928-8387)*

Knoxville: *(2817 E. Magnolia Avenue, Zip: 37914. Phone: 615/545-4680)*

Memphis: *(1835 Union, Suite 100, Zip: 38104. Phone: 901/722-2510)*

### National Cemeteries

Chattanooga: *(1200 Bailey Avenue, Zip: 37404. Phone: 615/855-6590)*

Knoxville: *(939 Tyson Street, Zip: 37917. Phone: 615/461-7935)*

Memphis: *(3568 Townes Avenue, Zip: 38122. Phone: 901/386-8311)*

Mountain Home: *(Zip: 37684. Phone: 615/461-7935)*

Nashville: *(1420 Gallatin Road, South, Madison, Zip: 37115. Phone: 615/327-5360)*

## TEXAS

### Medical Centers

Amarillo: More than 170 beds, with another 120 in nursing home unit. Substance abuse, vocational rehabilitation, cancer, and AIDS research. Ambulatory EEG monitoring, geriatric care, noninvasive cardiology. *(6010 Amarillo Boulevard, West, Zip: 79106. Phone: 806/355-9703)*

Big Spring: About 250 beds, with another 50 in nursing unit. Acute psychiatry, alcohol and drug rehabilitation, eye surgery, urologic surgery. *(2400 S. Gregg Street, Zip: 79720. Phone: 915/263-7361)*

Bonham/Sam Rayburn: More than 400 beds, plus another 100 beds in nursing care unit, 200 in domiciliary, 50 in intensive care, and 15 in substance abuse. Long-term rehabilitation, diabetic clinic, substance abuse. *(1201 East Ninth, Zip: 75418. Phone: 903/583-2111)*

Dallas: Almost 500 beds, with another 120 beds in nursing unit and 40 in domiciliary. Regional epilepsy center, AIDS, cardiac surgery, hemodialysis, post-traumatic stress, psychiatry, prosthetics. *(4500 S. Lancaster Road, Zip: 75216. Phone: 214/376-5451)*

Houston: More than 900 beds, plus more than 100 beds in nursing care unit. Adult day care, alcohol treatment, genetic counseling, prosthetics, seizure and movement disorders, spinal cord injury. *(2002 Holcombe Boulevard, Zip: 77030. Phone: 713/791-1414)*

Kerrville: More than 200 hospital beds, plus 150 in nursing care unit. Long-term rehabilitation and extended care. Intensive care, substance abuse, psychiatry, ambulatory care, post-traumatic stress. *(3600 Memorial Boulevard, Zip: 78028. Phone: 210/896-2020)*

Marlin: Nearly 200 beds. Rehabilitation of acute and chronically ill, plus medical care for aging. Psychiatric services. *(1016 Ward Street, Zip: 76661. Phone: 817/883-3511)*

San Antonio: More than 600 beds, plus more than 100 in nursing care. Spinal cord injury, geriatrics. Transplantion center for heart, lung, liver, and bone marrow. *(7400 Merton Minter Boulevard, Zip: 78284. Phone: 210/617-5300)*

Temple: More than 500 beds, plus more than 400 in domiciliary and 100 for nursing care. Outpatient substance-abuse program. *(1901 S. First, Zip: 76504. Phone: 817/778-4811)*

Waco: More than 800 beds, plus nearly 100 in domiciliary and 150 for nursing care. Specializes in long-term care and chronic care. Alcohol rehabilitation, hospice, post-traumatic stress, blind rehabilitation, female veterans. *(4800 Memorial Drive, Zip: 76711. Phone: 817/752-6581)*

## Clinics

Austin: *(2901 Montopolis Drive, Zip: 78741. Phone: 512/389-7101)*

Beaumont: *(3385 Fannin Street, Zip: 77701. Phone: 409/839-2480)*

Corpus Christi: *(5283 Old Brownsville Road, Zip: 78405. Phone: 512/854-7392)*

El Paso: *(5919 Brook Hollow Drive, Zip: 79925. Phone: 915/540-7811)*

Fort Worth: *(300 W. Rosedale Street, Zip: 76104. Phone: 817/335-2202)*

Laredo: *(2359 E. Saunders Avenue, Zip: 78043. Phone: 512/725-7060)*

Lubbock: *(4902 Thirty-fourth Street, Number 10, Zip: 79410. Phone: 806/796-7900)*

Lufkin: *(1301 Frank Avenue, Zip: 75901. Phone: 409/637-1342)*

McAllen: *(2101 S. Row Boulevard, Zip: 78501. Phone: 210/618-7147)*

San Antonio: *(9502 Computer Drive, Zip: 78229. Phone: 210/617-2645)*

Victoria: *(2710 E. Airline Drive, Zip: 77901. Phone: 512/572-0006)*

## Regional Offices

Bowie County: Served by regional office in Little Rock, Arkansas.

Houston: Serving counties of Angelina, Aransas, Atacosa,

Austin, Bandera, Bee, Bexar,
Blanco, Brazoria, Brewster,
Brooks, Caldwell, Calhoun,
Cameron, Chambers, Colorado,
Comaal, Crockett, DeWitt,
Dimitt, Duval, Edwards, Fort
Bend, Frio, Galveston, Gillespie,
Goliad, Gonzales, Grimes,
Guadalupe, Hardin, Harris, Hays,
Hidalgo, Houston, Jackson,
Jasper, Jefferson, Jim Hogg, Jim
Wells, Karnes, Kendall, Kenedy,
Kerr, Kimble, Kinney, Kleberg,
LaSalle, Lavaca, Liberty, Live
Oak, McCulloch, McMullen,
Mason, Matagorda, Maverick,
Medina, Menard, Montgomery,
Nacogdoches, Newton, Nueces,
Orange, Pecos, Polk, Real, Refu-
gio, Sabine, San Augustine, San
Jacinto, San Patrico, Schleicher,
Shelby, Starr, Sutton, Terrell,
Trinity, Tyler, Uvalde, Val Verde,
Victoria, Walker, Waller, Wash-
ington, Webb, Wharton, Willacy,
Wilson, Zapata, Zavala. *(8900
Lakes, Zip: 77054. Local:
713/664-4664. Statewide:
800/827-1000)*
Waco: Serves counties not listed
above. *(1400 N. Valley Mills
Drive, Zip: 76799. Local:
817/772-3060. Statewide:
800/827-1000)*

**Benefits Offices**

Dallas: *(Santa Fe Building, 1114
Commerce Street, Zip: 75242)*
Fort Worth: *(300 W. Rosedale Street,
Zip: 76104)*
Lubbock: *(Federal Building, 1205
Texas Avenue, Zip: 79401)*
San Antonio: *(3601 Bluemel Road,
Zip: 78229)*

**Vet Centers**

Amarillo: *(3414 E. Olsen Boulevard,
Suite E, Zip: 79109. Phone:
806/354-9779)*
Austin: *(1110 W. William Cannon
Drive, Suite 301, Zip: 78723.
Phone: 512/416-1314)*
Corpus Christi: *(3166 Reid Drive,
Suite 1, Zip: 78404. Phone:
512/854-9961)*
Dallas: *(5232 Forest Lane, Suite 111,
Zip: 75244. Phone: 214/361-5896)*
El Paso: *(Sky Park II, 6500 Boeing,
Suite 111, Zip: 75244. Phone:
214/361-5896)*
Fort Worth: *(1305 W. Magnolia, Suite
B, Zip: 76104. Phone: 817/921-
9095)*
Houston: *(503 Westheimer, Zip:
77006. Phone: 713/523-0884)*
Houston: *(701 N. Post Oak Road,
Zip: 77024. Phone: 713/682-2288)*
Laredo: *(6020 McPherson Road,
Number 1, Zip: 78041. Phone:
512/723-4680)*
Lubbock: *(3208 Thirty-fourth Street,
Zip: 79410. Phone: 806/792-9782)*
McAllen: *(1317 E. Hackberry Street,
Zip: 78501. Phone: 512/631-2147)*
Midland: *(3404 W. Illinois, Suite 1,
Zip: 79703. Phone: 915/697-8222)*
San Antonio: *(231 W. Cypress Street,
Zip: 78212. Phone: 210/229-4025)*

**National Cemeteries**

Fort Bliss: *(5200 Fred Wilson Road,
P.O. Box 6342, Zip: 79906. Phone:
915/564-0201)*
Fort Sam Houston: *(1520 Harry
Wurzbach Road, San Antonio,
Zip: 78209. Phone: 210/820-3891)*
Houston: *(10410 Veterans Memorial
Drive, Zip: 77038. Phone:
713/447-8686)*
Kerrville: *(VA Medical Center, 3600
Memorial Boulevard, Zip: 78028.
Phone: 210/820-3891)*
San Antonio: *(517 Paso Hondo
Street, Zip: 73202. Phone:
210/820-3891)*

## UTAH

**Medical Center**

Salt Lake City: More than 350 beds, plus nearly 50 in nursing care unit. Organ transplantation, especially heart transplants. Open-heart surgery, geriatric evaluation, lithotripsy, nuclear medicine, psychiatry, neurology. *(500 Foothill Drive, Zip: 84148. Phone: 801/582-1565)*

**Regional Office**

Salt Lake City: *(P.O. Box 11500, Federal Building, 125 S. State Street, Zip: 84147. Local: 801/524-5960. Statewide: 800/827-1000)*

**Vet Centers**

Provo: *(750 North 200 West, Suite 105, Zip: 84601. Phone: 801/377-1117)*

Salt Lake City: *(1354 East 3300 South, Zip: 84106. Phone: 801/584-1294)*

## VERMONT

**Medical Center**

White River Junction: More than 200 beds, plus about 50 for nursing care. Urology, neurology, psychiatry, radiology, prosthetics, dentistry, post-traumatic stress, hospice, respite care, geriatric evaluation. *(N. Hartland Road, Zip: 05009. Phone: 802/295-9363)*

**Regional Office**

White River Junction: *(N. Hartland Road, Zip: 05009. Local: 802/296-5177. Statewide: 800/827-1000)*

**Vet Centers**

Burlington: *(359 Dorest Street, Zip: 05403. Phone: 802/862-1806)*

White River Junction: *(Gilman Office Center, Building 2, Holiday Inn Drive, Zip: 05001. Phone: 802/295-2908)*

## VIRGINIA

**Medical Centers**

Hampton: More than 300 beds, plus 100 in rehabilitative nursing care unit and 400 in residential care domiciliary. Long-term spinal cord injury, hospice, program for homeless and chronically mentally ill. *(100 Emancipation Drive, Zip: 23667. Phone: 804/722-9961)*

Richmond: Nearly 700 beds, plus more than 100 in nursing care unit. Heart transplant, open-heart surgery, comprehensive cancer treatment, lithotripsy, spinal cord injury, prosthetics, geriatric evaluation. *(1201 Broad Rock Road, Zip: 23249. Phone: 804/230-0001)*

Salem: More than 500 beds, plus 100 in nursing care unit. Acute and chronic psychiatry, cardiac catheterization, geriatric evaluation, post-traumatic stress, respite care, sleep apnea, substance abuse treatment and detoxification. *(1970 Roanoke Boulevard, Zip: 24153. Phone: 703/982-2463)*

**Clinic**

Norfolk: *(6500 Hampton Boulevard, Zip: 23508. Phone: 804/444-5517)*

**Regional Offices**

Roanoke: *(210 Franklin Road, S.W., Zip: 24011. Local: 703/857-2109. Statewide: 800/827-1000)*

Northern Virginia: Counties of Arlington and Fairfax, plus cities of Alexandria, Fairfax, and Falls Church are served by regional office in Washington, D.C.

**Vet Centers**

Alexandria: *(8796-D Sacramento Drive, Zip: 22309. Phone: 703/360-8633)*

Norfolk: *(2200 Colonial Avenue, Zip: 23517. Phone: 804/623-7584)*

Richmond: *(3022 W. Clay Street, Zip: 23230. Phone: 804/353-8958)*

Roanoke: *(320 Mountain Avenue, S.W., Zip: 24016. Phone: 703/342-9726)*

Springfield: *(7024 Spring Garden Drive, Zip: 22150. Phone: 703/866-0924)*

## National Cemeteries

Alexandria: *(1450 Wilkes Street, Zip: 22314. Phone: 703/690-2217)*

Balls Bluff: *(Leesburg, Zip: 22075. Phone: 703/825-0027)*

City Point: *(10th Avenue and Davis Street, Hopewell, Zip: 23860. Phone: 804/222-1490)*

Cold Harbor: *(Route 156 North, Mechanicsville, Zip: 23111. Phone: 804/222-1490)*

Culpeper: *(305 U.S. Avenue, Zip: 22701. Phone: 703/825-0027)*

Danville: *(721 Lee Street, Zip: 24541. Phone: 704/636-2661)*

Fort Harrison: *(8620 Varina Road, Richmond, Zip: 23231. Phone: 804/222-1490)*

Glendale: *(8301 Willis Church Road, Richmond, Zip: 23231. Phone: 804/222-1490)*

Hampton: *(Cemetery Road & Marshall Avenue, Zip: 23669. Phone: 804/723-7104)*

Hampton: *(VA Medical Center, Zip: 23669. Phone: 804/723-7104)*

Quantico: *(P.O. Box 10, 18425 Joplin Road, Triangle, Zip: 22172. Phone: 703/690-2217)*

Richmond: *(1701 Williamsburg Road, Zip: 23231. Phone: 804/222-1490)*

Seven Pines: *(400 E. Williamsburg Road, Sandston, Zip: 23150. Phone: 804/222-1490)*

Staunton: *(901 Richmond Avenue, Zip: 24401. Phone: 703/825-0027)*

Winchester: *(401 National Avenue, Zip: 22601. Phone: 703/825-0027)*

## VIRGIN ISLANDS
### Vet Centers

Saint Croix: *(Rural Route 02, Village Mall, Suite 113, Zip: 00850. Phone: 809/778-5553)*

Saint Thomas: *(Havensight Mall, Zip: 00801. Phone: 809/774-6674)*

## WASHINGTON
### Medical Centers

Seattle: More than 400 beds, plus more than 50 for nursing care. Bone marrow transplant, spinal cord injury, prosthetics, geriatrics, open-heart surgery, dialysis, neurology, substance abuse, psychiatry. *(1660 S. Columbian Way, Zip: 98108. Phone: 206/762-1010)*

Spokane: More than 100 beds, plus about 50 for nursing care. Intensive care, pulmonary function, respiratory care, noninvasive cardiac services, GI endoscopy, ex-POWs. *(N. 4815 Assembly Street, Zip: 99205. Phone: 509/328-4521)*

Tacoma: About 650 beds, with another 70 in nursing home and 60 in domiciliary. Services for blindness, post-traumatic stress, drug and alcohol treatment, psychiatry, vocational rehabilitation. *(900 Veterans Drive, S.W., American Lake, Zip: 98493. Phone: 206/582-8440)*

Walla Walla: More than 100 beds, plus nearly 50 for nursing care. Chemical dependency, rehabilitation medicine, ambulatory surgery, intensive care, pulmonary function, psychiatry. *(77 Wainwright Drive, Zip: 99362. Phone: 509/525-5200)*

### Clinic

Yakima: *(Yakima Training Center, Building 156, Zip: 98901. Phone: 509/457-2786)*

## Regional Office
Seattle: *(Federal Building, 915 Second Avenue, Zip: 98174. Local: 206/624-7200. Statewide: 800/827-1000)*

## Vet Centers
Seattle: *(2230 8th Avenue, Zip: 98121. Phone: 206/553-2706)*
Spokane: *(W. 1708 Mission Street, Zip: 99201. Phone: 509/327-0274)*
Tacoma: *(4916 Center Street, Zip: 98409. Phone: 206/565-7038)*

## WEST VIRGINIA
### Medical Centers
Beckley: More than 200 beds, about 50 in nursing care unit. Hemodialysis, intensive care, oncology, respite care, substance abuse. *(200 Veterans Avenue, Zip: 25801. Phone: 304/255-2121)*
Clarksburg: More than 200 beds. Intensive-care unit, hemodialysis, cancer, psychiatry, post-traumatic stress, substance abuse. *(1 Medical Center Drive, Zip: 26301. Phone: 304/623-3461*
Huntington: Nearly 200 beds. Geriatric evaluation, cardiology, prosthetics, rehabilitation medicine, inpatient psychiatry. *(1540 Spring Valley Drive, Zip: 25704. Phone: 304/429-6741)*
Martinsburg: More than 300 beds, plus another 500 beds in domiciliary and 150 in nursing care unit. Brain injuries, intensive care, women's outpatient program, post-traumatic stress, substance abuse, homeless program, nuclear medicine. *(Route 9, Zip: 25410. Phone: 304/263-0811)*

## Regional Office
Huntington: Serves all counties except Brooke, Hancock, Marshall, and Ohio, which are served by the regional office in Pittsburgh, Pennsylvania. *(640 Fourth Avenue, Zip: 25701. Local: 304/529-5720. Statewide: 800/827-1000)*

## Vet Centers
Beckley: *(101 Ellison Avenue, Zip: 25801. Phone: 304/252-8220)*
Charleston: *(512 Washington Street, West, Zip: 25302. Phone: 304/343-3825)*
Huntington: *(1005 Sixth Avenue, Zip: 25701. Phone: 304/523-8387)*
Martinsburg: *(105 S. Spring Street, Zip: 25401. Phone: 304/263-6776)*
Morgantown: *(1191 Pineview Drive, Zip: 26505. Phone: 304/291-4001)*
Princeton: *(905 Mercer Street, Zip: 24740. Phone: 304/425-5653)*
Wheeling: *(1070 Market Street, Zip: 26003. Phone: 304/232-0587)*

## National Cemetery
Grafton: *(431 Walnut Street, Zip: 26354. Phone: 304/265-2044)*

## WISCONSIN
### Medical Centers
Madison: Nearly 250 beds. Cardiac catheterization, epilepsy center, hemodialysis, open-heart surgery, positron emission tomography, sleep lab. *(2500 Overlook Terrace, Zip: 53705. Phone: 608/256-1901)*
Milwaukee: More than 400 beds, plus 200 in nursing homes and nearly 400 in domiciliaries. Aging, spinal cord injury, female veterans, open-heart surgery, pain clinic, dysphagia program. *(5000 W. National Avenue, Zip: 53295. Phone: 414/384-2000)*
Tomah: More than 500 beds, plus 100 for nursing care. Post-traumatic stress, drug and alcohol treatment, ventilator-dependence program, long-term care, hospice.

Outpatient for mental hygiene and day treatment. *(500 E. Veterans Street, Zip: 54660. Phone: 608/372-3971)*

## Clinic

Superior: *(3520 Tower Avenue, Zip: 54880. Phone: 715/392-9711)*

## Regional Office

Milwaukee: *(5000 W. National Avenue, Building 6, Zip: 53295. Local: 414/383-8680. Statewide: 800/827-1000)*

## Vet Centers

Madison: *(147 S. Butler Street, Zip: 53703. Phone: 608/264-5343)*
Milwaukee: *(3400 Wisconsin, Zip: 53208. Phone: 414/344-5504)*

## National Cemetery

Wood: *(5000 W. National Avenue, Building 122, Milwaukee, Zip: 53295. Phone: 414/382-5300)*

# WYOMING

## Medical Centers

Cheyenne: More than 80 beds, plus 50 beds in nursing unit. Substance abuse, post-traumatic stress, native American veterans programs, chronically mentally ill. *(2360 E. Pershing Boulevard, Zip: 82001. Phone: 307/778-7550)*
Sheridan: More than 300 beds, including more than 100 psychiatric, nearly 100 alcohol abuse, and 50 for nursing care. Geriatric evaluation, post-traumatic stress, dialysis. *(1898 Fort Road, Zip: 82801. Phone: 307/672-3473)*

## Regional Office

Cheyenne: *(2360 E. Pershing Boulevard, Zip: 82001. Local: 307/778-7396. Statewide: 800/827-1000)*

## Vet Centers

Casper: *(111 S. Jefferson, Zip: 82601. Phone: 307/235-8010)*
Cheyenne: *(3130 Henderson Drive, Zip: 82001. Phone: 307/778-7370)*

# STATE VETERANS FACILITIES

The following state-supported facilities are devoted primarily to the care of military veterans. They operate under rules set down by the U.S. Department of Veterans Affairs, which periodically inspects the facilities.

Unlike VA nursing homes and domiciliaries, they charge a fee for their services. Typically, those fees are smaller than those at comparable private-sector facilities because of VA financial support.

Nursing homes are for patients who require assistance in daily living. Domiciliaries are for veterans who can take care of many basic needs. This list is based on 1994 statistics.

## ALABAMA

Alexander City: 150-bed nursing home. *(Bill Nichols, State Veterans Home, 1801 Elkahatchee Road, Zip: 35010. Phone: 205/329-0868)*

## ARKANSAS

Little Rock: 55-bed domiciliary, 60-bed nursing home. *(Arkansas Veterans Home, 4701 West 20th Street, Zip: 72204. Phone: 501/324-9454)*

## CALIFORNIA

Yountville: 820-bed domiciliary, 570-bed nursing home, 50-bed hospital. *(P.O. Box 1200, Veterans Home of California, Zip: 94599. Phone: 707/944-4500)*

## COLORADO

Florence: 120-bed nursing home. *(Colorado State Veterans Nursing Home, Moore Drive, Zip: 81226. Phone: 719/784-6331)*

Homelake: 130-bed domiciliary, 90-bed nursing home. *(Colorado State Veterans Center, P.O. Box 97, Zip: 81135. Phone: 719/852-5118)*

Rifle: 100-bed nursing home. *(Colorado State Veterans Home, 851 East 5th Street, P.O. Box 1420, Zip: 81650. Phone: 303/625-0842)*

## CONNECTICUT
Rocky Hill: 650-bed domiciliary, 350-bed hospital. *(Connecticut Veterans Home & Hospital, 287 West Street, Zip: 06067. Phone: 203/529-2571)*

## FLORIDA
Lake City: 150-bed domiciliary. *(Veterans Home of Florida, 1300 Sycamore Lane, Zip: 32055. Phone: 904/758-0600)*

## GEORGIA
Augusta: 190-bed nursing home. *(Georgia War Veterans Nursing Home, 1101 Fifteenth Street, Zip: 30910. Phone: 706/721-2351)*

Milledgeville: 290-bed domiciliary, 390-bed nursing home. *(Georgia State War Veterans Home, Vinson Highway, Zip: 30162. Phone: 912/453-4219)*

## IDAHO
Boise: 50-bed domiciliary, 140-bed nursing home. *(P.O. Box 7765, Zip: 83707. Phone: 208/334-5000)*

Pocatello: 70-bed nursing home. *(Idaho State Veterans Home, 1957 Alvin Ricken Drive, Zip: 83201. Phone: 208/233-6699)*

## ILLINOIS
LaSalle: 120-bed nursing home. *(Illinois Veterans Home, 1015 O'Conor Avenue, Zip: 61301. Phone: 815/223-0303)*

Manteno: 10-bed domiciliary, 300-bed nursing home. *(Illinois Veterans Home, One Veterans Drive, Zip: 60950. Phone: 815/468-6581)*

Quincy: 150-bed domiciliary, 630-bed nursing home. *(Illinois Veterans Home, 1707 North Twelfth Street, Zip: 62301. Phone: 217/222-8641)*

## INDIANA
West Lafayette: 190-bed domiciliary, 610-bed nursing home. *(Indiana Veterans Home, 3851 North River Road, Zip: 47906. Phone: 317/463-1502)*

## IOWA
Marshalltown: 110-bed domiciliary, 690-bed nursing home, 25-bed hospital. *(Iowa Veterans Home, 1301 Summit Street, Zip: 50158. Phone: 515/752-1501)*

## KANSAS
Fort Dodge: 230-bed domiciliary, 90-bed nursing home. *(Kansas Soldiers Home, Zip: 67843. Phone: 316/227-2121)*

## KENTUCKY
Wilmore: 300-bed nursing home. *(Kentucky Veterans Center, 100 Veterans Drive, Zip: 40390. Phone: 606/858-2814)*

## LOUISIANA
Jackson: 100-bed domiciliary, 140-bed nursing home. *(Louisiana War Veterans Home, P.O. Box 748, Zip: 70748. Phone: 504/634-5265)*

## MAINE
Augusta: 120-bed nursing home. *(Maine Veterans Home, Conry Road, RFD 2, Zip: 04330. Phone: 207/622-2454)*

Caribou: 40-bed nursing home. *(Maine Veterans Home, 39 Van Buren Road, Zip: 04736. Phone: 207/498-6074)*

Scarborough: 120-bed nursing home. *(Maine Veterans Home, 290 U.S. Route One, Zip: 04074. Phone: 207/883-7184)*

## MARYLAND
Charlotte Hall: 100-bed domiciliary, 150-bed nursing home. *(Charlotte Hall Veterans Home, Route 2, Box 5, Zip: 20622. Phone: 301/884-8171)*

## MASSACHUSETTS
Chelsea: 300-bed domiciliary, 60-bed nursing home, 170-bed hospital. *(Soldiers Home in Massachusetts, 91 Crest Avenue, Zip: 02150. Phone: 617/884-5660)*

Holyoke: 50-bed domiciliary, 260-bed nursing home, 30-bed hospital. *(Soldiers Home in Massachusetts, 110 Cherry Street, Zip: 01040. Phone: 413/532-9475)*

## MICHIGAN
Grand Rapids: 140-bed domiciliary, 620-bed nursing home. *(Michigan Veterans Facility, 3000 Monroe, Northwest, Zip: 49505. Phone: 616/364-5300)*

Marquette: 60-bed domiciliary, 180-bed nursing home. *(D. J. Jacobetti Home for Veterans, 425 Fisher Street, Zip: 49855. Phone: 906/226-3576)*

## MINNESOTA
Hastings: 200-bed domiciliary. *(Minnesota Veterans Home, 1200 East 18th Street, Zip: 55033. Phone: 612/438-8500)*

Minneapolis: 80-bed domiciliary, 350-bed nursing home. *(Minnesota Veterans Home, 5101 Minnehaha Avenue, South, Zip: 55417. Phone: 612/721-0600)*

Silver Bay: 90-bed nursing home. *(Minnesota Veterans Home, 45 Banks Boulevard, Zip: 55614. Phone: 218/226-3350)*

## MISSISSIPPI
Jackson: 150-bed nursing home. *(Mississippi Veterans Home, 4607 Lindberg Street, Zip: 39209. Phone: 601/354-7205)*

## MISSOURI
Cape Girardeau: 150-bed nursing home. *(Missouri Veterans Home, Route 2, Box 495, Zip: 63701. Phone: 314/290-5870)*

Mexico: 150-bed nursing home. *(Missouri Veterans Home, 920 Mars Street, P.O. Box 473, Zip: 65265. Phone: 314/581-1088)*

Mount Vernon: 100-bed nursing home. *(Missouri Veterans Home, 600 North Main, Zip: 65712. Phone: 417/466-7103)*

Saint James: 150-bed nursing home. *(Missouri Veterans Home, Zip: 65559. Phone: 314/265-3271)*

## MONTANA
Columbia Falls: 60-bed domiciliary, 90-bed nursing home. *(Montana Veterans Home, P.O. Box 250, Zip: 59912. Phone: 406/892-3256)*

## NEBRASKA
Grand Island: 35-bed domiciliary, 410-bed nursing home. *(Nebraska Veterans Home, Burkett Station, Zip: 68803. Phone: 308/382-9420)*

Norfolk: 30-bed domiciliary, 130-bed nursing home. *(Nebraska Veterans Home, P.O. Box 409, Zip: 68702. Phone: 402/370-3177)*

Omaha: 30-bed domiciliary, 160-bed nursing home. *(Thomas Fitzgerald Veterans Home, 156 W. Maple Road, Zip: 68116. Phone: 402/595-2180)*

Scottsbluff: 90-bed domiciliary, 50-bed nursing home. *(Western Nebraska Veterans Home, 1102 West 42nd Street, Zip: 69361. Phone: 308/632-3381)*

## NEW HAMPSHIRE

Tilton: 150-bed nursing home. *(New Hampshire Veterans Home, Winter Street, Zip: 03276. Phone: 603/286-4412)*

## NEW JERSEY

Edison/Menlo Park: 40-bed domiciliary, 350-bed nursing home. *(New Jersey Veterans Memorial Home, P.O. Box 3013, Edison, Zip: 08818. Phone: 908/603-3013)*

Paramus: 260-bed nursing home. *(New Jersey Veterans Memorial Home, P.O. Box 608, One Veterans Drive, Zip: 07653. Phone: 201/967-7676)*

Vineland: 300-bed nursing home. *(New Jersey Memorial Home, 524 Northwest Boulevard, Zip: 08360. Phone: 609/696-6400)*

## NEW MEXICO

Fort Bayard: 40-bed nursing home. *(New Mexico State Veterans Home, P.O. Box 36210, Zip: 36219. Phone: 505/537-3302)*

Truth or Consequences: 20-bed domiciliary, 160-bed nursing home. *(New Mexico Veterans Center, P.O. Box 927, Zip: 37901. Phone: 505/894-9081)*

## NEW YORK

Oxford: 240-bed nursing home. *(New York State Veterans Home, Zip: 13830. Phone: 607/843-6991)*

Stoney Brook: 350-bed nursing home. *(Long Island State Veterans Home, State University of New York, 100 Patriots Road, Zip: 11790. Phone: 516/444-8500)*

## NORTH DAKOTA

Lisbon: 110-bed domiciliary, 30-bed nursing home. *(North Dakota Veterans Home, Lock Box 673, Zip: 58054. Phone: 701/683-4125)*

## OHIO

Sandusky: 200-bed domiciliary, 350-bed nursing home. *(Ohio Veterans Home, S. Columbus Avenue, Zip: 44870. Phone: 419/625-2454)*

## OKLAHOMA

Ardmore: 35-bed domiciliary, 140-bed nursing home. *(Oklahoma Veterans Center, P.O. Box 489, Zip: 73402. Phone: 405/223-2266)*

Claremore: 350-bed nursing home. *(Oklahoma Veterans Center, P.O. Box 988, Zip: 74018. Phone: 918/342-5432)*

Clinton: 30-bed domiciliary, 145-bed nursing home. *(Oklahoma Veterans Center, P.O. Box 1209, Zip: 73601. Phone: 405/323-5540)*

Norman: 190-bed nursing home. *(Oklahoma Veterans Center, P.O. Box 1668, Zip: 73070. Phone: 405/360-5600)*

Sulphur: 30-bed domiciliary, 140-bed nursing home. *(Oklahoma Veterans Center, 200 E. Fairlane, Zip: 73086. Phone: 405/622-2144)*

Talihina: 210-bed nursing home. *(Oklahoma Veterans Center, P.O. Box 1168, Zip: 74571. Phone: 918/567-2251)*

## PENNSYLVANIA

Erie: 100-bed domiciliary, 75-bed nursing home. *(Pennsylvania Soldiers & Sailors Home, P.O. Box 6239, Zip: 16512. Phone: 814/871-4531)*

Hollidaysburg: 170-bed domiciliary, 350-bed nursing home. *(Hollidaysburg Veterans Home, P.O. Box 319, Zip: 16648. Phone: 814/696-5356)*

Spring City: 150-bed domiciliary. *(Southeastern Pennsylvania Veterans Center, Veterans Drive, Zip: 19475. Phone: 610/948-2400)*

## RHODE ISLAND
Bristol: 80-bed domiciliary, 260-bed nursing home. *(Rhode Island Veterans Home, Metacom Avenue, Zip: 02809. Phone: 401/253-8000)*

## SOUTH CAROLINA
Anderson: 220-bed nursing home. *(Richard M. Campbell Veterans Nursing Home, 4605 Belton Highway, Zip: 29621. Phone: 803/261-5350)*
Columbia: 150-bed nursing home. *(South Carolina Veterans Pavilion, 2200 Harden Street, Zip: 29203. Phone: 803/737-5302)*

## SOUTH DAKOTA
Hot Springs: 275-bed domiciliary, 50-bed nursing home. *(South Dakota State Veterans Home, 2500 Minnekahta Avenue, Zip: 57747. Phone: 605/745-5127)*

## TENNESSEE
Murfreesboro: 120-bed nursing home. *(Tennessee Veterans Home, 345 Compton Road, Zip: 37130. Phone: 615/895-8850)*

## VERMONT
Bennington: 20-bed domiciliary, 185-bed nursing home. *(Vermont Veterans Home, 325 North Street, Zip: 05201. Phone: 802/422-6353)*

## VIRGINIA
Roanoke: 60-bed domiciliary, 180-bed nursing home. *(Virginia Veterans Care Center, 4550 Shenandoah Avenue, N.W., Zip: 24017. Phone: 703/982-2860)*

## WASHINGTON
Orting: 50-bed domiciliary, 150-bed nursing home. *(Washington Soldiers Home, P.O. Box 500, Zip: 98360. Phone: 206/893-2156)*
Retsil: 145-bed domiciliary, 270-bed nursing home. *(Washington Veterans Home, P.O. Box 698, Zip: 98378. Phone: 206/895-4700)*

## WEST VIRGINIA
Barboursville: 200-bed domiciliary. *(Barboursville Veterans Home, 512 Water Street, Zip: 25504. Phone: 304/736-1027)*

## WISCONSIN
King: 145-bed domiciliary, 590-bed nursing home. *(Wisconsin Veterans Home, Zip: 54946. Phone: 715/258-5586)*

## WYOMING
Buffalo: 120-bed domiciliary. *(Veterans Home of Wyoming, 700 Veterans Lane, Zip: 82834. Phone: 307/684-5511)*

# VETERANS HELPING VETERANS

By the time most people are ready to leave active duty, they're convinced they've heard a large percentage of the world's total collection of acronyms. They may be right.

There's one acronym, however, that isn't heard much on active duty, but that is very important to many veterans. It's "VSO."

That's veteran-speak for "Veterans Service Organization." These are groups that have special authority under federal law to represent veterans in cases before the Department of Veterans Affairs or any VA body.

A VSO service officer is a professional. That's what he does for a living. He's been specially trained by his organization to represent veterans. He understands the law and the administrative processes.

VSOs must offer their services, without charge, to any veteran. You don't have to be a member of their organization.

VA rules even have provisions that enable veterans to appoint an entire VSO, not just one service officer from a VSO, as the veteran's representative. That permits veterans to draw on the full resources of an organization, especially the VSO facilities in Washington.

Not every VSO is equally effective. Not all of their representatives, or service officers, are equally skilled. Here are the VSOs that are legally entitled to represent veterans before the VA:

**American Defenders of Bataan**
P.O. Box 12052
New Bern, NC 28561
(919 / 637-4033)

**American Ex-Prisoners of War**
3201 East Pioneer Pkway, Suite 40
Arlington, TX 76010
(817 / 649-2979)

**American GI Forum**
1017 N. Main, Suite 200
San Antonio, TX 78212
(512 / 223-4088)

**American Legion**
1608 "K" St., N.W.
Washington, DC 20006
(202 / 861-2700)

**American Red Cross**
17th & "D" St., N.W.
Washington, DC 20006
(202 / 639-3586)

**American Veterans Committee**
6309 Bannockburn Dr.
Bethesda, MD 20817
(301 / 320-6490)

**AMVETS**
4647 Forbes Blvd.
Lanham, MD 20706
(301 / 459-9600)

**Army and Air Force
Mutual Aid Association**
Fort Myer
Arlington, VA 22211
(703 / 522-3060)

**Army and Navy Union**
1391 Main Street
Lakemore, OH 44250
(216 / 733-3113)

**Blinded Veterans Association**
477 "H" St., N.W.
Washington, DC 20001
(202 / 371-8880)

**Catholic War Veterans**
419 North Lee St.
Alexandria, VA 22314
(703 / 549-3622)

**Congressional
Medal of Honor Society**
40 Patriots Point Rd.
Mount Pleasant, SC 29464
(803 / 884-1471)

**Disabled American Veterans**
807 Maine Ave., S.W.
Washington, DC 20024
(202 / 554-3501)

**Fleet Reserve Association**
125 N. West Street
Alexandria, VA 22314
(703 / 683-1400)

**Gold Star Wives**
540 N. Lombardy St.
Arlington, VA 22203
(703 / 527-7706)

**Italian American War Veterans**
122 Mather St.
Syracuse, NY 13203
(315 / 479-8315)

**Jewish War Veterans**
1811 "R" St., N.W.
Washington, DC 20009
(202 / 265-6280)

**Legion of Valor**
92 Oak Leaf Lane
Chapel Hill, NC 27516
(919 / 933-0989)

**Marine Corps League**
8550 Lee Highway, Suite 201
Fairfax, VA 22031
(703 / 207-9588)

**Military Chaplains Association**
P.O. Box 42660
Washington, DC 20015
(202 / 574-2423)

**Military Order of Purple Heart**
5413-B Backlick Rd.
Springfield, VA 22151
(703 / 642-5360)

**National Amputation
Foundation**
12-45 150th St.
Whitestone, NY 11357
(718 / 767-0596)

**Navy Mutual Aid Association**
Arlington Annex, Room G-070
Washington, DC 20370
(703 / 614-1638)

**Non Commissioned Officers
Association**
10635 IH 35 North
San Antonio, TX 78233
(512 / 653-6161)

**Paralyzed Veterans of America**
801 Eighteenth St., N.W.
Washington, DC 20006
(202 / 872-1300)

**Pearl Harbor Survivors
Association**
Drawer 2598
Lancaster, CA 93539
(805 / 948-1851)

**Polish Legion of
American Veterans**
5413-C Backlick Rd.
Springfield, VA 22151
(703 / 354-2771)

**Regular Veterans Association**
2470 Cardinal Loop, RVA Bldg., 212
Del Valle, TX 78617
(512 / 389-2288)

**Retired Enlisted Association**
1111 S. Abilene Ct.
Aurora, CO 80012
(303 / 752-0660)

**Swords to Plowshares:
Veterans Rights Organization**
400 Valencia St.
San Francisco, CA 94103
(415 / 552-8804)

**United Spanish War Veterans**
P.O. Box 1915
Washington, DC 20013
(202 / 347-1898)

**Submarine Veterans
of World War II**
862 Chatham Ave.
Elmhurst, IL 60126
(708 / 834-2718)

**Veterans of Foreign Wars**
406 West 34th St.
Kansas City, MO 64111
(816 / 756-3390)

**Veterans of World War I**
P.O. Box 8027
Alexandria, VA 22306
(703 / 780-5660)

**Vietnam-Era Veterans**
250 Prairie Ave.
Providence, RI 02905
(401 / 521-6710)

**Vietnam Veterans of America**
1224 "M" St.
Washington, DC 20005
(202 / 628-2700)

**Women's Army Corps
Veterans Association**
P.O. Box 5577
Fort McClellan, AL 36205
(205 / 820-4019)

# NONMILITARY VETERANS

Not everyone who is officially a veteran actually wore the uniform of one of the U.S. armed forces. The federal government has extended special "veterans status" to select groups of people who rendered service to the U.S. military without having ever been on active duty themselves. This "veterans status" makes members of these groups eligible for many VA programs, especially medical treatment.

To begin receiving benefits, these people must first receive an official set of discharge papers from the Department of Defense. A local VA benefits office can help veterans through the application process.

Following are the groups that have earned many VA benefits by their service to the United States. Although this list is subject to change, it's unlikely that any groups will lose their veterans status. To be put on the list, they have had their wartime records carefully screened by a Department of Defense panel over a period of several years. It is very likely, however, that additional groups that performed wartime service to the U.S. military may be added to the list in the coming years.

- Women's Air Forces service pilots.
- Signal Corps female telephone operators unit of World War I.
- Engineer field cadets.

- Women's Army Auxiliary Corps.
- Quartermaster Corps female clerical employees with American Expeditionary Forces during World War I.
- Civilian employees of Pacific naval bases at Wake Island who participated in defense during World War II.
- Reconstruction aides and dietitians in World War I.
- Male civilian ferry pilots.
- Wake Island defenders from Guam.
- Civilians assigned to the Secret Intelligence element of the Office of Strategic Services.
- Guam Combat Patrol.
- Quartermaster Corps vessel *Keswick* crew on Corregidor during World War II.
- U.S. civilian volunteers in defense of Bataan.
- U.S. merchant seamen who served on blockships in support of Operation Mulberry during World War II.
- U.S. merchant seamen in oceangoing service from December 7, 1941, to August 15, 1945.
- Civilian Navy IFF technicians who served in combat areas of the Pacific from December 7, 1941, to August 15, 1945.
- U.S. civilians with the American Field Service overseas from August 31, 1917, to January 1, 1918.
- U.S. civilians of the American Field Service who served overseas under U.S. armies and U.S. army groups between December 7, 1941, and May 8, 1945.
- U.S. civilian employees of American Airlines overseas under a contract with the Air Transport Command from December 14, 1941, to August 14, 1945.
- Civilian crewmen of U.S. Coast and Geodetic Survey vessels in areas of immediate military hazard during operations with U.S. armed forces between December 7, 1941, and August 15, 1945.
- Honorably discharged members of the "Flying Tigers" who served between December 7, 1941, and July 18, 1942.

- U.S. civilian flight crews and aviation ground support employees overseas under a contract with the Air Transport Command from December 14, 1941, to August 14, 1945.

- U.S. civilian flight crew and aviation ground support employees of Transcontinental and Western Air, Inc., overseas under a contract with the Air Transport Command between December 14, 1941, and August 14, 1945.

- U.S. civilian flight crew and aviation ground support employees of Consolidated Vultee Aircraft Corporation overseas under a contract with the Air Transport Command between December 14, 1941, and August 14, 1945.

- U.S. civilian flight crew and aviation ground support employees of Pan American World Airways, its subsidiaries and affiliates, overseas under a contract with the Air Transport Command from December 14, 1941, to August 14, 1945.

- Honorably discharged members of the American Volunteer Guard, Eritrea Service Command, between June 21, 1942, and March 31, 1943.

- U.S. civilian flight crew and ground support employees of Northwest Airlines who served overseas under a contract with Air Transport Command from December 14, 1941, through August 14, 1945.

- U.S. civilian female employees of Army Nurse Corps who served in defense of Bataan and Corregidor in 1942.

# OFFICIAL WARTIME PERIODS

Some veterans benefits are restricted to people who served on active duty during times of war. For example, wartime service is needed to qualify for a VA pension, and it's sometimes a factor in determining priority for care in a VA medical facility.

When wartime service is needed to qualify for a benefit, veterans should pay attention to the fine print. Sometimes the rules for a benefit require a specific length of wartime service.

Reservists and National Guardsmen during periods of wartime can usually qualify as "wartime vets" if they spent at least one day on active duty for training.

It's important to note that for the Persian Gulf War, the Vietnam War, the Korean War, and World War II, you need not have served in a combat region to qualify as a wartime vet. Service in the states or anywhere in the world is sufficient to establish you as a wartime veteran, so long as you were in the military during the prescribed period.

Some World War I veterans can qualify as wartime veterans if they were stationed in Russia after the normal wartime period for World War I.

And Mexican War veterans must have served in Mexico, along the border, or in adjacent waters during the period of war to qualify as wartime veterans. People who were on active duty during that time but who weren't stationed near the war zone cannot qualify as wartime veterans of the Mexican Border War.

The official periods of wartime are specified by federal law and are as follows:

*Mexican Border War:* From May 9, 1916, through April 5, 1917. Service must have been in Mexico, on the Mexican border, or in adjacent waters.

*World War I:* From April 6, 1917, through November 11, 1918. For people who served in Russia, the period is April 6, 1917, through April 1, 1920. In order to help World War I veterans qualify for benefits that require a certain number of days in uniform during wartime, Congress extended the official wartime period to July 2, 1921, for veterans who had already spent at least one day in the military between April 6, 1917, and November 11, 1918.

*World War II:* From December 7, 1941, through December 31, 1946. To help World War II veterans meet the minimum time-in-service-during-wartime requirements for loan guaranty, vocational rehabilitation, and educational programs, Congress enlarged the official wartime period to run from September 16, 1940, through July 25, 1947. That extension applies only to veterans with at least one day in the military between December 7, 1941, and December 31, 1946, who apply for one of the three programs mentioned above.

*Korean Conflict:* From June 27, 1950, through January 31, 1955.

*Vietnam Era:* From February 28, 1961, through May 7, 1975.

*Persian Gulf War:* From August 2, 1990. The end-date for the official wartime period hadn't been established when *Veteran's Guide* went to press in mid-1997.

# Two Centuries of Veterans: Some Statistics

### American Revolution (1717–1784)

Participants . . . . . . . . . . . . . . . . . . . . . . . . . . . . . . . . . . . . . . . . . . . . . . . . . . . 290,000
Deaths in service . . . . . . . . . . . . . . . . . . . . . . . . . . . . . . . . . . . . . . . . . . . . . . . . 4,000
Last veteran died, April 5, 1869 . . . . . . . . . . . . . . . . . . . . . . . . . . Age 109
Last dependent died, April 25, 1911 . . . . . . . . . . . . . . . . . . . . . . . Age 90

### War of 1812 (1812–1815)

Participants . . . . . . . . . . . . . . . . . . . . . . . . . . . . . . . . . . . . . . . . . . . . . . . . . . . 287,000
Deaths in service . . . . . . . . . . . . . . . . . . . . . . . . . . . . . . . . . . . . . . . . . . . . . . . . 2,000
Last veteran died, May 13, 1905 . . . . . . . . . . . . . . . . . . . . . . . . . . Age 105
Last dependent died, March 12, 1946 . . . . . . . . . . . . . . . . . . . . . . Age 89

### Indian Wars (Approx. 1817–1898)

Participants . . . . . . . . . . . . . . . . . . . . . . . . . . . . . . . . . . . . . . . . . . . . . . . . . . . 106,000
Deaths in service . . . . . . . . . . . . . . . . . . . . . . . . . . . . . . . . . . . . . . . . . . . . . . . . 1,000
Last veteran died, June 18, 1973 . . . . . . . . . . . . . . . . . . . . . . . . . . Age 101
Spouses (drawing VA pension) . . . . . . . . . . . . . . . . . . . . . . . . . . . . . . . . . . . 3
Children (drawing VA pension) . . . . . . . . . . . . . . . . . . . . . . . . . . . . . . . . . . . 2

### Mexican War (1846–1848)

Participants . . . . . . . . . . . . . . . . . . . . . . . . . . . . . . . . . . . . . . . . . . . . . . . . . . . 79,000
Deaths in service . . . . . . . . . . . . . . . . . . . . . . . . . . . . . . . . . . . . . . . . . . . . . . . . 13,000
Last veteran died, September 3, 1929 . . . . . . . . . . . . . . . . . . . . . . Age 98
Last dependent died, November 1, 1962 . . . . . . . . . . . . . . . . . . . . Age 94

### Civil War—Confederate (1861–1865)

Participants . . . . . . . . . . . . . . . . . . . . . . . . . . . . . . . . . . . . . . . . . . . . . 1,000,000
Deaths in service . . . . . . . . . . . . . . . . . . . . . . . . . . . . . . . . . . . . . . . . 133,821
Last veteran died, March 16, 1958 . . . . . . . . . . . . . . . . . . . . . . Age 112

### Civil War—Union (1861–1865)

Participants . . . . . . . . . . . . . . . . . . . . . . . . . . . . . . . . . . . . . . . . . . . . . 2,213,000
Deaths in service . . . . . . . . . . . . . . . . . . . . . . . . . . . . . . . . . . . . . . . . 364,000
Last veteran died, August 2, 1956 . . . . . . . . . . . . . . . . . . . . . . Age 109

### Civil War—Dependents, both sides

Spouses (drawing VA pension) . . . . . . . . . . . . . . . . . . . . . . . . . . . . . . 2
Children (drawing VA pension) . . . . . . . . . . . . . . . . . . . . . . . . . . . . . 22

### Spanish-American War (1898–1902)

Participants . . . . . . . . . . . . . . . . . . . . . . . . . . . . . . . . . . . . . . . . . . . . . 392,000
Deaths in service . . . . . . . . . . . . . . . . . . . . . . . . . . . . . . . . . . . . . . . . 11,000
Last veteran died, September 10, 1992 . . . . . . . . . . . . . . . . . . . . Age 106
Spouses (drawing VA pension) . . . . . . . . . . . . . . . . . . . . . . . . . . . . . 1,131
Children (drawing VA pension) . . . . . . . . . . . . . . . . . . . . . . . . . . . . . 425

### World War I (1917–1918)

Participants . . . . . . . . . . . . . . . . . . . . . . . . . . . . . . . . . . . . . . . . . . . . . 4,744,000
Deaths in service . . . . . . . . . . . . . . . . . . . . . . . . . . . . . . . . . . . . . . . . 116,000
Living veterans . . . . . . . . . . . . . . . . . . . . . . . . . . . . . . . . . . . . . . . . . . 13,000
Parents (drawing VA pension) . . . . . . . . . . . . . . . . . . . . . . . . . . . . . . 4
Spouses (drawing VA pension) . . . . . . . . . . . . . . . . . . . . . . . . . . . . . 78,909
Children (drawing VA pension) . . . . . . . . . . . . . . . . . . . . . . . . . . . . . 8,295

### World War II (September 16, 1940–July 25, 1947)

Participants . . . . . . . . . . . . . . . . . . . . . . . . . . . . . . . . . . . . . . . . . . . . . 16,535,000
Deaths in service . . . . . . . . . . . . . . . . . . . . . . . . . . . . . . . . . . . . . . . . 406,000
Living veterans . . . . . . . . . . . . . . . . . . . . . . . . . . . . . . . . . . . . . . . . . . 7,433,000
Parents (drawing VA pension) . . . . . . . . . . . . . . . . . . . . . . . . . . . . . . 6,019
Spouses (drawing VA pension) . . . . . . . . . . . . . . . . . . . . . . . . . . . . . 327,885
Children (drawing VA pension) . . . . . . . . . . . . . . . . . . . . . . . . . . . . . 22,128

## Korean Conflict (June 27, 1950–January 31, 1955)

Participants . . . . . . . . . . . . . . . . . . . . . . . . . . . . . . . . . . . . . . . . . . . 6,807,000
Deaths in service . . . . . . . . . . . . . . . . . . . . . . . . . . . . . . . . . . . . . . . 55,000
Living veterans . . . . . . . . . . . . . . . . . . . . . . . . . . . . . . . . . . . . . . . . 4,499,000
Parents (drawing VA pension) . . . . . . . . . . . . . . . . . . . . . . . . . . . . . 3,782
Spouses (drawing VA pension) . . . . . . . . . . . . . . . . . . . . . . . . . . . . . 71,616
Children (drawing VA pension) . . . . . . . . . . . . . . . . . . . . . . . . . . . . 5,317

## Vietnam Era (August 5, 1964–May 7, 1975)

Participants . . . . . . . . . . . . . . . . . . . . . . . . . . . . . . . . . . . . . . . . . . . 9,200,000
Deaths in service . . . . . . . . . . . . . . . . . . . . . . . . . . . . . . . . . . . . . . . 109,000
Living veterans . . . . . . . . . . . . . . . . . . . . . . . . . . . . . . . . . . . . . . . . 8,273,000
Parents (drawing VA pension) . . . . . . . . . . . . . . . . . . . . . . . . . . . . . 9,425
Spouses (drawing VA pension) . . . . . . . . . . . . . . . . . . . . . . . . . . . . . 90,683
Children (drawing VA pension) . . . . . . . . . . . . . . . . . . . . . . . . . . . . 18,807

## Persian Gulf War
## (August 2, 1990– November 30, 1995)

Participants . . . . . . . . . . . . . . . . . . . . . . . . . . . . . . . . . . . . . . . . . . . 3,700,000
Deaths in service . . . . . . . . . . . . . . . . . . . . . . . . . . . . . . . . . . . . . . . 6,526

## Two Centuries of Veterans

Veterans . . . . . . . . . . . . . . . . . . . . . . . . . . . . . . . . . . . . . . . . . . . . . 41,746,000
Deaths in service . . . . . . . . . . . . . . . . . . . . . . . . . . . . . . . . . . . . . . 1,087,526
Living war veterans . . . . . . . . . . . . . . . . . . . . . . . . . . . . . . . . . . . . 20,169,000
Living veterans . . . . . . . . . . . . . . . . . . . . . . . . . . . . . . . . . . . . . . . 26,198,000
Parents (drawing VA pension) . . . . . . . . . . . . . . . . . . . . . . . . . . . . . 23,406
Spouses (drawing VA pension) . . . . . . . . . . . . . . . . . . . . . . . . . . . . . 612,743
Children (drawing VA pension) . . . . . . . . . . . . . . . . . . . . . . . . . . . . 70,501
Veterans (drawing VA compensation) . . . . . . . . . . . . . . . . . . . . . . . 2,668,576

---

As of July 1, 1995
Compiled by Department of Veterans Affairs

# INDEX

# NOTES

# NOTES

# NOTES

# NOTES